# *You*-niquely HER
## *Hurt. Empower. Reign.*

A true story of deceit, lies, and manipulation

Kema Banks Johnson

Fulton Books, Inc.
Meadville, PA

Published by Fulton Books 2021

ISBN 978-1-63860-825-7 (paperback)
ISBN 978-1-63985-845-3 (hardcover)
ISBN 978-1-63860-826-4 (digital)

Printed in the United States of America

There is a little *you* in HER.

To a woman who never lied to me, who told me the truth even when it hurt. My angel on earth, now in heaven.

When I hugged you, I felt loved. Your touch instantly let me know what heaven feels like. Every time we hugged, I cried in your arms, and you would say, "Come on, Nikki, you're going to make me cry." And we would both cry together. The power of unconditional love!

She told me what I was going through as a woman was nothing new.

She said, "I went through it, my mother went through it, and many more women will continue to go through it. Women are scared to tell their story because they are scared to be labeled stupid. Tell your story for other women who have been through what you have been through. They will see how we are all one and the same. The journey to heartbreak is inevitable, but the experience is what makes it unique."

This book is dedicated to my Nana.

# Acknowledgments

---

Special thanks to those who inspired me throughout my writing process, especially my husband, Thomas Johnson, for all his support.

I thank my mother, father, and kids; Bishop, Nila, and Breyana; Rose Moore, aka Roxxane in the book, the other half of my heart; Cheyenne Lynch, for pushing me to keep going when I felt like giving up and for reading unedited pages, giving helpful commentaries; Keidarrien Carr-Daye, for creating a beautiful picture from a few words and a rough draft idea (thanks, K-Baby!); and Moriah Jeffers at MNPhotographyco for my photo collage; and most importantly, the WOMEN in my life and around the world.

# Let Me Introduce Myself

---

My name is Joss Love.

I'm a single independent black woman with two kids, successful in my own little way. I was content with life, but I knew something was missing—the desire to be in love. I wanted a man to fill my heart and my bed.

I was maintaining my own home and car. I was holding down a management position, on third shift at my job. I worked every day, and I enjoyed what I did for work.

I'm five feet, nine inches, with long legs, caramel skin, and a smile that can melt even the hardest individual's heart. I'm free-spirited when it comes to life, believing everything happens for a reason. I didn't give two cents what people thought about me.

I handled my business, and I did it responsibly. I didn't like drama, nor did I go looking for it. On top of it all, I love the Lord. Knowing him created values in me that were nonnegotiable, and one of those values is marriage.

I met these men on different platforms and at different ages and stages of my life. These men took me through different levels of happiness and drama—each relationship being more drama filled and intense than the one before it, each story resonating with a woman, who is or was in a relationship, just like mine, one way or another.

This proves I was destined to not be any different from any other woman who experienced heartbreak in the love department. I found myself involved with men who chose me to be the woman they led their double lives with. Making the life I thought I had with them out to be a *lie*!

I was in the right place at the right time for all these men to interact with me. I wasn't looking for any of them, but they somehow found me, unknowingly opening the door to manipulation and deception. Some of these guys weren't my type, but they had charm and charisma, and they knew how to make love. That made it easy to fall for them, see past their faults, ignoring the deception while allowing them all to manipulate, lie, and deceive me in the end.

Through music, I was able to heal. Listening to other women sing about their experience with love helped me. They helped me to realize I wasn't alone in my experience, and I will survive. To reign freely. Undefeated by love!

# Hi, My Name Is...

It was 9:00 p.m., and my alarm went off for work. It was the middle of the week, and I needed to be at work before ten.

I was the third-shift trainer in my department, and I had new trainees coming in tonight. Every year my job had a peak season, in which we did extensive hiring throughout the whole building, and we got new folks twice a week. And tonight was one of those nights.

Things weren't going so well at home between my boyfriend Marcus and I. I wanted to stay at home with him to smooth things over from the argument we had earlier that day.

After a brief fifteen minutes of hesitation, I got up and began to get ready.

While I dressed, I asked Marcus if we could talk about our disagreement in the morning when I got off. He agreed and went back to playing his video game.

Marcus and I had been together for nine and a half years. Things had been slowly taking a turn for the worst in our relationship. I experienced a lot of pain in our relationship, and within months, we stopped talking to each other, then the arguments increased.

A few weeks ago, Marcus and I had a pretty bad fight that ended in domestic violence. I packed what I could and left for a couple of hours. The tension between us became so intense I knew we were about to cut our losses and go our separate ways soon.

In no way was I mad about the idea of us parting ways. Marcus had become my best friend, and I genuinely believed we were better friends than lovers. We both knew our relationship was running its last course.

I told Marcus goodbye and headed out the door for work.

I clocked in to work with enough time to get the training room together for my new people. I gave the operators a crash course of what we did within The Warehouse (the name of the place where I work). Later that night, they transitioned to the production floor to start doing live orders. The night was going by quickly. The trainees picked up the information and were ready to work on their own, as I watched over their work.

The department I worked in produced customized items for specific brands or teams. We received the brand information from another department, and once it reached my department, we produced the finished product. Simple work.

As the group was settling into their job, I was able to monitor them from a different angle of the production floor as well as get materials for them to complete their orders. The night was going well, and I was ready to get it over with, to get home to Marcus.

It was almost break time when one of the newbies needed some extra materials. I quickly made my way to the department that housed the materials the operator needed.

This department was small. The area had eight employees working within it. The picking area consisted of one wall containing three hundred logos on both sides. I was looking for the materials I needed, and I happened to walk by one of the pickers. I didn't pay him any mind as I made my way around him. On my way back past him, he said, "Hey!"

I looked at him and said, "Hi."

Another trainee needed a logo by the time I made my way back in my area. I quickly turned around to make another run to the picking area. I pulled my phone out to adjust my music while I headed to the department.

The Warehouse had a no-phone policy other than listening to music, and you had to ask for approval to change music stations.

I quickly attempted to change my music when the picker who addressed me just minutes before said, "You know we can't be on our phones, right?"

I looked up at him, and I told him I was allowed to adjust my music. I said, "Matter of fact, I'm one of the people you have to come to, to get approval to turn your phone." I saw his phone on his picking cart, so I jokingly asked, "Are you approved to have that out?"

He looked at me, smiled, and then said, "Yes!"

I wanted to know who this guy was, but before I could say another word, he reached his hand out and said, "My name is Drew."

I smiled back at him while extending my hand back at his. "I'm Joss."

"Nice to meet you, Joss."

I smiled. "Likewise, Drew." I told him I had work to do and that I would speak to him the next time I came back through the area. He nodded his head and laughed as I walked by.

I went back to my area to continue training my new folks. The night was still going smooth, and there were no major issues with training. After about an hour or so from the last material run, I had to go back over to the picking area for materials again.

I made my way around the corner, and Drew was standing right there. He said, "I was wondering if I was going to see you again tonight."

I replied, "It's up to whether or not the operators needed materials or not."

"So, what if I wanted to talk to you, say, outside of work. How would I do that?"

While he talked, I pointed in the direction of my department. "While at work, you can catch me right over there. Outside of work, that's not going to happen."

He politely asked, "What if you just gave me your number so I can call you?"

"I don't give out my number, and I have a boyfriend."

"I'm involved with someone too. I just want your number to talk as friends."

I didn't think anything of it. I wrote my number in the palm of his hand and proceeded to my work area. It didn't take him long to call my phone. I activated my headphone microphone and said, "Hello."

"Hello, new friend. I'm on break, and I wanted to make sure you didn't give me a fake number."

I laughed. Drew instantly started telling me about himself. He came off as fun and friendly.

He said, "I'm from the Boro. I don't know anyone from this county. I couldn't find a job in the Boro, so I decided to try some places outside of the area. I lucked up and ended up here, at The Warehouse."

Drew made me laugh, making jokes about different situations he saw throughout the night. He had something funny to say about everything. I laughed at all his jokes and comments. I sounded like a schoolgirl the way he had me laughing and giggling.

I said, "You're hilarious, Drew."

He said, "I hope so. I do comedy shows outside of working a nine-to-five. I DJ on the side too."

Drew was thirty-three years old, the same age as me. He was close to six feet tall. His skin was caramel colored, not too dark and not too light. He was of muscular build with a temple-fade haircut. And from what I could tell, he knew how to dress. He was dressed like he was headed to a casual nightclub.

He had a cunning smile with a clean-cut goatee. He was nice to look at, resembling David Banner in some ways. His full name was Drew Johnson, but he liked to go by his initials, DJ, but I liked to call him Drew. He was an up-and-coming actor, entertainer, and DJ in his local area.

I loved Marcus, and I didn't plan for anything to come of Drew and I talking as friends. He said he was looking for a friend, and he liked to network through women.

Drew and I talked on the phone while on the production floor. I was making my conversations discreet because we weren't allowed on our phones, and I suspected Drew was doing the same, until my supervisor approached me telling me he needed to fire someone for being on their phone.

Drew was listening as my supervisor described him to me. I got scared. I assumed Drew was going to snitch and tell my supervisor he was on the phone with me. I thought I was about to lose my job as well. My supervisor headed over to the area where Drew was picking.

He said, "How does he know I'm on my phone? I've been working this whole time, and he wants to come and harass me for no reason. Don't hang up, Joss. No matter what."

I said, "Okay!"

I listened on the other end of the phone. I wanted to hear what was going on. But I felt bad for Drew. He was getting fired for talking to me on the phone, and there was nothing I could do. Drew was given the reason for his termination. I heard Drew say thank you and then some ruffling of papers.

He said, "Are you still there, Joss?"

Relieved he didn't snitch, I said, "Yeah, I'm here. Someone had to tell on you, Drew."

"Yeah, and I know who it was. But it's okay. She will get her due. I was just beginning to like this job, and now I'm on to the next one. I'll be all right though. I just don't want to go home to tell this woman I lost another job. I'm glad I got a gig this weekend."

Drew's tone turned sad. I felt bad for him. He said, "I gotta go. I'll be calling you sometime, Joss."

We said bye to each other, then we hung up.

Drew called the next morning. "Hey! I hope I'm not calling too early?"

I said, "Nah, my boyfriend just left for work. I have a few minutes to chat. Are you okay?"

"Yeah, I'm good. I'm really glad we met, and I hope you are serious about us being friends. I don't have any real friends outside of family, and I need a new friend in my life. And I hope she is you! I just came from my daughter's school, dropping off a change of clothes. She had an accident."

"Is your girlfriend her mom?"

He quickly said, "Nah, my daughter and her don't get along. My girlfriend has two daughters, and my daughter isn't her priority. She does for her sometimes, but she doesn't pay attention to my daughter like that."

"Why are you with someone that doesn't treat your kid like her own?"

I could tell something was wrong with their relationship by the way he said "this girl" last night and what he was telling me now. "Life is too short to be unhappy, Drew."

"You hit the nail on the coffin. I've been trying to get out of this relationship for years, but I don't seem to get very far. Our relationship was a mistake since we started, and she knows it too, but neither of us does anything about it. It's a relationship of convenience at this point."

"That's sad, Drew. It's also not healthy for your daughter."

He agreed, saying, "I know, I know."

Drew and I talked on the phone for a while longer. He always dreamed of being a DJ and an actor. He sent me pictures of him with different celebrities. He performed on the weekends at least once a month. He had a couple of friends that were in the acting business, and he was involved in a couple of projects that were going to get him to the big screen. He had his own UK following, where he held a high number of fans.

I could tell he was going to do big things. Talking to him was like a bit of fresh air. It felt good to talk to someone new outside my small circle of friends and family. Before we hung up, Drew promised to call me again.

Later that night, I took a nap before work. I was asleep on my stomach, and Marcus played his video game between my legs while I slept, occasionally using my butt as his pillow. He was playing a shooter game while online with his friends.

I was getting annoyed by the noise he was making. When he got up to use the bathroom, I took advantage of the moment to readjust myself in the bed. He sat back down and placed his head back on my butt. Suddenly, the room went silent, and he said, "I will never marry you."

"What did you say?"

Marcus shifted himself slightly toward me, turning his head toward me. "I will never marry you!"

I didn't know where the statement came from, but it was sudden and random, and with the way he repeated it, he wasn't playing. I rolled over, causing his head to fall to the mattress. I rearranged my pillow, and I fell back asleep. I didn't want to think about what he said; I had to work in a few hours.

My sleep was the same as any other night. When my alarm went off, Marcus was still playing his game. I got up and started preparing to leave the house. I kissed him goodbye and headed to work. I went to work like I did every night before, but as I pulled into the parking lot of my job, "I will never marry you" popped into my head.

I didn't know why Marcus felt the need to say those words to me at that moment, especially after we smoothed out our disagreement. With him coming right out he wasn't going to marry me, I knew I was wasting my time being with him. A feeling took over my body I couldn't describe. I remembered what I told Drew in our phone conversation the day before.

"Life is too short to be unhappy, Joss," I told myself.

I decided that night I would leave Marcus. When I got home the next morning, I reminded Marcus what he said to me the night before.

He said, "Joss, I said what I said. And I'm serious. You're a good woman, but I can't see myself settling down."

His words were all I needed to hear to confirm what I needed to do next. Within the week, my daughter and I moved in with my mother. My son stayed with his father. I didn't want to spend any more time in a deadbeat relationship that wasn't going anywhere.

I gave Marcus every piece of me. I helped him raise his daughter and help him get a house, but I wasn't good enough to marry. I had to let go of dead weight and make room for happiness.

Moving back in with my mom wasn't a step forward for me, but it was a step I needed to move forward from the situation I was in with Marcus. I came up with a plan to advance in life, for me and my kids.

Three weeks later, I saw Marcus in the store with another woman. He had his daughter with him, the daughter I helped raise. He didn't bring just anyone around his daughter, so I knew he intended to keep the woman around.

It was hard walking away from our relationship, and I cried some nights trying to figure out how I was going to live without him.

But after seeing him in the store with another woman so quickly after we separated, I felt closure. I felt even more weight lifted off my shoulders, not having to worry about how he was getting along without me.

Marcus was no longer mine, and the sooner I got it through my head, I was going to be okay. I didn't intend to go back to him. He knew it when he looked up at me and then lowered his head in shame as I walked by them in the store. His daughter, with her head lowered too, didn't say a word to me either.

A week later, while sitting in my car getting ready to go in for the night shift, I received a text message from my supervisor, Johnny. I assumed he was texting about the new hires we were getting tonight.

He said, "Heads up. One of the new hires is the guy I just walked out of here about a month ago for being on his phone. Don't expect too much from that one."

I asked, "How is that even possible for him to be back if we fired him?"

I knew exactly who my supervisor was talking about. I sat up in my seat. I looked in the rearview mirror to check my face for anything that shouldn't be there. I patted my hair, stepped out of the car, adjusted my clothes, and I walked into the building. I couldn't wait to see Drew.

Drew greeted me with a warm tight hug as soon as I walked through the security door. He looked better than I remembered. He smelled good, and he was excited to see me.

Excited, I said, "Hey, Drew! How are you back here again?"

"I had to come back. I had to come back to see you."

"Me? Why me?"

"We can talk about that later. But long story short, I came in the first time through a job placement company, but this time I got hired by The Warehouse through the door. I officially work here. With you, my friend."

I was excited to have a male friend to talk to again. I knew he was just coming back, and a lot had changed for me in the past month. I had plenty to update Drew on. Having him in my area this time meant I could keep a better eye on him so he didn't get fired this time around.

We talked nonstop. He told me he broke up with the girlfriend, and he was doing better with his DJ gigs. He was excited to tell me the steps he was making toward being happy. He took my advice and made life better for him and his daughter.

I updated Drew on my current relationship status. I told him I moved in with my mother, and everything I went through was worth it.

I didn't get much work done because every chance I could, I was cutting up with Drew. I felt attached to Drew, and I enjoyed being in his presence.

The next night, Drew and I took our breaks together so we could talk some more. We hopped in my car and drove around the building. We didn't want folks knowing we were breaking together. When we got back to the parking lot after the first break, we sat in the car for a second before going inside.

He said, "Can I kiss you?"

I turned my head toward him, surprised he was coming on to me. I smiled and laughed at the same time. "Now isn't the time, Drew. Maybe later when we aren't in the parking lot. Why don't we talk about it at lunch?"

"All right, I'm going to hold you to lunch later. I can't wait to taste your pretty little lips."

I punched him on the arm, and we went back inside the building.

Lunch came quickly, and I was nervous. I hadn't kissed another man in over ten years. I was confident in myself and my skills, but I was nervous considering any kind of a relationship with another man, let alone kissing one.

All the women at the job were interested in Drew. He was one of The Warehouse's eye candy. But I was the one holding his attention. I didn't know if I was ready, but I wasn't going to turn him down. I needed to get ready for my kiss with Drew.

We didn't talk about kissing while we walked to my car. I hoped he had forgotten about it. When we finished buckling our seat belts, Drew leaned closer to me and said, "I can't wait to kiss those lips."

I smiled.

We had a forty-five-minute lunch break. We rode around to keep folks from watching what we were doing.

I said, "I don't want to drive around the whole break. We needed to find somewhere to park and talk."

I thought about going to my cousin Roxxane's house, which was less than a mile from the job, but I didn't want her to know or see Drew just yet. I knew my mom was at work because she worked for The Warehouse too. We headed over to my mom's house since she lived three minutes down the road. I pulled into her driveway and cut the car off. I left the music playing on low.

I pushed my seat back. I wanted to have room to turn and face Drew. I sat back into the seat to relax. Drew grabbed my hand. He said, "Can I kiss you now?"

I made the first move, going straight for the kiss. I needed to get over my nervousness. I wanted to show him kissing was my secret weapon. Our lips met, and I felt the heat from his lips. We kiss slow and soft. I sucked his bottom lip as he lightly sucked on my top lip. Kissing him sent vibes throughout my body. I pushed him away to regain myself.

He looked at me seductively from the passenger seat. His body language told me he wanted me. He leaned back in to continue kissing me. Placing his hand between my legs, he rubbed up and down on my jeans, hard enough for me to feel the pressure on my yoni. The moisture came alive between my legs. And we continued to kiss. Drew grabbed on my breast, just how I liked it, and it turned me on even more.

He said, "Can I undo your jeans?"

I hesitated for a short second, then I unbuttoned my pants myself. Drew's excitement increased. He kissed me again as his hand slid down my pants and he entered me with his fingers. I had to stop kissing him to catch my break. His fingers felt good inside of me. He was lighting the flame that lived inside of me, and it was getting hot inside the car.

I stopped him to open the car door. The light on the inside of the car came on, and I could see Drew was very excited by the look of his jeans. I touched it, softly rubbing his member outside of his pants. "Do you have a condom?"

He replied, "Yup."

Seductively I said, "Come get it while it's hot."

Drew got out of the car and walked over to my side of the car. I turned my body to face him. I lifted each leg as he helped me out of my pants. He kissed each thigh gently. Anxiously waiting for what was coming next, I positioned my feet on the car's doorstep, laid back, and waited for him to take me.

He lowered his body and positioned himself on top of me. We were face-to-face with each other. He lowered his head to kiss me. He lifted my shirt, softly kissing my breast. His lips met my lips again, and I felt him slowly enter me. He watched every twitch my face made as he filled me. Once, he was completely inside of me, I felt his body relax. He was amazed at the heat my yoni gave off.

Drew shifted, finding his position. He thrusted inside of me slow and hard. Short bursts, with deep impacts. It sent trembles through my body. He pulled out, slowly caressing my clit with his member, teasing it, teasing me. The sex he was giving me sent me somewhere else. My body wanted to shake, but it didn't know what it wanted to do. He lifted my leg slightly, causing him to gain another inch inside of me. I felt his growth, and he could tell by the moans I softly let out. I called his name as he powered in and out of me, treating me to a feeling I had never felt before.

I was in my mother's driveway at three in the morning on my lunch break, having the hottest spontaneous sex I had ever had in my life. I didn't care about work. All that mattered was that moment, how my body was feeling, how he was grinding, how I was moaning. How each thrust made me feel something different.

We were five minutes late from lunch, and neither of us cared. We laughed about the whole experience.

As he headed to his workstation, he said, "You felt wonderful, Joss."

I went to my desk with so many thoughts rushed through my head. The after-experience embarrassment set in. Even though I knew the experience was out of this world, I thought maybe he wasn't going to want to talk to me anymore because he thought I might be easy. I wasn't easy; I just wanted the release.

My thoughts were running away from me. I started having flash-backs to what he did to me in the car a few minutes ago. I inhaled as if I was right back in that moment.

That morning, while Drew drove home, we talked about what we did. He told me he never did anything like that before, and I told him I never had sex in a car before then. Before hanging up the phone, he told me I was special.

Things progressed between Drew and I quickly. I told my supervisor about us just in case someone said they saw us together. I didn't know what kind of position being with Drew was going to put me in, but I was willing to see. We agreed if either of our jobs were on the line because of our relationship, then he would leave The Warehouse instead of me.

I was officially going to introduce Drew to my mother and my older brother. They both worked at The Warehouse so they already knew about him, but they weren't formally introduced to him. They liked him the moment they were introduced. My mother liked him so much she made him breakfast the first day he came over to the house.

Drew came to my mother's house every morning before going home. Sometimes my mother would cook breakfast for us, and some-times we would just sleep. Other times Drew and my brother would play video games, or we would watch a movie. I was thirty-three years old, and I had to keep the door to my bedroom open because that was the only way my mother would allow Drew in my room. I didn't mind; it was her house, her rules.

I didn't know if we were in a relationship or not, but we talked and spent time together every day. Working at the same job helped make it possible. We had sex a couple of times since the first hookup, but we never spent the weekend together and we never went on dates.

\*\*\*\*\*

My brother pressured me into creating a social media page in order to see pictures of my new niece. I didn't want any other social media accounts except for the Gram, but I was a new auntie, and my brother wanted to share my niece's milestones with me on the book. I didn't have any friends on my page, because I didn't intend to use the page other than to see pictures of my niece.

I started getting messages in my inbox within days of creating my page. Folks at my job told me it was normal for people to send random messages to your inbox. One day a random guy from Florida hit my inbox. He asked me if I was single, and without thinking about it, I replied, telling him I was single by choice. I didn't know what Drew and I were. I knew we weren't fully committed because neither of us said anything to the other about a relationship.

One night, Drew and I had been texting back and forth. He wanted me to come over to his workstation for a second when I had a chance.

Minutes later, I was happily strolling into his work area. He handed me my first love letter of the night. We started writing each other love letters to keep from texting at work; we sent emails as well to each other to keep all lines of communication open.

As I was about to walk away, Drew stopped me. "Can I use your phone to listen to music? Mine is about to go dead soon. You're not going to be able to listen to music tonight anyways."

"You can use my phone. Music will probably be the only thing that can help you get those numbers up anyways."

I unlocked the phone screen then handed the phone to Drew along with my headphones. I needed to get back to my side of the area to check on a machine. I gave him everything he needed to access my phone.

Before next break, Drew walked over to me with my phone in his hand. He placed the phone in my hand. Then he walked away.

He appeared to be mad about something. I was confused. I didn't understand why he was mad if he was, in fact, mad.

We took our breaks together, but Drew walked away so fast he acted as if he didn't want to be bothered this break. I unraveled the earbuds from around my phone to text him and to find out what was going on with him.

Before I could start texting, Drew was already walking toward me. His face looked noticeably mad. I watched him as he got closer to me. When he got close enough to whisper low enough for me to hear, he said, "I don't want to talk to you ever again." Then he walked away.

My mind did a double take. I knew I heard him correctly. I didn't know why he said what he said, but I needed to find out. I wanted to know why he said what he said. In the middle of my thoughts, my supervisor yelled for me to come help him with a machine. I wanted to go talk to Drew, but I had a job to do. I texted him instead.

I asked, "What's wrong, Drew? Did something happen? I can't make it over to you at this moment, but please text me back."

He never texted me back.

I spent the longest fifteen minutes trying to get the machine I was working on up and running. As soon as everything with the machine cleared, I walked over to the area where Drew was working. He lowered his head and proceeded to work, ignoring me as I approached. His actions had me worried. I didn't know what was going on, but Drew was obviously pissed.

I asked, "What's going on, Drew? Why are you angry?"

He quickly said, "You tell me, Joss!"

"What are you talking about, Drew? I don't know what you are talking about."

With an attitude, he replied, "I went through your phone and I saw your text to that guy, telling him you were single by choice! So, you're single, Joss?"

Shocked by his comment, I said, "Oh, wow, you're mad about that? I don't know that man. He asked me a question, and I answered. There was nothing behind the message at all. We never made anything clear about what 'we' are."

He said, "Joss! Stop fronting on me. I read the message. You told the guy you were single. You told him in your own words. It seemed like you were trying to lead him on. I'm not going to get hurt by another woman, so I'd rather leave you alone than go through that pain again."

I said, "I'm telling you, Drew, there is nothing to that message. I don't want that guy. I want us officially to be together more than anything else."

He said, "What do you mean officially? You have me officially. I already come to your house every morning, and everyone in this building knows we're together. How much more official do you want to be, Joss?"

I said, "Drew, you act like we sat down and said we were in a relationship. I'm not going to assume anything, no matter how much I want it to be true."

He immediately said, "Joss, I need to get to work. I'll see you around."

I said, "So, you're telling me you are done with whatever we have for no reason?"

Drew said "Yup!"

He proceeded to put his earbuds in his ear while getting back to work. I felt humiliated for some reason. I still had a whole day at work to hold my feelings in. I went back to my work area feeling like I wasted my time with Drew.

Before the shift ended, Drew sent me a text message asking if we could meet up somewhere to talk about the situation. I told him meeting up would be a good idea. We met at a local park right after work. When we got to the park, Drew told me how he felt about the message. "Joss, I feel like you told that man you were single because you want to be single. I think because you just got out of a long relationship, you want to spread your wings to other men. I don't want to be the person standing in the way of you trying to find your happiness with someone else."

"You're thinking way too hard about one simple message. I told the guy I was single by choice, meaning I'm single because I want to be. I didn't think I was lying to him because we never sat down and

25

talked about what we were. Some guys don't do titles. And I was not going to assume I was in a relationship, and I'm not."

"I need to think about what we can be going forward. I don't want you going around telling people you are single by choice, letting them think they might have a chance with you. I'll let you know on Monday how I feel."

Drew told me my actions hurt him. He said what I did, painted a different picture of me, and he needed to think about whether or not he really wanted to be in a relationship with me. It was Friday morning, and that meant I had the weekend to think about Drew and if we had a relationship or not.

I didn't hear from Drew all weekend. Sunday night, at work, Drew was already parked next to my normal parking spot. I didn't know if I should approach him or if I should wait for him to speak to me. All weekend he had me feeling some kind of way. I kept trying to figure out why he took a simple comment so far out of proportion. His behavior didn't seem normal.

I questioned everything I felt for Drew. I didn't realize I cared for him as much as I did. I didn't think my response was inappropriate or out of the way. I knew I did nothing wrong, but Drew had me feeling like I committed the worse sin ever.

It mattered to me if Drew wanted to have a relationship with me, but I told myself I wasn't going to get bent out of shape if he didn't want to be with me. And after my relationship with Marcus, I wasn't sure I wanted to be in a relationship myself.

Drew's car door slammed shut. I looked up to see him cross over to my side of the car. He said, "Hey, beautiful."

"Hey to you too. You seem extra chipper, seeing how we left things at the park on Friday. I take it you had a good weekend. I didn't have a good weekend. I cried about you this weekend, like I was a kid. You called me out on something you took the wrong way, and then when time came to put a title on our relationship, you tell me you need to think about it over the weekend, like I'm some option. No, sir, that's not me. I'm no one's option."

He said, "Joss! That's why I came over here. I want to be in a relationship with you. I'd be stupid to let a woman like you walk out of my life. Over the weekend, I realized I needed you in my life. The weekend was rough for me too, baby. I'm sorry for making you feel like I did. And I didn't mean to not call you either. Things got busy for me, and I simply forgot. I wanted to tell you in person I love you and I want to be in your life as your man but nothing less than a friend."

At that moment, Drew didn't realize he made me the happiest woman in the world. I said, "Yes," as if he just asked me to marry him. I was ready for everything our relationship could be.

As time went on, Drew's attitude was changing and not for the better. Every week we were arguing over something stupid. And with each argument, it meant less communication from him. Drew would act like I always had an attitude, and then he would avoid me afterward. Sometimes for hours. Sometimes even days.

Drew had a way of winning me over with his sob stories. He had a notion that life was bound to always be against him because he struggled for everything in life. He never knew his father, his mother abused him, and his sister didn't like him. His relationship with his daughter's mother was traumatic for him and his daughter. I listened to his stories, and I empathized with him. His burdens ran deep.

I made excuses for his behavior and attitude. I chopped most of his behavior up to him not having someone to have his back. I knew he was the kind of person that needed reassurance in life. I wanted to be that something different for him. I didn't think his attitude was worth me leaving. His working and his lack of communication was another story.

Red flags started arising when he started disappearing on me. I knew his career choice involved serious trust. Knowing he was in the clubs every weekend, hanging around pretty women, it wasn't easy for me to think positive. Drew was attractive, and I knew women tried to get with him constantly. I wanted to trust him, and I didn't have trouble trusting him until he proved otherwise.

I accepted the good with the bad in our relationship. When we were together, things were good. I took the quality over the quantity. I decided, in time, everything else could be worked on.

A typical morning after work for Drew and I would always consist of breakfast. After breakfast, Drew and I would chill, laugh, and talk. He would stay at the house for a different amount of time, but he was always gone by noon.

He would always promise me a weekend together, sometimes telling me he would come right back after he handled whatever business he had going on for that day. Drew would leave me on Friday, and I wouldn't see him again until Sunday night a few hours before work.

My hopes for spending the weekend with Drew quickly died. I made the most of the time he gave our relationship and the time frame we had to make it possible. We didn't hesitate to get it in when it came time to get busy. We were good in the pleasure department.

Drew would get anxious some morning at my mom's house, wanting sex, but out of respect for her home, we tried not to be sexual there. Every chance he could, he was trying to seduce me. Drew and I would make love wherever we could. That would sometimes mean in the car, at the park, or at work in the parking lot. Sex with Drew was always spontaneous. He kept me with a spontaneous bag, which included condoms, lotions, wipes, and a blanket. I was ready for him at any time and any place.

Drew had a healthy sexual appetite. He was ready to go at any time. I never had any doubt he desired me. Every time he was near me, he couldn't keep his hands off me. His excitement for me, indescribable. When my body had an itch (no matter where it was), he was willing to scratch it. He was a passionate lover, taking his time when he needed to. He was spontaneous in where he gave his loving, and he didn't care where that happened to be. If he wanted it at that moment, he went for it. He aimed to please, and I was always satisfied.

Everything was going well for us until a couple of weeks later. Drew started short-texting me, which wasn't normal for him.

On Friday, after he would leave me, he would text me back-to-back, and then instantly he would stop. He would reply hours later, if he texted back at all. Drew would go hours without texting. I would call his phone nonstop sometimes, sometimes getting lucky and other times I'd get his voicemail. Sunday nights before work, when he pulled in my mother's driveway, he knew I wasn't a happy camper.

He had an excuse for why he couldn't communicate every weekend. It became normal on Fridays to say goodbye until Sunday. He would get angry with me for saying until Monday, but we both knew it was the truth.

He'd say I was jealous of his work as an entertainer and should always expect the unexpected when it comes to his job.

Sometimes I cared what he said, and other times all I could think about was always being alone on the weekend. I was tired of being alone on the weekend when I had a man to go out with.

I made plans for Drew and I every weekend. I knew Drew would more than likely have a DJ gig, but it didn't stop me from trying. Some weekends Drew would encourage me to make plans for us. Most of those weekends I'd end my night with a wine cooler and a dry-ass phone because Drew either got too busy to call or cancel or some outlandish bullshit accident happened to him.

Every Sunday night we'd end up arguing about whatever bullshit lie he came up with. Sometimes by midshift, I didn't know if Drew and I were still together or if we were broken up for the umpteenth time. Drew was the one always breaking us up, always reading too much into a comment or a gesture. He had a way of throwing everything back at me. He told me I was selfish because I wanted too much attention from him when he was just trying to get his career started. I was the one that wasn't being patient or understanding of his career.

My thirty-fourth birthday was approaching, and I was excited. I was officially free from my ex Marcus, and I was feeling my independence. And I was on my way to a promotion on my job. My son was in college, and my daughter was blossoming into a beautiful young queen. Drew was still around. And my world felt complete.

To celebrate my new milestone, I wanted to throw myself a tiki-themed party. I wanted tikis illuminating the yard, with a bunch of tents with different themes happening inside each of them. I planned to ask Drew to be the DJ for the party.

With his busy schedule, I wanted to make sure to plan my party around a time I knew he would possibly be free. I didn't want a gig or one of his shows to fall on the same day as my party. I wanted him present for the party, and I was going to make sure of it.

I texted him and asked, "What do you have planned for mid-April [which was almost two months away]? Hopefully you're free."

Drew said, "Nothing, I don't think. Are you up to something, Joss?"

Excited, I said, "It's good to hear you will be free. I want to hire you to do something for me. Are you down for the task, Mr. Johnson? I don't think I should have to pay you, but I'm sure we can work something out."

"Yes, baby, anything for you, as long as I'm not booked. You know I need every booking I can get."

"I'm sure you will be free. I'm asking you now so you don't have an excuse later. I'm going to plan it around you to make sure you are free and available to spend my whole birthday weekend with me. That's what I want from you for my birthday, Drew. A whole weekend together, just you and me. No car issues, no kids, no gigs, or shows, nothing but us."

"Okay, Joss, I can do that!"

I told him the date and what I needed him to do. I didn't plan on paying Drew money for his services, but I planned to give him something he could feel. I told him I was going to make hotel reservations for us that weekend as well. I wanted everything to be perfect.

I knew if I got Drew away from the area, especially in my car, he wouldn't have any way to get back to a so-called emergency with his daughter or his mother. They were a part of some of the excuses he gave each time he disappeared or couldn't show up to something.

The party came and went it off without a hitch. I received my first lap dance from my friend Bella, and it was amazing. Friends I hadn't seen in years while with Marcus came out to celebrate with me. I enjoyed the vibes from the whole night, and I was ready to get to the hotel to get my birthday sex on and poppin'.

Despite my suggestions to drive one vehicle, Drew drove his car anyways. Not surprisingly, the following morning, he had to leave me to get his daughter because she supposedly pushed his mother. His mother left several messages telling him to come get his daughter.

He promised me he was going to come back after he worked everything out. I made him swear to return to me, and he did. It was Saturday morning, and we still had until Sunday at the hotel. Drew promised to go handle his daughter and return to the hotel to be with me.

He called me an hour and a half later. "The car has been over-heating, and I'm stuck in the Boro, baby. I don't think I'm going to make it back to you, but I'm going to try. I'm sorry, baby. Good thing is, I know what's wrong with it. The piece is like a hundred and twenty dollars, and I don't have that right now. I got someone that can fix it, but I don't have the money to pay him until payday. I'm sorry, I messed up your birthday."

I felt bad about his car, but I was upset because I knew there was going to be some reason he wouldn't be able to spend time with me like I desired. I wanted to cry. I refused to be unhappy on my birthday, and I didn't want to spend the nights at the hotel alone on my birthday weekend. I wanted him with me.

I said, "I'll give you the money, Drew! Give me a minute and I'll get it sent over to you within the hour. I want you here with me, and the only way that can happen is if your car is working. It's still early. Maybe you can get it done and make your way back to me."

"Baby, I love you! You're the freakin' best, and I can't wait to get back to you to show you how much I appreciate you. I'm going to make all this up to you, I promise."

I had the money sent over to him in less than thirty minutes. While I was out, I grabbed us some dinner for later to ensure we didn't have to leave the room. I told Drew to call me as soon as the car was fixed so I'd know when to expect him. I knew that meant he should be in my arms no later than eight o'clock tonight.

I returned to the room to relax. I was still tired from the night before, so a nap was on the agenda before Drew returned. I set an alarm to make sure I was up around the time Drew should be calling. I also wanted enough time to prepare myself for Drew's return.

When my alarm went off, I realized Drew hadn't texted. I called and texted him nonstop. Despite all the calls and texts to Drew's phone, I didn't get a response. I made the most of the night trying not to think of Drew's disappointment.

When he finally called, it was eleven o'clock that night. He said, "I still haven't gotten the car fixed."

I said, "It's all good. I knew you weren't going to come back when you didn't answer my calls. I already packed up the room, and I'm leaving. I'm not going to be alone on my birthday weekend. I'm heading to Roxanne's house."

When I told Drew my plans, he got upset. "Man, Joss, you don't ever have faith in me. I don't want you to leave the room because I might get back to you. And you don't need to be at her house drinking."

"You don't have the authority to tell me what I could and shouldn't do. I'm over your shit and your so-called emergencies. I'll see you Sunday night." I hung up the phone.

Drew and I didn't speak the rest of the weekend. I knew if I texted him, I would be disappointed. He didn't message or call me either, and he was fine playing the MIA game.

When I got to work on Sunday, I was surprised to see Drew's name on the callout list. I texted him immediately. "Are you okay? I'm at work and you're not here, and you didn't text me to let me know you weren't coming in."

To my surprise, Drew texted me right back just as quickly as I could hit Send on my second message. "I'm about to call you!"

A few seconds later, he was calling my phone. "Hey, I couldn't come to work because the car is out of gas. When I got the car out of the shop, I went to do a gig, and the people stiffed me. I needed the money for my gas tank. They only paid me forty damn dollars for three hours of DJing. You don't understand, I needed that money. I knew you were going to call as soon as you learned I wasn't coming to work. I may be out until Wednesday if I don't get some gas money."

While he talked, I felt sorry for him. Drew couldn't afford to be out of work, especially not until Wednesday. Selfishly, I wanted to see him because I hadn't seen him since Saturday morning when he left me hanging. I wanted to be the bigger person, and I wanted some of his loving.

"I'll fill your tank up if you can get to me tomorrow before work."

Drew's tone turned to excitement. He said, "I'll see you early tomorrow so we can spend some time together before work."

I knew that meant we were going to get some action in before our shift. I realized after we hung up the phone I had given Drew half of my birthday money. I was giving Drew money every pay week. If it wasn't a piece for his DJ equipment, it was a high-dollar emergency. He always offered to pay me back, but I never saw a dime.

Drew broke up with me more times than I could count. It was always around the start of the weekend. He dedicated a song to me every time he screwed up, and his favorite song to send was "I only want what's Best for You" by Trey Songz. The song mostly followed a breakup to imply he wasn't good enough for me and I deserved better. Almost every weekend I was single. Or at least it felt that way.

Drew passed out one night at work. Since everyone knew we were dating at this post, they came to get me in my department to help with him. I was scared because I didn't know what was going on with him. He didn't tell me he wasn't feeling well that day.

My supervisor called the ambulance, and he was taken to the hospital. I followed behind the ambulance in my car.

At this point in our relationship, almost a year and a half in, I had not once been introduced to a family member or a friend. I've had people say hi to me over the phone, but I never physically met anyone that knew Drew. He mentioned places he frequented and a couple of street names some family members resided on. I also knew he stayed with his mother sometimes, but I didn't know exactly where he stayed because I never been to his house. I didn't know anyone to call if I needed to call someone for him.

During intake, the nurse asked Drew a question about where he lived. He asked me to hand the nurse his ID out of his wallet. While handing the nurse his license, I glanced at it. I read the address on it and memorized it. When the nurse handed it back to me, I put it back into his wallet but not before I glanced at it again to make sure

I got the address completely right in my head. Drew was really sick, and he didn't notice anything.

I was relieved to have an address just in case something happened, but I noticed it wasn't the address to his mother's house. I put the address in my phone under his contact information, along with the other address he told me he lived at.

After Drew's medical scare, it seemed he realized that I was down for him. He became more aware of his lack of communication. He started spending every Wednesday with me with no time limits. He didn't rush to leave the house by noon. He stayed with me and dedicated time to us.

He texted me more than he ever did before. I was loving it all. Drew's trip to the hospital was a much-needed blessing in disguise. He still wasn't spending weekends with me, but he was calling during gigs when he had a chance.

In November, I decided to treat my mom to a concert with a couple of her favorite R&B artists performing. I wanted the night to be special, so I invited Drew. The event was on a Friday night, so it was a stretch catching him free. He surprised me by accepting the invite. He was free until 11:00 p.m. that night of the concert. He had to be at the club to set up for the night. I took what I could get.

The concert started at 6:00 p.m. I planned for us all to go to dinner and then the concert. I previously rented a room for myself with hopes after the night's plans, Drew would come back to the room with me to celebrate.

The day of the concert, my mom, Drew, and I went to dinner to waste time before the concert. We were excited for the concert, my mother especially. She was about to see Joe and Kem on the same night. We ate our food then sat around talking for a few minutes to buy us time before the concert.

I caught our server's attention to ask her for a favor. I secretly pulled a ring box from out of my pocket without Drew noticing. I handed it to the server and asked her could she bring it back on a dessert tray for me. She got excited and hopped off toward the kitchen. A few short minutes later, she arrived back at the table with the box on a plate. She stood closer to Drew's side of the table.

I looked at Drew and then the box, drawing his attention to the box. His eyes widened as he looked at me with his mouth open. I grabbed both of his hands and proceeded to ask him to marry me from across the table. We had an audience of customers, and my mother kept saying yes repeatedly for him.

He said, "Yes, Joss, I will marry you!"

Everyone clapped while Drew got up to kiss me. Everything at that moment felt perfect. And we still had a concert and a hotel room to get to.

The concert was beautiful. Our seats were right in front of the stage. I wished Kem or Joe would have invited couples on the stage, like Keith Sweat did at his concert, so we could have had the chance to announce our engagement in front of the crowd. I was satisfied with the night. I was newly engaged, and my mother got a chance to hold Joe's hand to the point he desperately started shaking her off while calling for security.

The night was perfect. And to top it off, Drew came back to the room with me. He had a couple of hours before he had to be at the club, and he spent those couple of hours with me.

When we got back to the room, I handed Drew a letter my daughter wrote for him. She and Drew got along like father and daughter. They even swapped sneakers from time to time because they were both sneaker heads. She wanted to be a part of the proposal, so she wrote Drew a letter asking him to be her stepdad. My daughter was the only person that knew I was going to propose to Drew that night. He called her after reading her letter and told her he would gladly take the title of being her stepfather.

After the phone call, Drew made his way over to me. He said, "I can't believe we are engaged, baby! Tonight was magical. And you proposing to me made it one of the best days of my life."

Deep down, I knew if Drew and I were married, everything else we were dealing with could easily be worked out. I wanted to be something good in his life. I wanted to help make his life happier by agreeing to be there for him, completely.

Drew kissed my lip, my neck, and then my breast. His hardness stood at attention, reaching out for my yoni. He kissed and touched me all over. I slowly raise my leg to place my foot on the bed. I wanted him to take me while we stood. I want him inside of me more than ever. I closed my eyes, desperately wanting him to take me. The feeling of him sliding his fingers inside of me took my breath away. My wetness soaked his fingers as he slowly moved them in and out of me.

He had sensations running through my body that made me exhale with each of his motions. I wanted to cum. I wanted to show him how much I loved him. I wanted to give him me.

Drew removed his fingers and turned me around toward the hotel mattress. His hands slowly glided from the base of my neck, down my spine to my lower back. His hands massaged my body. He wanted me to ask for it; he wanted to tease me until I couldn't take it anymore. He caressed and touched on my body until I gave in, telling him to make love to me.

Drew grabbed my hip and slowly entered my heat. He made love to me like no other time. He felt different, tasted different, even moved different. I was glad I was going to be able to have this feeling for the rest of my life. He was not just my boyfriend anymore; he was my fiancé, soon to be my husband.

The couple of hours we had came and went quickly. Drew prepared to leave me for his gig. I didn't want him to leave. I didn't want the night to end. I wanted us to keep celebrating our engagement.

"I'll be back, Joss. I promise this time. I'm not going to let this night end on a bad note. I want us to remember this night forever. I know you probably don't have any hope that I will return, but I'm going to show you."

Drew kissed me on the forehead then grabbed one of the hotel keys, and he walked out the door. I convinced myself to not call or text him while he was gone. I was going to dwell on the good of the day. If he came back, it would be a surprise for me.

Drew was walking back into the hotel room around four in the morning. My heart completely sank. I was surprised he came back. I knew he really loved me. And him coming back like he promised proved that.

Drew undressed. He jumped into bed behind me, and he massaged me with his hands until he was ready to pick up where he left off before he had to go to work.

He was up promptly the next morning at 8:00 a.m. It was Saturday morning, and I knew he had rehearsal for a play he was in at 9:00 a.m. I was glad he came back like he said. I wasn't going to be greedy and make him promise to come back. I wanted him to come back on his own.

*****

Drew never spent the holidays with me. My family is close-knit, so we were always getting together to do something to celebrate anything. We always had family functions, and a lot of them were out of town. Drew could never come. On occasion we would have a party in town, and he would promise to come or to make an appearance. Each time he would have a gig or an excuse. He'd call or text to say he would be late, but he would never show. It took longer than it should have for my family to be introduced to him.

My family was having Christmas dinner at my mom's house one year. Drew was invited to come through with the music as well as to finally meet my family members. I wasn't too hopeful that he would show, but he came first thing that morning to help get the house decorated and ready for guests. My mother and I were both shocked by his presence. My mom was more excited than me. He had a gig for Thirsty Thursday at the club that night, so he wasn't going to be able to stay the whole dinner.

Since the morning after the concert until a few days before Christmas, Drew went back to his old ways. He still went MIA on the weekends, and he was constantly breaking up with me for no reason at all. Sometimes he would give me the ring back, or I'd catch him not wearing it. There were times I didn't know where we stood as far as a couple or if we were still engaged. The ups and downs in his behavior had me taking things day by day.

With everything that led up until now I didn't expect much from Drew. I didn't tell anyone how much crap Drew was putting me through emotionally but my cousin Roxanne. He was making me look foolish, but I prayed for things to get better. My love for him was causing me to turn a blind eye to his actions. I had hopes that he was going to get better. I saw many signs of things not adding up right, but I chose to ignore them. Roxanne tried to help open my eyes as well, but she knew I loved him, and it didn't matter what she had said.

I never thought he was with other women, but he loved what he did as a DJ. It took trust and understanding. I believed Drew had something serious going on with him, and he was desperately holding it deep inside. It was time for me to get down to the bottom of his behavior. With him showing up early for Christmas dinner, he had me wondering if he was trying to show me he wanted to get married. He knew he had to do better.

Drew was introduced to all my family members, and the evening progressed nicely. They accepted him as my fiancé and as a new member of our family. I took the opportunity as another way to solidify our relationship. I didn't want to think he had anything to hide, and I wanted to believe we were eventually going to get married. He stood in front of my family praising our engagement. He invited everyone at the party to our soon-to-be destination wedding on a tropical island—plans he and I never made. Shortly afterward, he was heading out to his DJ gig.

*****

When I needed time away from my mother's house, I would get a hotel room downtown. On occasion, Drew would show up at the room, promising to spend the weekend with me. I knew otherwise. He wasn't going to have the opportunity to stay, or he was going to be late. Sometimes he would show up late, and other times he'd only stay for a couple of hours, or he never showed at all.

One random weekend, I got a room. I invited my fiancé to join me. He promised he would come visit, but the night crept on by and there was no sign of Drew. My calls went straight to voicemail, and I was felt like I was being ignored again. I told myself I was going to enjoy my weekend, so I decided not to get wrapped up in whether Drew was coming to the room or not.

Around six in the morning, I heard a knock on the hotel room door. I assumed it was Drew, so I got up to answer it. He stepped in the room with no concern; he was a day late, and he never bothered to let me know if he was coming or not. He started taking off his clothes while talking.

He said, "Were you sleep?"

I stood there watching him undress. "I don't have time for your stupid questions this early in the morning, Drew. I was up all night waiting for you to answer my calls. You're a day late, and I'm sick of you standing me up."

He gave me another excuse for why he was late. I listened as we got into bed.

"I don't ever mean to hurt you, Joss. I just get caught up trying to get my career off the ground, and I'd rather sacrifice now than later. Over time I'll be able to take you to Maui [both of our dream vacation spot]. Things are going to get better, and I just need for you to be patient."

Drew made love to me that morning before falling asleep. He was out like a light. I was tired of his behavior and of his excuses and possible lies. The only way I was going to find out what Drew had going on was through his phone.

Something about Drew's actions wasn't adding up for me. I had to get to the bottom of it all. There was no way he had so much going on after all these years and he couldn't spend one damn weekend with me. Something didn't sit right with me, and the only way I was going to find out was by going through his phone. I was tired of his excuses. He was hiding something from me, and I was going to be uneasy about our future until I found out what it was.

While Drew slept, I eased out of the bed. When he came into the room, I watched him and his every move. I saw where he hid his pants after he took them off. I saw where he placed his car keys. I quietly checked each of his pant pockets. My heart sank as I couldn't find his phone. He never went anywhere without his phone. He always had his phone, and I recently gave him the money for his current phone, so I knew it was around somewhere.

I grabbed the keys to his car and quietly left the room to check his car for his phone. I didn't care if he got up after I walked out of the room. I was on a mission, and because he had his phone in the car, it intensified my need to get to his phone. I was getting anxious knowing he might have purposely tried to hide his phone in his car to keep me from finding him out.

To my surprise, the phone was in the armrest of his car. I grabbed the phone, and I walked to the driver's side of my car for cover. I felt myself lose my breath. The anxiety of possibly finding something out was making me nervous and nauseous. I prayed he wasn't playing me. I prayed everything he told me over the past couple of years was the truth.

No sooner than I unlocked his phone and clicked on his messages, the door to the hotel room opened and Drew's head emerged from the door. I didn't know what to do. The only thing I saw in the instant I had his phone was a message associated with a photo from someone named Juicy. The picture was of a set of breasts. I placed the phone behind me in my shorts, nervously playing everything off, telling Drew I needed some air.

In the room, I couldn't sit still. The little bit of info I saw had me anxious for answers. I couldn't take it anymore. I grabbed the phone from my shorts, throwing it on the bed next to him. "Who's Juicy Drew? And why is she sending you pictures of her breasts?"

"What the fuck, Joss? Why do you have my phone? I can't believe you have stooped this low as to go through my phone, Joss."

"Hold up! You're not about to turn this back on me. You're hiding something, Drew, and I know it. And I didn't go through your phone. You came outside before I had a chance to, but I saw enough. Is there something you need to tell me? Who is Juicy, and why is she sending you pictures of her breasts?"

"I'm not answering that question, Joss. You're wrong for what you were almost about to do, so you say. You're wrong for trying to go through my phone."

While we argued. I kept demanding answers. Drew got dressed instantly. He was planning to leave. I didn't want him to go, but I knew he was leaving anyways. I didn't know what he was thinking. I just knew he was angry. As he left the hotel room, he said, "Bye!"

I knew it was over between us because Drew never said, "Bye!" He didn't like to say bye because it sounded final to him. He always said "later" or "I love you," but he never said bye.

I tried to call him to get him back to the room, but he didn't answer. I texted, asking if we were officially over. I pointed out he said "Bye" to me, and I needed to know if that was a true and final goodbye. My text went ignored. I didn't hear from Drew for over a week. The Warehouse fired him for no call, no show. Two weeks later, he texted me.

He said, "Hey, Joss, I had to disappear to Charlotte for a while. My mom had the cops looking for me over something stupid."

At this point, I stopped caring about the reasons he couldn't or had to do this or that.

He added, "My insurance is going to lapse at five o'clock today if I don't pay it. My plan is to stay in Charlotte with my best friend until I get on my feet. I don't know where that leaves us, but I need space to think about everything. Especially since you still don't trust me."

I texted back, "After all this time, you could have at least called to let me know what's been going on with you. It's been two weeks, Drew. If you're really in Charlotte, tell me where you are. Tell me exactly where you are, and I will send you the money for your car insurance."

He said, "I'm at my best friend's house in Charlotte. She stays by the big shopping center downtown. Now are you going to send me the money or not?"

I sent him the money as promised. I texted him to give him the information on the money transfer. I told him I was on my way to Charlotte to see him.

He said, "Why are you going to come here? I won't be in the same spot by the time you get here, so don't come here, Joss. I'll be heading to another friend's house soon. Plus, I don't want to see you right now."

"I don't care about the money, Drew, but I do want answers for the picture and Juicy as well as how long you have been lying to me."

He said, "I'll come see you later. After I get the insurance taken care of. I promise! You deserve answers. And before I completely walk away from you, Joss, I will come see you."

It was getting dark. Hours had gone by, and there was still no Drew. I texted his phone, threatening him and going off. I emailed him as well. I knew he was reading my messages.

I was angry at him but mad at myself for letting him play with my emotions all these years. He didn't care about me or our relationship. I was his walking, talking piggy bank and sex machine. I wanted to find Drew. I wanted some kind of revenge.

"I need you to stop lying to me and tell me where you are, Drew, and what the fuck is going on with you!"

He said, "You're doubting me, and I don't like that. This is why I'm going to end up breaking it off with you. You don't trust me at all. I'm not messing with other women, Joss. I'm faithful and loyal to you. So, please stop acting this way toward me!"

I gave him an ultimatum. "You have until the end of the night to come see me. Take it or leave it."

I was tired of his neglect, and he needed to be honest with me about what was going on with him. Drew hung the phone up in my ear. I looked at my phone in shock and proceeded to hit redial.

A few seconds later, I received a text message from Drew. "I will not talk to you while you are upset. I'll call you tomorrow."

I instantly became angry. Drew was hiding something. He was keeping something from me. I mentioned to him in the past, after one of his MIA weekends, that I would show up at his house as a joke. At this point, my life was no laughing matter, and I need to show up at his house. He wasn't in Charlotte. I wanted to find Drew.

I wrote down all the information Drew told me about his family, his sister's full name and the street he mentioned she lived on and his mother's full name and where she lived as well. I googled their names and searched for their current and past addresses. I needed to use what information I had to find out where he could be.

I waited until three o'clock in the morning to set out on a Drew hunt. After the club, I knew he would go straight home. If he stayed at any of these locations, his car would be in the yard. I set out on a drive to locate Drew, to let him know how crazy I was. I wasn't going to wait for him to come see me; I was going to find him first.

I drove to every location on my list. I visited the clubs he frequented and a house that used to belong to his grandparents. I went by an old address listed for his sister, and I went to his mother's house. His car wasn't in the yard. I sat outside her house for a while. Last I knew, he was living with her.

I got out to put some pictures I had of Drew and I in the mailbox. I didn't care at this point. My actions were reckless, but I wanted Drew to see how crazy he was making me. I wanted to find him. But that was if he even lived there.

I remembered the address I got off his license while he was in the hospital. I entered the address into my GPS and prepared for my next stop. I wasn't going in the direction of Guilford County; I was headed to a whole other county all together—another lie by Drew.

My heart raced as I drove to my destination. After discovering the man I am engaged to, the man I loved, had layers of secrets unfolding one after the other, I needed to calm down. I had to pull over. I had to think about what I was going to do if his car was in the yard. It was six thirty in the morning, and I was in the middle of nowhere. I was sitting at a store that was less than a mile away from total emotional destruction. I needed to prepare myself for the worst.

I sucked up my anger and courage and headed in the direction of the address. At first glance, as I drove by, I didn't see Drew's car. I slowly drove by the front door of the address. When I reached the end of the road, I turned around to take another look at the house. I wanted to make sure I didn't miss anything. I knew if I kept looking for something, I was going to eventually find it.

While heading back toward the house, I looked in the direction of the front door. A little girl was standing at the door as if she were about to come outside. I drove slower. I was able to get a better look at the little girl as I approached the house. The little girl's face was familiar. She waved at me as I drove by. Getting a better view of her face, I saw it was Drew's daughter, Neveah. The girl was his daughter. I was sure she was the girl in the pictures Drew showed me of his daughter. She was speaking to someone in the house before she started walking down the steps. I wondered who she was talking to. Was he home? Where was the car?

I drove the next street over in order to give myself a better view of the house as well as the little girl. I quickly snapped a picture, and I headed home. I called Drew's phone as I drove home. He never answered.

My mind was trying to process what I just saw. Better yet, what I just learned. I was getting blindsided by all things Drew. The little girl I saw didn't look like the difficult child Drew always described to me. He said she was always sad, but this girl looked happy. She was running to the mailbox with a huge smile on her face. Drew was definitely hiding something.

*****

Drew's disappointments were no longer fazing me. I didn't wait for a call. I didn't expect him to answer when I called. On the weekends I spent time with friends and family. I stopped asking him to come see me.

The disconnect from the relationship was happening. It took longer than it should have, but it was happening. Drew's lies were catching up to him, and he was losing me in the process.

My mother and my daughter were questioning his whereabouts. I knew they wanted to ask why he was no longer around. I didn't want people to know the truth about our relationship because I was still trying to figure out the truth myself. I was messed up on the inside. I made up excuses for him and his absence. I wasn't proud of myself and what was taking place in my relationship with Drew.

Drew didn't answer any of my texts or calls. I couldn't think. I didn't want to go to work. I wanted revenge, and I wanted him to hurt. I wanted him to hurt like he was making me hurt. I didn't know what to think about his behavior. Emotionally, Drew was breaking me down.

I sent him a long email telling him exactly how I was feeling. I told him he could have at least said bye, like he said he was if he was going to walk away from the relationship. I didn't let him know what I had found out about him. I felt a sense of relief once I hit Send on the email. In that moment, I realized I dodged a situation that could have been much worse. It was like God didn't want me to marry Drew because his secrets were spilling out right on my lap.

A couple of weeks later, I received a response from my email to Drew. I was impartial to the email, but I was eager to find out what excuse awaited me. Three weeks had lapsed since I last heard from Drew. And that meant his excuse was going to be out of this world. The longer he stayed away, the more extreme the excuse would be.

In the email, Drew stated since the last time him and I spoke, he and his mother got into a really bad argument. She called the cops on him. He went to jail, staying locked up the remainder of the weekend because he got arrested on a Saturday.

He claimed he didn't have anywhere to go when he got out, so he called his ex-girlfriend. He said she was the girl in the photos. His ex-girlfriend was Juicy. She sent the picture in an attempt to get him back. She agreed to let him stay at the house until he found another job. He said he wasn't happy, and he was sleeping on the floor. He wasn't allowed to touch anything, and she gave him a curfew. He said he did what he had to do. He said because of the way he and I left things, he didn't think he could call me. He claimed he had a mental break after being back home for a week. His ex-girlfriend called his mom, and they rallied together to get him committed.

He claimed, yet again, he was in a facility in Virginia, and he's been there for almost two weeks. He didn't have access to his phone because he threw it in a lake. He said he couldn't get in contact with me. He said he had to bribe a nurse to let him check his emails. That was how he was able to send me an email. He said he would never say bye to me and he would be in contact as soon as he was released.

I was mind blown from all the crazy details Drew described in his email. I realized how good of an actor he really was. I suddenly wished he never responded. There was more to his story, and I wasn't interested. He lost me when he called his ex instead of calling me. I deleted the email and went on about my life.

A few days later, one of the older women at the job I call Ninja walked up to me, telling me she saw Drew.

I said, "You didn't see Drew. He's been committed."

"Joss, he is—"

And as she was finishing her sentence, another one of my younger ladies, Oneida, yelled, "Joss, Drew is at security wanting to see you! He's up there looking like Lucious Lyons from *Empire*." She laughed.

She said, "That boy has got to be crazy!"

I laughed, but I was in shock. I didn't expect to hear from Drew, let alone see him. I wanted to know what she meant, by him looking like Lucious Lyons. I thought he made it, possibly signed a movie deal.

I walked up to security. As I turned the corner to the guard shack, I saw Drew standing outside the security door. He was wearing an oversize floor-length maroon robe, a pair of silk pajama bottoms, a pair of house slippers with a durag on his head. He looked like a cheap Lucious Lyons that smelled good. He appeared sad in the face, but I wasn't focused on his face as much as his flashy bedroom outfit he chose to wear to my job at three in the morning.

He said, "You look mad."

"How should I be, Drew? I haven't seen you in I don't know how long, and you show up at my job drawing attention to yourself looking like you stepped out of a *GQ* magazine. The last I heard from you was an email telling me you had been committed. Should I be shocked instead of mad?"

Drew was an animated person. He was a good actor as well. He had costumes and other items to help him successfully act out his roles. He paid attention to all details, including his story and lies.

He once told me he was going out of town for a week for an audition in a movie starring Samuel L. Jackson. He mentioned I may or may not be able to reach him while he was away auditioning. I was happy for him, but I also thought he was trying to cover up some bullshit.

He had his evidence and proof to document his whole trip. He had a voicemail from a producer, giving him details about the role and audition. When he got on the plane, I received pictures of him on the plane and of him at an event. He even called to tell me when he was headed into the audition and asked to pray for him. With all his proof, I didn't think twice about his audition.

My mother and I were excited for him. My mother especially, because she was a big fan of Samuel L. Jackson. Drew returned home with a tan and more pictures of an event that turn out to be a DJ's conference. He never auditioned for any movie, and he went to Georgia, not Los Angeles.

That truth came out when I pressed him about the role and the name of the movie. At which point I had already looked up what Samuel L. Jackson was working on at the time, and he had just finished *Django*. That couldn't have been the movie he auditioned for because it was coming out in a few weeks. Drew just returned from his trip three weeks prior. I knew he was lying; I knew production didn't happen that fast.

He said, "There you go. I shouldn't have come here. The way you recount what I told you happened to me sounds like you don't believe me. You never believe me about anything, Joss. When I tell you my life is hell, I'm telling you the truth. You are the only good thing in my life, and I am messing it up. I broke out of that place because I needed to see you. I'm only happy when I'm with you. You showed me what love is."

"Broke out, huh? Now I really don't believe you, Drew."

He said, "Baby, my life has gone to shit in less than a month. You are the only thing that is constant, and I need you!"

I wanted to give Drew the benefit of the doubt, but he was only consistent with disappearing and lying. I asked Drew to meet me at my mom's house after work because I needed to get back to work. "Drew, we need to talk about our relationship and how we are going to move forward."

"Well, can you help me get a phone? It doesn't have to be a phone from a vendor, maybe a prepaid from Walmart. I need to find out where my daughter is."

I went to my car to grab Drew some cash. I gave him a hundred and fifty dollars for a phone. Then I went back to work.

Drew never showed up at my mother's house. I emailed him a couple of times to see if he was okay, out of concern. I was experiencing a different kind of hurt this time because he only came around to get money. I was present for the hurt and pain, but deep down I was numb. I didn't want to believe I was going through this crazy drama. Reflecting on the past few years, I realized none of it was worth it.

Mint Condition was coming to town for a concert, and everyone was talking about going. I wanted to go to the concert myself, but I had to work. I thought of Drew because they were his favorite R&B group. I wished for a chance for us to go together, but Drew was missing in action as always, and I knew our relationship was officially over. Against my own better judgment, I emailed Drew. I wanted to see if he was going to the concert. Surprisingly, I received a reply instantly.

He said, "I miss you, baby, and no, I'm not going to the concert. And I'm doing okay. I recently started a new job, and I won't be able to make the concert this time. Hopefully, I'll see you soon, baby. I love you!"

A couple of days later, my coworker Oneida approached me. "Girl, I saw Drew at the concert last night. He was sitting behind me with his arm around another woman's chair. I didn't know if it was him at first, and I didn't want to be nosey. But I'm sure it was him."

I said, "Can you describe the woman? Better yet, were they there together?"

"I can do you one better. My girlfriend took a picture of me and my husband, and she had to have gotten got him and the woman in the picture. I'll ask her to send the picture to me. I'll let you know when she sends me the picture."

I waited for what seemed like forever for her to tell me she received the picture. I wanted to see this other woman. I wanted to see Drew. I wanted to see if they looked like they were at the concert together.

She said, "It's him, Joss."

Anger built in me as I examined the picture. Drew said he wasn't going to the concert. He said he didn't have the money to go, plus he had to work. I knew he wanted to go, and it was his favorite band. Somehow, I knew he would go.

I called Drew. I begged him to come see me. I told him I missed him, begging him to come scratch my itch. I turned on my charm, and I sweet-talked him into coming to see me after work. I told him it would be like old times when we shared breakfast.

Drew was at my mother's house waiting for me when I arrived from work. I said, "I need to run to the store. Can you ride with me?"

I wanted Drew to get in the car with me. He was hesitant, but he got in. Little did he know I wasn't going to the store. For what I was planning, I needed Drew in my presence. If I confronted him while at the house, he was going to get in his car and leave, and I would never get any answers.

I drove to an area where I knew Drew wasn't familiar with. I pulled to the side of the road, put my car in gear, and turned to face him. I started spewing everything I found out about him at him. I told him all the lies and stories he told me didn't add up.

Instead of Drew fessing up to any of the information, he demanded I take him back to his car. He got out of my car and began walking. He didn't know where the hell he was. I was amused by his attempt to walk. I drove next to him while he walked, demanding answers. I wanted the truth. He didn't say a word. He stopped walking long enough to look in the window. "Can you take me back to my car, please!"

I was fed up. No answers from him was my answer. Drew was lying to me about a lot of things, and he wasn't going to tell me anything. I told Drew to get in the car. I took him back to my mother's house. He quickly got out of my car, hopped in his car, and took off. I called his phone, and he didn't answer. A few minutes later, he called me back. "Joss, I need to tell you something. I don't know how to tell you this, but you're smart, and you already started figuring things out for yourself. It's hurting me to keep hurting you. I can see the anger in your eyes. I honestly got scared, and I know it's time for me to tell you the truth. I have been lying to you this whole time."

My body went totally numb. A sensation ran through me I couldn't explain. I instantly became nauseous. My gut told me Drew was hiding something from me, but his words hit me so hard I couldn't respond.

"I'm married, Joss. I've been married the whole time we've been together. The pictures you saw of Juicy is my wife. She is Juicy. She is the ex-girlfriend, or should I say wife—whatever you want to call her at this point. I'm sorry, and one day I hope you can forgive me. I can't keep lying to you. I want you to know I don't love her. I love you, and I really wanted to marry you. I don't know how to fix this, Joss. All I know is I need to get a divorce."

"Wow! So, it was your wife that went with you to the concert you told me you weren't going to? I know because Oneida from the job saw you with her. She told me everything. Even down to you holding your wife's coat for her as you left the coliseum."

He said, "It wasn't what she thought she saw. We didn't plan to go to the concert together. My wife stole some money out of my wallet one night when I got paid, the same morning you gave me the money for the phone. She brought a ticket for the show after she found out I brought one."

He admitted to getting a ticket for himself with some of the money I gave him to get a phone. He said he didn't know she got the ticket until he got back to the car from buying his ticket at the ticket master's office. She told him she had to go inside to pee; she came back out with a ticket laughing. He said he looked at her ticket, and she was seated right next to him. That was why he was glad I couldn't go.

"Something is wrong with you, Drew. You say all this so freely, wanting me to believe it's the truth, even though I know goddamn well it's all bullshit. A+ acting at its finest. I don't give a damn what it looks like to anyone. You lied and deceived me for years. This is some double life–living type of shit, and you have destroyed so many people's lives by lying like this. I'd rather you had left me alone. I don't have any words for you right now, but what I do know we are over. You cheated on me, and I don't mess around with married men, Drew. You put me in the middle of an affair I didn't know I was in."

He said, "Joss, for the record, there were no other women. I didn't cheat on you. I just happen to have a wife."

I didn't bother to respond. I told Drew to have a nice life, and then I hung the phone up.

In that moment, I wanted to die. I felt like an idiot because I knew all the signs pointed to him being deceitful about something. I didn't believe half of the excuses he came up with, but I gave him the benefit of the doubt. In the end, I ended up getting played hard. He was someone's husband. Nothing about our relationship could be fixed. The damage had been done.

I went into the house, and I told my mother everything. She was in total shock. She didn't believe any of what I was telling her. I reminded her of some of the crazy excuses he told me in the past, telling her everything about Drew was a lie and he would no longer be coming around any longer.

I wasn't in the talking mood. I was upset, but I didn't want my mother or daughter to see me hurt. I went in the bathroom, and I cried. Emotionally messed up, I thought about everything. Thoughts of not getting married. Memories that were built on lies and deception. I wondered about his wife and whether she knew about me. I wondered what went wrong in their marriage for him to go as far as living a lie.

Everything Drew put me through had to be a lesson learned. I gathered my emotions and nursed my wounds. There was no taking any of it back. I had to deal with it all and move on. My heart was going to be guarded from here on out. I loved Drew despite everything he put me through, with his lies, lack of communication, and now a wife. Getting over him wasn't going to be easy, but I had to let him go.

*****

Six months had gone by since I had my life uprooted by love. I wasn't dating, just working and taking care of my kids. I was at a happy point in life. There were times I sat back and thought about Drew. Like what was he doing? Was he okay? Is he thinking about me? Sometimes I wished he didn't tell me about his real life, especially the part about him having a whole wife.

I thought back to every time Drew disappeared and wondered what he was really doing versus the overly exaggerated lie he told me. I wondered how he and his wife spent their weekends together as I desperately sat waiting for him to show up to be with me. I felt stupid for being so blind to all the things he did. Really stupid because I missed him. I missed him and everything about him.

An unknown number had been calling my phone for two days straight. It stood out because I didn't answer telephone numbers I didn't know. I waited each time for the caller to leave a message before I attempted to call the number back. I got annoyed seeing the number show up on my phone for the third time that day. The call was interrupting my music as well as my workout.

Whoever was calling finally got the hint and left me a voicemail. I started up the voice message. A warm sensation went up my spine. I recognized the voice, but I didn't know why he was calling. It was Drew, and I was confused.

I was excited and anxious to hear the complete message. We didn't end things nicely, and his repeated calling was making me wonder as to why he has been calling. I missed him dearly, but I was still wondering why he was calling.

I started the message from the beginning, and I held my breath while I listened to his deep, raspy voice say my name. "Hey, Joss, I finally got the nerve to call you. I didn't expect you to pick up the phone, but I thought it was worth a try to call you and apologize for hurting you. These past six months had me doing a lot of thinking and growing up. I realized I hurt the person that loved me more than any person in this world. I messed that up, and I regret hurting you. I don't ever regret meeting you. I hope you can someday forgive me. This is my number. Call me sometime. You may be seeing me around soon anyways. I'll be back at The Warehouse in a couple of weeks for the next busy season, and I didn't want you to be surprised when you saw me."

I listened to the message a few times to hear him say my name and to see if there was a hint of him missing me in his voice. I saved his number in my phone, then I proceeded with my workout.

Drew wasn't lying this time when he said I'd see him soon.

The following Monday, Drew was standing less than five feet away from me on the production floor at The Warehouse, again. He was looking and smelling good. He did it all to catch my attention. He was going to try to find something to get my attention while he worked with me. I acknowledged him with a head nod, and he smiled back at me.

I tried to avoid Drew as much as possible at work. My attempts weren't going to last long because I was the lead in my department, and he worked in my area this time around. There was no way around avoiding a conversation with him. After the initial conversation of "how you been" and "what have you been up to," it was going to be all business for me, even though it was going to be hard not to want something more from him.

Drew made it a point to make himself known every night. He gave me a hug at the start and end of every shift. It was cute, and I welcomed it. It was good to see him, but the hurt he did on my heart was still fresh, and I didn't know how I was going to get past it to even attempt to let him in as a friend.

Since Drew was back at the job, *again*, he and I agreed to try to rekindle our friendship. He informed me of everything he was going through with his wife, and a possible divorce was looming in the future. He moved in with his uncle until the separation period was over, and his uncle was going to help him get back on his feet.

He said, "That's why I'm back here. Being with you gave me the strength to leave her. I was in a bad space with that woman, and I let her control me. I knew eventually I was going to make my way back to you, Joss. One way or another."

"Umm, so you come back to my job for the third time to be close to me. Some people would call that stalking, Drew."

We talked off and on at work as friends. He told me he changed. His career as a DJ picked up. He was now contracted to DJ at the weekly ball games on Saturdays.

I was in the process of moving into my own house in a couple of weeks, and I was focusing on my well-being and my kids. I was free from drama. I was happy for Drew, and he sounded like he was in a good spot in life too.

I remembered I needed some help moving into my new place. I asked Drew if he could help me and my manager Johnny move my stuff into my place on the coming up Friday. In times past, he always had a problem with Fridays and weekends, but to my surprise, Drew said he would help.

That Friday morning, we started moving my things into my new house. When we were done, my manager went home to get some sleep, and Drew stayed behind to help me organize the furniture. I made him something to eat, and we went in my new bedroom to eat and talk.

He said, "I'm happy for you, and I'll come visit whenever you need me to."

I laughed and said, "And you can stay the night sometimes. If you need to, that is."

I didn't know why that comment slipped out, but I figured the cat was out of the bag. I wanted him to know I was willing to give us another shot as long as he was really getting a divorce.

I stopped laughing, and I asked, "You're really getting a divorce, right? And you don't live with her anymore, right?"

"C'mon, Joss! You think I'd lie to you like that again? Give me a little slack this time around."

"Well, we didn't have many days where we woke up to each other. It would feel good to fall asleep and to wake up to you."

He said, "Why are you bringing up old stuff? Can we look toward the future and none of that past stuff? I want to make things work for us this go-round. I want to be with you, Joss."

A couple of days later, Drew and I hooked up sexually. While he sexed me, he told me how much he missed me and missed being inside of me. I admitted to him I missed him as well. I wanted the divorce to come as soon as possible so Drew could finally be all mine. I didn't want the regret of his marriage looming in our relationship.

Drew was on the phone with me more often than before. He also responded to my texts and calls regularly. The only thing I questioned was his connection at his uncle's place. Sometimes we would be in a deep conversation, and then his video or chat would disconnect. He said it was from his uncle staying out in the middle of nowhere, but I remembered the house I visited was out in the middle of nowhere as well. I didn't want to think Drew was that conniving to try to hurt me again. He was showing a real change in behavior from before.

A few weeks after Drew and I hooked up, I started wondering why he hadn't stayed with me yet. That raised a red flag for me. I didn't want to go down that road with him again, so I made mention of it to Drew in our next conversation.

It wasn't long after our conversation when Drew started slacking. I'd text him, and he wouldn't respond for hours. When he was at his uncle's house, he always went to bed at the same time. No matter the conversation or if we were in the middle of a topic, he rushed to get off the phone suddenly because he was tired or needed to go to sleep.

I confronted him about all the suspicious things he was doing, some of which didn't add up, but he had his explanations as always. He said he hadn't stayed at my house yet because he was busy working, and time hadn't afforded him the opportunity to do so yet. And as far as his sleep schedule, his body would know when he was tired, and he just wanted to sleep when his body would tell him to sleep. As far as the texting back, well, that was the signal's fault.

One weekend, my daughter was going out of town. I invited Drew to stay the weekend with me, and he happily accepted. The weekend came quickly, and Drew was a no-show. I called and texted him. Both attempts went ignored. It got late in the evening, and I knew he wasn't going to come. I cut my losses and went out on the town by myself.

I knew the truth was apparent, and I needed to address it. I didn't want Drew to think he could wiggle his way back into my life while he still carried his lies. He was lying to me about being separated from his wife, and I now was sure of it. I was sure he told me they were separated to convince me to take him back. Drew was an actor, but I guess this time around he couldn't keep his lie going. He knew with me having my own place, it was going to be a challenge to hide his lies. He knew I was going to want him to stay the night. That was why he was ignoring my calls. He knew, I knew, he wasn't free. Drew was still at home with his wife.

Drew went MIA the entire weekend he was supposed to stay with me. He eventually showed up at my house that following Monday afternoon. He didn't call or text. When he walked into my house, I didn't acknowledge him. I was mad; he had the nerve to show up at my house. The excuse was going to be good, but I wasn't falling for it. I didn't even want to hear it.

"Why are you here, Drew? Why even bother showing up after three days? You're back to wasting my time and lying, and I know it."

Drew instantly got angry. He said, "You don't trust me, and you probably won't ever trust me again. Why did you let me make a fool of myself trying to get you back when you were never going to trust me?"

"Why should I, Drew? First, you lie to me about being married for over three years, and then you proceeded to allow me to propose to you. You had the nerve to say that! You come to my job practically every year for three years stalking me. You lied to all your family members including your kids. You made me look like a fool to my family, and you took advantage of my love and the trust I did have for you. And now you're walking around plotting to get me back as if it were going to be easy. You told me things were going to be different because you left your wife and moved in with your uncle, but you're still avoiding calls and text messages just like you did before. Honestly, I don't think you're at your uncle's house. I think you're still at home with your wife. And you want me to trust you? Hell nah, Drew, you're not worth the headache this time. We need to end whatever it is we were trying to save and just salvage what we have left and remain friends."

"I agree," he said.

"Drew, I know you're still with your wife, and that's why you can't stay with me. You lied to me yet again, Drew, when you could have just left me alone."

My emotions got the best of me, and no matter how much I told myself not to cry, I broke down. Tears started streaming down my face. The hurt from the inside was resurfacing, and I couldn't hold back. "I gave you every bit of me, and you had me thinking you were going to be my future. You lied about everything, and everything was a lie. You took money from me, and you even had my daughter angry because you betrayed her love as well. Then you sit here in my face, accusing me of not trusting you all the damn time. The winner is you, Drew, for actor of the year. You hurt me, then you return to peel the scab off, only to pour alcohol on the wound all over again. I'm stupid to keep falling for your mess. But not anymore."

He lowered his head while I spoke. He didn't look me in my face, not once. He knew everything I was saying was the truth, and I wasn't blinded by love enough to be a fool this time around. I walked him to my front porch and told him I'd see him around.

He walked away slowly. He turned back to me and said, "For the record, Joss, I never cheated on you. I cheated on my wife with you!"

I laughed as he got in his car. He really was a good actor, and that line hit like a double-edged sword. He never cheated on me, but he voluntarily forced me into an affair—an affair I didn't even know I was a part of. Drew apparently thought I was supposed to give him credit for not cheating on me. I laughed as I walked in my house.

Drew pointed out off work by the end of the week. He never came back to The Warehouse.

Drew's career helped him in his journey to deceive me. He told me he never meant to hurt me and the love he had for me was real. He never expected to fall in love with me, and once he did, he didn't know how to live with this truth. For over three years, he lived a double life with me, building a whole new family while he had a family at home, including a wife—someone he married legally.

# Hey, Shorty...

I was glad to finally get the year behind me. I was living with my mother, working long crazy hours and trying to get over a three-year relationship that resulted in betrayal. I felt defeated for a while, but I regained myself. I had to gather myself for me and my kids. My son starting his first year of college, and my daughter was a freshman in high school. I haven't had any fun in a long while, but the holidays were looking hopeful.

It was New Year's Eve, and The Warehouse was closed for the night. I didn't have any big plans to usher in the New Year, but I planned to spend most of my night at my cousin Roxanne's house.

My sister-in-law arrived in town a few days before, and she was posted up at a hotel in town. She didn't know anyone in town, and she didn't want to bring in the New Year by herself, so I brought her along with me to Roxxane's house.

Roxanne had a couple of people over to celebrate the new year. We were all having a good time. We had music playing, alcohol flowing, and some folks were smoking on that Barry White. There were some future dating prospects at the gathering, even a gentleman that had a long-standing crush on me. I was having fun and flirting hard. I didn't want a relationship; I just needed someone to help me get over Drew.

Drew and I ended our communications with each other after he told me he was married. Getting over him wasn't easy. Mentally I was over him, but emotionally I was hurt. I wanted to trust men again. I was openly ready to usher love into my new year. I wanted it to be safe for me to date, but I also didn't think I was ready.

A few minutes or so before the New Year's clock was to strike twelve, my sister-in-law stopped having fun and wanted to go back to her room. I was finally enjoying myself, and her wanting to go home was putting a damper on my night. I had thirty minutes to drop her off and get back to the gathering before the ball dropped.

We got situated in the car, and I started heading toward the hotel. She kept apologizing for ruining my night. I wanted to drop her off and get back to the party. She broke my train of thought by asking me to stop at the store next to the hotel.

I wasn't looking my best, but I was cute. I had the black knee-high boots on, along with some skintight jeans, with a red long-sleeve sheer top. My hair was slayed with curls and bangs that swooped perfectly across my right eye. I was looking and feeling cute.

I pulled up to the pump to park. I needed to grab some more alcohol for the party. My sister-in-law went one way, and I went toward the beer section. As I approached the beer cooler, I noticed a guy wearing a brown leather vest, Timberland boots to match the vest, black jeans, a black long-sleeve shirt, and a black ball cap. He was facing the beer but quickly turned to me, making eye contact.

I could tell by his facial expression he was going to say something to me. He wasn't ugly, but I didn't want him to talk to me. I was feeling good from the party, and I just wanted to get the alcohol, drop my sister-in-law off, and get back to Roxxane's before the New Year rang in.

The guy looked at me and said, "Hey, shorty! Can I get your number?"

I tried to come off as if I weren't bothered by his approach. I laughed slightly. Then I said, "I don't give my number out to strangers."

"I'm not a pervert or anything. I just want your number so I can call you. To possibly take you out on a date in the coming new year."

I wanted the conversation to be over. I didn't enjoy men approaching me, let alone asking for my number. I told myself to do what I always did, and that was to give him a fake number. To get him off my back and out of my face.

In the past, I would give men who asked for my number my actual number, but I'd change the last digit. The men never questioned if it was a fake number or not.

I looked at him and said, "I'm going to say my number once. If you miss a number, it's on you."

I said my number as quick as possible. As soon as I said the last digit, I stopped talking and shook my head. I accidentally gave him my real number. I hoped he didn't memorize the number. I stepped around him to grab the beer. I was ready to get out of there.

I was angry with myself. I was trying to forget about Drew, who kept popping up to lie to me. I had a couple of other guys who had my number who wanted to go on dates with me, but I wasn't trying to be bothered with men like that. I didn't need another dude to ward off. I wanted to drop this woman off, get back to the party, and forget I made the dumb mistake of sharing my actual telephone number with someone I wasn't interested in sharing it with.

I passed the guy again as I was leaving the store. He was in the back seat of a car. I immediately thought to myself he was a scrub. Sitting in the backseat of someone else's ride. I looked him in his eyes as I walked by. I couldn't help it; I gave him one of my smiles. He yelled from the car, "You will be mine."

When I got in the car, I told my sister-in-law about the transaction. She laughed and said, "Can't take you anywhere."

We both laughed. I said, "My dumbass gave him my real number by accident, trying to be smart."

"What? I can't believe you did that! What were you thinking?"

"Yeah, I know right?"

After saying bye to my sister-in-law, I headed back to Roxanne's house. I had twelve minutes to get back to her house before the ball dropped. I wanted to bring in the year celebrating and enjoying myself. I pulled out of the hotel parking lot when my phone started to ring. I didn't recognize the number, but I answered the phone anyways. It was the guy from the store. He said, "Hi!"

"Hi back atcha. Was my number burning a hole in your pocket?"

"I had to call to make sure you didn't give me the wrong number. My cousins bet me that you gave me the wrong number. I had to prove them wrong. I also wanted to hear your voice. And after hearing it now, your voice does something to me. But yo, my name is Sawyer. Everyone calls me Saw for short. What's your name, beautiful?"

I laughed. "My name is Joss."

We talked long enough for me to get back to Roxanne's house. I told Sawyer, Saw for short, I had to get back to what I was doing before I bumped into him at the store. I said have a good and safe night. Then I hung up.

The next day, the unknown number from last night popped up on my phone. I smiled to myself before answering it. "Hello, Sawyer."

"Damn, you sound good on the phone. Ha." He made a slight "Ha" sound after every statement or comment he made. It was a tic or something. I first thought he was asking me a question after every comment, but it was the way he talked. I don't think he knew he was doing it.

Sawyer was attractive in the way he carried himself. He looked good enough for me to say he could get it. I didn't know how long I intended to make him wait if I did decide to give him the yoni. I had to find out what he was all about him before he got any of my goodies because I didn't give away my yoni to just anyone.

He was five feet, eleven inches, with a high yellow skin tone. He was almost a red bone. His voice was rough and raspy. His body was well taken care of, minus a small beer gut. His arms were full of muscles. He had a slight old-school thug appeal, but his demeanor was sweet. I could tell his patience was short but in an attractive way. He said he was thirty-nine years old and single. He had his own car, as well as his own apartment, that he shared with his little cousin. He had a son, and he worked the night shift six days a week, only off on Sundays. He worked whenever he could because he liked having money in his pocket.

He said, "It was luck seeing you the other night because I'm normally at work. Why are you single, Joss?

I replied, "I'm single because I work hard as a mother for my kids. I don't have time for the games people play in relationships these days. It's safer to be single."

I didn't bother to tell him about my relationship with Drew and the unbelievable drama I went through with him. I in turn asked, "Why are you single?"

"I'm single because I work too much. And women cost too much money. I like my money too much to spend it on a woman. I want to work and drink my beer every day without someone telling me what to do. I'm content with my life."

I felt the sincerity in his tone. I also respected the fact he knew what he wanted. He and I talked on the phone for a couple of hours. Sawyer had a dry sense of humor, but it was enough to make me laugh.

Our conversation was a breath of fresh air, for Drew was still fresh on my mind, and I needed a distraction to keep me from wanting him, from wanting to hear his voice. It had only been a few months since I found out his secret, but it still hurt like it happened yesterday. I knew I had to let Drew go. I knew I had to get him out of my mind because he was married and there was no way for us to be together. And Saw didn't act like other men, and that was comforting. The direction our conversations went, the route seemed safe. I agreed to let Saw call me again.

Saw started calling me every morning after work like clockwork. He got excited each time I answered. He'd say, "Girl, your voice does something to me. Ha." I thought to myself, if he were this excited about my voice, the rest of me would have him obsessed. He and I talked all week. On Friday, he asked me If I'd like to go to his cousin's house on Saturday for some drinks.

I asked, "What about work?"

"I'll miss a day for you. You must know you gotta be something special if I'm willing to miss money for you."

Before we hung up, I agreed to go with him, and I gave him the directions to my mother's house.

Saturday afternoon arrived, and I was excited to see Sawyer. I was nervous to be around his family. I didn't know them, and I didn't know what to expect. I had a cool demeanor about myself. Being chill, laid back, and funny, so I wasn't too worried. He wore a fresh fade haircut, a white oversized T-shirt, and a pair of black jeans. He pulled in the driveway in his older model silver Cadillac. He looked good.

I got in his car, and he leaned over and kissed me. I was shocked by his gesture. The whole experience of him picking me up and acting like a gentleman was new to me. I had two long-term relationships totaling twenty-three years under my belt, and one started while I was in high school. He made me realize I never had someone take me on a real date my entire life. Even though Drew and I dated for some time, I didn't count him because he never took me out on a date let alone spend a weekend with me.

When we arrived at his cousin's house, everyone was already slightly lit. Saw introduced me to everyone, and I was greeted with surprise. Everyone was glad to meet me, but they were surprised Saw took the day off to party. I took a seat in the living room and attempted to enjoy myself. If someone made small talk, I joined in. I chatted with the woman of the house most of the night. Saw occasionally looked over at me and smiled. He saw I was okay around his people and I was having a good time.

We left his cousin's house around three o'clock in the morning. I was expecting my mom to say something when I got home because it was early in the morning. I didn't care. I was caught up in Saw because he was caught up in me. His attention was on my every move, and I enjoyed how he was acting toward me. I enjoyed getting some much-needed attention.

When we pulled into my mother's driveway, Saw wanted to talk. We sat in the car listening to music and revisiting some of the things we talked about during the week. He told me what he wanted in a woman, and even though he had just met me, he knew I was what he wanted. He said, "I like a woman that works, cooks, and takes care of a home. And she has to like sex."

When he was done talking, he leaned over to kiss me. For ten minutes things got a little intense for us. The way his hands groped my breast while he kissed up and down my neck, I could tell Saw wanted me sexually. I wanted him as well. I stopped him to tell him we needed to call it a night. He was disappointed, but he understood.

The following week Saw and I made plans to get a hotel room for the weekend. He was a respectable man, and he never came off rude in any way. Our phone conversations were mainly about work and future plans.

He wanted to start his own business with a cousin he was close to. He wanted to take care of his mother because she was getting older. He said he was a simple man who wanted simple things. Every so often something sexual would come up, but he would quickly say, "I'm just playing."

I knew he wasn't playing, but I respected him for not having a 24-7 perverted mind. We were grown adults, and we knew what the next agenda on the list would be. I needed some sexual attention, but I didn't want him to know how eager I was to get it. I wanted Friday to arrive so bad. I was ready for my weekend with Saw.

On Friday, when I arrived home from work, Saw was already calling my phone. When I answered, he said, "I'm on my way to come get you so we can get the room."

I was amused by his gestures. I was about to spend the weekend with a gentleman, and he was treating me like no other guy had treated me in my past. He was doing everything right.

He beeped his horn letting me know he was outside. I grabbed my wallet and keys and headed out the door. I got in the car, and to my surprise, Saw handed me the money for the room. I was used to paying for everything, especially when I was with Drew. I took the money and said, "Thank you!" I was mentally tripping over Saw and how he was so different from all the other men I dated.

I got out to get the room when we got to the hotel. Saw parked his car. I expected him to come in, but he stayed outside smoking. For a moment I second-guessed whether I should stay with him. After checking in, I asked the Lord to keep me safe and to not let any hurt, harm, or danger come my way. Saw was finishing up his cigarette when I stepped out of the building. He said, "Are we good to go? Where's the room located?"

I replied, "Yup, and our room for the weekend is on the top floor in the corner."

Saw lifted his finger to point in the direction he assumed I was talking about. I said, "Yes, over there."

"We might as well walk. I can leave the car where it is and move it later."

I looked around as soon as I walked in the room. We had a typical hotel room with a microwave and fridge. We had a small round table, a king-size bed, and of course, a TV on the dresser. The room was nothing to brag about, but it was enough for us to be comfortable during our stay.

Saw asked if I was hungry, and I said I was. He pulled out his wallet and handed me a couple of twenties and the keys to his car. He said, "Can you go grab us some biscuits?"

I was shocked he trusted me with his car. I left to get the biscuits and came back to Saw on his phone. He was talking to his cousin whom he was planning to start a business with. Saw had his phone on speaker. He told his cousin he had to go because I was back. His cousin said, "Treat her right," and then there was a click.

I said, "Dang, how many people did you tell we were getting a room?"

"I tell my cousin everything."

"Everything, Saw?"

"Nah, not like everything, but every time I go somewhere, I tell him. If something happens to my mom or something, I want to be reached. Ha."

"Okay, Saw, that's understandable. But you're telling your family about me already though? It's only been a couple of weeks, and you're just happy because you think you're going to get some booty this morning. That's why you were rushing to get to this room."

I walked over to the small table as I talked. And Saw laughed. "I wasn't rushing to get the room so we could have sex. I wanted to make sure you were going to stay the weekend with me. I'm trying to make sure everything is to your liking. I wasn't rushing anything. I would like to get a nap in before we start our day together. I'm tired, and I know you're tired. Rest was on my mind, at least for right now."

His response wasn't what I expected.

He said, "Joss, I'm not like them other young clowns. I know how to treat a woman as long as she acts like a woman and she's not just with me for my money."

I laughed. But I was also relieved. After dealing with Drew's mess and deceit, I had to find a way to understand all men weren't the same. I was lucky enough to find Saw. We ate our breakfast, then we watched TV until we fell asleep.

That afternoon, Saw took me back to my mother's house to get the stuff I packed for our weekend getaway. We grabbed something to eat for dinner as well as some junk food for the fridge in the room.

I asked, "Are you planning to stay with me the whole weekend?

He said, "I have to go in to work Sunday evening, but other than that, I'm going to be right here with you."

We laughed, joked, and played around with each other. When it came time to call it a night, we both showered, and I went first. While he showered, I lay on the bed, clicking through the channels, trying to find a music station to play in the background of whatever we might be doing later.

Saw came out of the bathroom buck naked. His light cara-mel-colored skin tone glistened as his muscles showed in his arms and legs. His third leg hung with no shame in his game. He walked over to me happy and smiling. He didn't say anything as he eased his body between my legs until he was face-to-face with me.

He asked, "Are you okay?"

I told him yes.

He kissed me on my lips and then all over my breasts. He was patient and gentle. He took his time searching and memorizing my body. My heat was rising inside of me, and I was ready for him to break me open.

Saw dropped down to the side of me, and I rolled closer to him, laying my head on his arm. We continued to kiss. I drew my knee up and slowly opened my legs. His hand went from rubbing my breasts to between my legs. His fingers played with the outside of my yoni. I wanted him inside of me. I moaned with anticipation, and in between our kisses, I whispered, "Take me."

Saw used two fingers to enter me. His fingers glided inside me while I exhaled with pleasure. I could feel the wetness erupting from inside of me, soaking his fingers. Saw was excited for his chance to feel my wetness with his member. Each time his fingers moved inside me, he would say, "Mmm. You're so wet, and I can tell you're ready for me."

He slowly rolled on top of me, but he backed up and sat up between my legs. I watched him as he watched what he was doing to me, moving his fingers in and out of me. His excitement, standing firm, was waiting for its chance to feel my juices. Saw removed his fingers then nudged forward, and he entered me.

His member filled me, and I moaned. I felt my yoni get wetter as he entered me. He grabbed my legs and placed them on his shoulders. He reached under me, grabbing my ass, pulling me slowly into him, moving in and out of me. He gasped with each of his motions. He moved and moaned.

His member moved in and out of me slowly, as he rotated, opening and closing my legs. He rotated watching what was happening between our private parts. He stroked me as his excitement continued to rise. Lowering my legs and positioning himself perfectly between my legs. He ground until he found the spot inside of me he wanted to dig out until he struck gold. His movements were gentle but aggressive. I could tell he was holding back, but what he was doing was working for me and my body. When we were done, I went to the bathroom to grab a hot rag to place on his member.

He said, "No woman has ever done this to me before. I must have felt good to you. Ha."

I said, "Don't get a big head, or you wouldn't get any more."

We both laughed.

Saw was attentive to me and my body. We talked and played around the whole weekend. He was rough and rugged on the outside but was a softie when it came to love. He stayed with me the entire weekend. We didn't leave the room until he left for work that Sunday. Saw asked, "Hey, baby, do you want something to eat before I leave?

"I could eat, but I want something good. You can pick the place."

"Okay, I'll be right back."

An hour had gone by, and I hadn't heard from Saw. Everything in me told me I was tricked for some yoni. Saw didn't give me that impression, so I assumed something came up and he couldn't let me know. All kinds of crazy thoughts popped into my head.

I called myself so many names, blaming myself for giving him the yoni too early. I felt like he was the worst kind of man, sexing me then leaving me stranded at a motel. I wanted to cry; I wanted to find out what the hell was going on.

I called Saw's cell phone, and to my disappointment, it went straight to voicemail. I waited a little longer. After another hour of waiting, I was breaking down emotionally. I cursed savageness on every man I came into contact with. I wouldn't trust another man ever in life. I cried, and I prayed. My heart was turning cold.

After my mini breakdown, I called Saw's phone again. I was ready to leave a message, giving him a piece of my mind. I was beyond angry. He still didn't answer the phone. I called my mother to ask her to come get me in the morning. She didn't ask any questions.

I ordered a pizza. While I waited for the pizza, I took a shower. I wanted to feel less dirty. I was mad at myself for allowing myself to be used by another man. I kept revisiting old conversations in my mind between Saw and I, trying to recall any signs he was this kind of a person. His actions didn't match his personality. I wanted to call my cousin Roxanne, but I didn't want her to know. I didn't want to feel any more embarrassed than I already felt. I knew she wouldn't judge me, but I wanted to keep my embarrassment to myself. I was tired of being heartbroken.

I was on my second movie of the night when I heard the room door jiggle open. It was Saw walking toward me with a death grip on a McDonald's bag and a giant drink cup. He had an excited look on his face, and I wondered why. I was shocked he had the nerve to show up, but I knew if he was in the room with me, he had an award-winning excuse like Drew always had, and I was ready for it.

Excitedly he said, "Baby, are you okay? Man, I couldn't wait until lunch to get here to you. I didn't stand you up, baby. I went to get your food, and the line was around the building. I waited in line as long as I could, and it was getting late. I had to get to work. I was going to call you while I was on the way to my job, but I never charged my phone after we…you know! And it was dead. I was late getting to work, so I had to wait for break to find my charger. On break, I charged my phone, but I couldn't leave to bring you food or to tell you what happened until lunch. I brought you some McDonald's. It was on the way. I heard your voicemails. I knew you were mad, and I wanted to get here as soon as possible to show you I'm not playing games on you. You're still mad, aren't you?"

"Hell yeah, I'm mad, Sawyer. Everything you just told me sounds like some bullshit. I don't have time for drama or bullshit. I've had enough of that from my last relationship, and I don't need it or want it in my life going further. I thought you were different, but you got some shit up with you too!"

He said, "No, Joss! No, no, no! I'm not like other dudes that try to get over on women. I'm interested in you, and I want to know you for the rest of my life. I just had some bad luck today communicating with you, and I want to say I'm sorry! I'd rather leave you alone than hurt you, Joss. Please forgive me."

His words were sincere, and his body language went from excited to worried. He was concerned about how I was feeling.

"I hope you can forgive me, baby. I have to get back to work. My phone is at fifteen percent charged."

He showed me his phone. I glanced at the battery life. I believed him, but I wasn't going to tell him that.

He added, "I'll be right back here in the morning as soon as I get off."

"No need, my mother is picking me up."

"Why would you do that? I brought you here, and I have no problem bringing you home. I don't want your mom to think anything negative about me. Please let me take you home."

I wanted to trust him. I wanted to give him a fresh slate. I didn't want to think he was picking up where Drew left off. I decided to give him a chance to redeem himself. "I'll text my mother, but you better be here in the morning, Sawyer."

"Sure thing. Ha." He walked over to me, kissed me on the forehead, and then added, "Don't be thinking about giving my stuff away [referring to my yoni]." He kissed my lips, and he headed back out the door.

I was left feeling overwhelmed. I didn't know if I could take another messed-up relationship so soon after Drew. It's only been a few months since I last spoke to Drew. I was supposed to marry him. I was in love with him, but he turned out to be playing games. No matter how much Drew said he loved me, I couldn't be with a married man. Morally, that wasn't the type of woman I wanted to be in life. If I ever got married, I wouldn't want anyone sleeping with my husband.

Getting over Drew was going to be hard, but I wanted to give Saw a chance. I was going to watch him for red flags. I was going to build my wall of emotional comfort until he showed me it was okay for it to come down.

Saw walked into the hotel room fifteen minutes after his shift ended, at seven fifteen on the nose. I looked at the clock and then in his direction and proceeded to lie back down. He was happy to still see me in the bed asleep. He went into the bathroom, and the shower came on. A few minutes later, Saw was getting under the blankets scooting closer to me. His member reached me before the rest of him did. He slowly rubbed the side of my leg. "Are you asleep?"

I ignored his gestures and his question. I didn't want him to know I was awake. My body on the other hand was reacting to his member and the rubbing on my leg. I let out a slight moan, and Saw took that as an invitation to wake my yoni.

Saw lifted my leg slightly, wide enough for him to fit his member to slide between my ass cheeks. His member found its destination, and he pushed through my wetness. He slowly grooved forward, each thrust pushing me toward the edge of the bed.

Once we reached the end of the bed, he entwined his leg with mine, reaching over me with his hand. Grabbing a handful of the mattress, holding on tight, he used all of his weight to thrust inside of me. My head lightly hit the headboard as he continued to thrust inside me repeatedly. His strong grip across my body kept me right where he wanted me to be.

I moaned in pure excitement. Saw was giving me hood lovin', and I welcomed every thrust. He softly rocked my head into the headboard until he came. His stamina was amazing for someone who worked all the time. He knew what he could do, and he knew he did it well, even if he was aggressive with it. We fell asleep until right before checkout. Later that afternoon, Saw took me home.

*****

At work, it was the same shit, different week type of vibe. Saw and I talked every day. We made plans to get another hotel room the following weekend. We started getting a room every weekend. We took turns paying for the room and spoiling one another. I was always excited for Friday afternoons. We spent the weekends at hotels and hanging out with his cousins.

I didn't expect much from Saw after the hotel incident. I was in need of some male companionship to forget someone I didn't care to ever see again. He was different from Drew. He called me on the regular, and the weekends were our time. He was attentive to me, calling me pet names. He always made sure I ate. His attention was on me. When I called, he answered. Things were blissful.

In the bedroom, Saw was different. He loved sex. He had sex as if he were never getting any more yoni in his life. He had his moments when he would be sensual, and other times, he showed his true fucking style. He was an aggressive lover, or what I call a pounder. A pounder aggressively falls into the yoni, pounding away. He didn't always rely on rhythm, just sliding in the yoni and pounding away. The size of his member helped him out when it came to pleasure; it hit all the right spots. He was more satisfied with our sexual sessions than I was, but I didn't walk away disappointed.

Saw was conservative in public. He expected a woman to be respectable in public as well. He wanted to keep the bedroom stuff in the bedroom, other than a little PDA here and there. He liked I was nasty (in a sexy way). He told me I smelled like a good porno. The

71

kind he enjoyed watching. The kind where the girls were beautiful and sexy in their performance. One where he would finish and be satisfied. Saw was happy having someone to have sex with. He also liked to watch.

He told me he was turned on by smart women, and he loved that I was about my shit in everything I did. By this time, I was applying to be a supervisor at my job. The only person that could get in the way of my success was myself. He knew I'd rather be single than deal with a deadbeat man.

I made it a point after my last long-term relationship to try to never have bad sex. I found something exciting about every sex session I participated in. I didn't mind making my own moves when it came to pleasure, whether that was introducing a toy, grinding to my own rhythm, or moaning to my own tune. Most of the time, I didn't cum, but I was always satisfied. I didn't hold it against him or any of the other men I slept with.

One weekend we got a room. Sawyer had to work, so I had time to relax and take care of my mental. He returned to the room after he got off work. I was dressed in a white cami top and lace white panties. I had the lights dimmed to make the room romantic. Saw was amazed when he walked in and saw me lying on the hotel bed seductively waiting for him.

Sawyer was still in his work uniform looking manly and attractive. He walked to the bed and laid on top of me. He made the hunching motion a couple of times, and then he got up. He walked over to the chair next to the table and sat down. He lit a cigarette, and he watched me.

I said, "Tell me what you want?"

Saw sat up in the chair and looked over at me. "Please yourself."

I positioned myself to where my yoni faced him. I wanted him to see everything I was about to do to myself. I lay back, bent my knees, and spread my legs.

I patted my yoni a couple of times before I took my fingers to part my yoni lips. I rubbed my clit until I felt the moisture coming from my yoni. I wanted him to know I was wet. I played with my yoni until he heard my wetness. I gracefully moved my fingers across my honey spot. Grabbing on my breast with my free hand, I traced my yoni lips with the wetness from my fingers. I glided my fingers in and out of me in a wave of pleasure. The heat flushed through my body as my arousal built up in me.

Watching him watch me had me on a different level of ecstasy. I was excited inside and out. I was ready to make myself cum. I wanted him to see my face when I came. I approached my moment of release. My body shifted upward. I moaned soft and loud as I faced Saw's dark silhouette finishing off his cigarette while he sat in amazement of the pleasure I just gave myself.

After my release, Saw came over to me. He grabbed my breast with one hand as he undid his pants with the other. He pulled his pants off and removed his work shirt. He reached between my legs, and with two fingers, he entered me. He felt my heat as my head fell back with perfect ease, revealing my neck. Saw kissed my neck while his fingers danced inside of me. My hips were grinding with his every move. I moaned as his fingers played. My hips gyrated to the motions of his fingers. Tension was building, and things were getting intense. I could see Saw's excitement, and I knew he felt mine. I wanted him inside. I wanted him to be engulfed by the heat of my love. I was ready for my pounding session.

Saw and I spent all our free time together. Every chance we could be together we were. We were in and out of hotels every weekend for almost two months. Sometimes I spent nights at the room by myself because he had to work, but when he was off, he was sharing my space. He was showing me how he felt about me, and I was enjoying every moment of it.

One Friday morning, Saw arrived to pick me up to take me to the hotel. I was ready for a much-needed break from people. I was ready to be alone with him. He told me he didn't want to do anything or go anywhere; he just wanted to stay in and enjoy each other. I was fine with whatever he wanted to do.

By Sunday, Saw started acting weird, and I could tell something was bothering him. I didn't bother to tell him what I could see. I wanted to wait for him to talk to me, so I didn't bother to pressure him. We went to dinner, and he took me home. As I stepped out of his car, he grabbed my hand, letting my hands gently slip through his.

He said, "I love you, Joss Love!"

I suspected he had feelings for me, but I wasn't expecting him to just come out with it. I looked inside the car, and I told him I loved him too. I wasn't in love with him, but I knew I cared enough to love him as a friend. That wasn't important at the moment; I didn't want to leave him hanging. Saw had the ability to make me fall in love with him, and that feeling wasn't far off. I walked in the house smiling, feeling confident in where our relationship was headed.

The next morning, I headed to the laundromat to wash my work clothes for work. I hated doing laundry at the laundromat, but I knew things would go by quickly because I had Saw to talk to while I waited for my clothes.

Saw called my phone every morning like clockwork. As I waited for my morning call, I realized it was past the time he would normally call. I called him instead. His phone went straight to voicemail. I assumed he had to be on the phone with one of his cousins, so I waited for him to call me back. I was almost done with my laundry before my phone rang.

He said, "Hey, baby."

I was happy he finally called. I said, "I've been waiting for your call."

"Yeah, I knew you were. Look, man."

I could tell something was wrong with him. I thought he was going to tell me something about one of his family members.

"Joss, I don't know how to tell you this shit, but I need to tell you because I love you and I don't want to hurt you."

"Sawyer, what are you talking about hurting me?"

"Listen! Every time we spend time together, you show me I'm worth something. You never put me down, and you never used me for my money. You helped pay for stuff. I was just trying to be happy. I didn't think I would end up falling for you. I need to tell you I haven't been honest with you this whole time we have been hanging out."

"What is it, Saw?"

I thought he was going to tell me he had HIV or something. I was nervous. The anticipation was building inside of me, and I wanted to know what could have him professing his truths to me.

He said, "Joss, please believe me when I say I love you and I hope one day you can forgive me. Ha."

Annoyed, I said, "Saw, just say whatever it is that you're trying to say, please."

"I'm with someone. And before you ask, no, I'm not happy. I realized that after being with you."

I sat in my car gazing out into traffic. I knew I heard him correctly, but I was wondering, how? How could he be with someone if he spent all his time talking to me and working? We spent every weekend together. He took me around his family. How was he with someone? Maybe he moved on to the next or it was all just a game. All I knew I was over love.

I returned to reality. I asked, "Saw, why are you coming clean now, and how long were you planning on leading me on?"

"Joss, baby, I never wanted to lead you on. I was just trying to be your friend and maybe get some booty. But I never intended to hurt you. I have been trying to get out of this relationship with her for years, but she won't go anywhere. I never slept with her while we were hooking up either. I only want you. I needed to tell you because it was hurting me to see you happy, and I knew I was hurting you. You deserve better than me and what I did to you."

I was fuming, and I was trying to keep myself under control. Reality struck me again, and I was losing faith in love. I lost Drew and Saw in less than three months. I was going to be guarded for sure. I cleared my throat and said, "I appreciate you not letting the relationship drag on while you had someone else. I'm glad you told me, and I'm guessing this will be the last time we talk."

"We can be friends."

"I'd rather not!"

I quickly hung up. I was hurting inside. I was trying to do everything right, and I was still left standing with nothing. I had plenty of questions to ask Saw, but I didn't care. He belonged to someone else, and that wasn't going to change. The damage was done, and there was no way I could trust him. I had to get over him too!

I finished my laundry, deleted Saw's number as well as our text messages, and cried on my way home. I wanted to get all my tears out before then. I didn't want my daughter to see my pain, and I didn't want to tell my mother what just happened. I didn't expect to ever hear from Saw again.

*****

A couple of months later, I went to the park to walk the track. I loved the crisp smell of spring. Everything started to blossom in its own way around this time, and it was relaxing to see.

I walked a couple of laps before I walked to my car to get a sip of water. On my walk to the car, I noticed there were three other vehicles in the parking lot, but I was the only one walking the track. As I got closer to my car, I heard, "Ay yo!"

I hated when guys hit on me like that. I continued walking to my car without acknowledging the comment. I sat down in my front driver seat and cracked open my bottled water. I had my door open with one leg in the car and the other leg outside of the car.

A figure appeared to be approaching my car from the back passenger side. I quickly stood to let whoever it was know that I see them and I was ready for whatever. The track was out in the open, so I didn't think it was anything crazy about to happen.

It was four o'clock in the afternoon, and I assumed whoever it was just wanted something. When I stood up, I turned to face the direction in which the man was approaching. When I looked up, it was Saw. He was grinning at me from ear to ear. He said, "I called you a second ago, and you didn't answer. Ha."

I replied, "I don't answer to 'Ay yo!' That's not my name!"

"I see you haven't changed. You're still that secure woman you were when I first met you. Why are you at the track? You already look good. Ha. You got a minute to talk?"

"It's good to see you too, Sawyer. The last time I heard from you, you were telling me you had someone and you didn't want to lead me on. I'm on the way back to the track to finish my walk."

I didn't have any ill will toward Saw, but I didn't want to get caught up in any mess he was in. He didn't go into details when he told me he had someone. I didn't know how long they had been together, nor did I ask him what she was to him.

He asked, "Can you walk with me to my car at least?"

I did.

He said, "Girl, I missed you. I didn't think I'd ever see you again, but then again here you are. It's like fate wanted me to come to the park today to see you! Just like at the store. I went to work early today, took an early lunch, and I came to the park to get away from the job to breathe. I was online looking at cars until I looked up and saw you. How have you been, baby?"

As he talked, I listened. I had to admit, it was nice to see him. "I'm doing okay! I'm out and about trying to stay active. I'm still doing the same crap I've always done. Go to work and go home."

"You still ain't got no man? Ha."

"Nope! Every time I try, they seem to already have someone. I stay to myself, and I'm still single."

I didn't want to tell him about the brief moment I tried to rekindle my relationship with Drew. Drew showed up at the job to work again a couple of months ago. He helped me move in my house. Then we had a not-so-friendly exchange, and that was the end of that. I knew Drew and I could only be friends going forward. And emotionally I was over him.

He said, "Can I call you and possibly take you out to eat? I would like to do something nice for you if you will let me. I'm on my break now, but I can call you later when I get off, maybe catch up. Ha."

"My number is still the same, Sawyer, if you still have it from before?"

"I deleted it! Cause if I didn't delete it, Joss, I would have kept calling you."

That quickly reminded me to ask him about his situation. I asked, "What about your situation with your somebody? How's that going?"

"Oh yeah, that shit is over. After I told you everything, I told her the truth. She agreed to forgive me, but I kept bringing you up, and she got tired of hearing about the things you did versus the things she didn't do. We had a bad argument, and her son broke the argument up. Things weren't the same after that. So, yeah, I'm single!"

I was relieved to hear he was single. I wrote my number on his hand, and he walked me to the track. He asked, "Can I get a hug?"

I moved into him to let him know he could hug me. I didn't mind. I wasn't seeing anyone, and it was going to feel good to have him wrap his arms around me. I hugged him back. His arms wrapped tight around me like he genuinely missed me. Memories of our hotel stays crept into my head. I could feel my yoni getting excited. I could feel he was getting excited as well.

I stepped away from him to keep things from going somewhere I wasn't prepared for it to go. When I stepped back, he said, "Why you are running? Ha. You had this before. You can see I missed you. Ha."

I replied, "I can tell something missed me."

He reached in, kissed me on the cheek, and started walking back toward his car. He yelled, "I'm going to call you later. Seriously."

I smiled as I headed back to my walk. I didn't know how to feel. It felt good to feel like a woman again, to feel alive in the most intimate of ways. I didn't keep company with men. I didn't go on dates. The only men I ran into were my coworkers and Drew. I welcomed the feelings he was giving me.

I wasn't sure if I wanted to revisit what Saw and I had. He was a good guy who loved to work. He was honest with me, and I gave him credit for that. His sex was good. But I wasn't sure if he was what I needed in my life. I didn't know what to do, but I also didn't know if I had the right to think about having anything with him.

I continued my walk around the track with a little oomph in my steps. Maybe it was fate giving me another chance with Saw—a chance for him to be all mine. I was going to see where it all was going to go. My thoughts were premature, and I needed to wait for him to call or better yet if I answer when he would call.

Most of the day had gone by, and I kept looking at my phone waiting to see if Saw was really going to call. I assumed his work schedule was still the same, so I knew I had until the next morning for the call to happen. I wasn't going to torture myself looking to see if I had a message every few minutes. I continue with my normal duties. I'd worry about my next move with Sawyer when the time came.

The next morning, my phone rang. I said, "Hello!"

He said, "Hey, baby! I know you missed me because I missed you."

I laughed. "I haven't thought about you, Sawyer, so why would I start now? I've been busy getting my life together, and you were the furthest from my mind. Sorry to disappoint you there. I moved! I stay around the corner from my mom's house."

"I got my own spot too. Ha. My little cousin and his girl stay with me, for real this time. Maybe you can come over to my place sometime."

"Maybe!"

He told me where he lived, and if he was telling me where he lived, he had to be telling the truth about being single. He asked, "Have you eaten anything, baby?"

"Nope."

"Well, do you want to have breakfast with me?"

I quickly said, "Nah, I'm good, Saw."

"C'mon, Joss! Ha. You already know who I am, and you're treating me like a stranger. You must be scared to be around me."

"I'm not treating you like a stranger. I don't want men around my house. I work the nights, and I have a daughter I have to protect. I don't play about my kids, and I don't trust no man around my daughter. I'd rather not have male company at my house."

"I understand, and I'm sorry."

"Sorry for what this time, Sawyer?"

"I didn't know you felt like you did about men being around your house. I think I'm in your yard. You said you stayed around the corner from your mother, so I drove around a couple of streets that were around your mother's area, and I noticed your car in the driveway. I knew this was your car. I think I'm outside your house right now."

"You gotta be kidding me! I hate to tell you this, but you're appearing mighty desperate!"

"Nah, nothing like that. I just know I gotta do something different in order to get you back and to keep you. Ha."

I exhaled and mumbled under my breath, "I'm hanging up now. Give me a minute to get myself together and I'll let you in. You're lucky my daughter is at school."

I threw my phone on the bed, grabbed a headscarf, then grabbed my robe. I went to open the door for Sawyer. As soon as I opened the door, he grabbed me and engulfed me in a hug. He said, "I missed you, baby."

Since Saw took it upon himself to invade my house with his presence, I decided to make him breakfast. I loved to cook, and I was getting hungry myself. I wanted him to see I was a true woman that knew how to cook as well as keep a clean house.

I cooked while Saw and I played catch-up. He was still working long hours and extra days. He told me about his apartment and how he was happy to have his own spot. Afterward we ate.

Some time had passed, and I went into my bedroom to grab an incense. Saw walked in my room behind me, closed the door, then locked it. He walked up to me as I turned around. He was looking at me with pure lust in his eyes.

He grabbed me and slowly opened my robe to grab my breasts. My body melted in his hands. I didn't want to give in to him. I didn't want him to think it was going to be this easy for him—to bump into me at a park, show up at my house, and have his way with me.

Saw moved me closer to my bed as he kissed me. He removed my robe. And with what little room I had between him and the bed, I backed away from him. "I don't know if you are the same person I met and spent time with before. I need to be able to trust you before I just give in to you."

He kissed my lips then looked me in my eyes. "I'm going to show you. You can trust me."

He removed his pants while he stared at me. Saw walked closer to me then spun me around to face my bed. My body instantly went weak. He was about to do some things to me I was going to enjoy. He pushed me forward, and he slid his member around my yoni. I didn't want to give in. I wanted to push him away; at the same time I wanted him to take me.

Saw penetrated me from behind. He started off slow, but his excited rhythm took over. I felt my moisture release all over his member. I gave in, and I let him have his way with me. He turned me around, and he gave me amazing pain with his pleasure. When we were done, he whispered in my ear, "This time you're going to be all mine."

We talked while he dressed. He was tired from work and the session we just had. He said, "I'll call you later, baby."

I lay in my bed hoping I didn't get myself back into a situation I didn't want to be in. I hoped he wouldn't start playing games with me all over again. He was honest with me about his situation the first time, and I was sure he knew I wasn't going to agree to be any man's side chick. I missed him and the fun we had.

Sawyer called me as soon as he got home. "I missed you so much, and I'm glad we ran into each other again. Ha. I'm glad the day went the way it did."

I said, "I don't need a reminder of our hit-and-run session."

We both laughed. He said, "Yeah, it's funny now, but I really didn't mean to hurt you, baby."

We talked on the phone until Saw fell asleep. We talked about how the past few months were for the both of us, how he ended up getting his own place, and how he worked all the time to stay out of trouble. He said he thought about me every day, especially on the weekend.

I, in turn, told him how I ended up getting my house. I was up for a supervisor position at work. I didn't tell him about Drew because I considered Drew to be a weak moment he (Saw) played a part of happening. If we didn't go our separate ways, I would have never allowed Drew back in. I didn't ask him about the someone he was with. I wanted him to volunteer that information.

Saw agreed to call me when he got up for work. I answered the phone with a giant smile on my face when he called.

He said, "Hey, baby! I dreamed of you."

I asked him, "What did you dream about?"

"It was about you being my woman."

"Do you have the right to belong to me and only me?" I was opening the door for him to speak on the someone he spoke of a few months ago. "I'm no one's side chick, and I never intend to be."

"You won't be my side chick."

We talked until he arrived at his job. He told me to have a good night and he'd talk to me in the morning.

My work night was crazy and hectic, and I was ready to go. I was getting a migraine, and it was going to be around for a while. I needed to destress quick, fast, and in a hurry. My night was so stressful I had forgotten about Saw and I reconnecting.

When I got home, I walked straight into my bathroom, turned the water on super hot, removed my clothes, and let the heat soak up the last nine hours of stress. While I was calming my mind, thoughts of Saw popped into my head. I smiled thinking about how he handled me the morning before.

I wondered if he was thinking about me as well. I wasn't going to call him because I wasn't desperate. I didn't want him to think he had me sprung in any kind of way.

When I was finished with my shower, I went straight to my phone to see if I missed a call from Saw. To my surprise, I did miss a call from Saw. I called him back without thinking twice. He answered on the second ring.

I said, "Hey, you called?"

He said, "Yes, ma'am, I did. I thought you was tired of me already. I didn't know what to think, so I waited until you called me back. Do you want to come over to give me some of that good stuff you have between them legs?"

I laughed. "Is that all I'm good for? An invite to your house is one thing, but giving you some of me is another. I don't know where you been or what you have been up to for me to keep jumping in bed with you. I did it yesterday, but that was a weak moment and I needed some male member just as much as you wanted some yoni."

"You're right, Joss! You deserve better from me. Can I rephrase my invitation?"

"If you want to, Saw."

"I want to." He proceeded with rephrasing his invite. "Hey, pretty lady! I would like for you to come over to my house to talk, and maybe you will let me have some."

I knew he was trying to be funny, so I laughed.

He said, "Seriously, Joss. Do you want to come over and chill with me this morning?"

"Yes, I'll come over until it's time to pick my daughter from school. She has early release today."

"Cool, Imma text you the address."

Going to his house meant I got to check out his surroundings. I didn't know what I was walking into. I thought we were moving too fast again, and I didn't want that.

Saw didn't live that far from me, roughly three miles away. His apartment was a two-bedroom, one-bath apartment. When you walked in, you step directly into the living room, and straight ahead was the kitchen. Saw's bedroom was immediately to the right, and the bathroom separated the two rooms.

In his room, he had a queen-size bed without a headboard pushed up against the wall with the only window in the room. There was a dresser with a small TV on the corner and a small table next to the bed that had empty cartons of cigarettes on it. He had his clothes in a small hamper that sat on the floor by the dresser.

I asked about the other room and why the door was shut, assuming it was his cousin's bedroom.

He said, "Woman, let me show you before you start thinking I got another woman living here. My little cousin lives with me for the moment. I'm hopeful he will be moving out soon because he can never give me his half of the rent on time. I get tired of reminding him. And his girlfriend, I can't stand her. You might meet them before you leave."

I went back into Saw's bedroom while he ran to the kitchen to get his beer. While I waited, I continued to look around for anything that looked out of place. He came in the room as I sat down on his bed.

I said, "So tell me about this someone you were messing with."

With ease, he said, "She's no one, really. An older woman I happen to be with since her kids were young. She has an older son, and she let his grown ass move in with us. That was the end of us. He is grown and old enough to get his ass kicked. He is rude and disrespectful to me, his mom, and his girlfriend. We got into a physical altercation, and she chose him over. She and I have been apart for over two months. She's been over here once, but that was to bring the grandkids [her son's two kids] to see me. She tried to sneak over here to see if I had someone here about a month ago. She is crazy, and I'm glad she isn't in my life anymore. There was one other girl, but she just wanted my money. She was always asking me to buy her this and that, and when we went out, she spent a lot of my money. I wasn't down for that, so I dove back into work. I'm free to be with you, though."

Saw never gave me deceitful behavior vibes. His feelings for me were genuine because he reassured me about everything. I relaxed on my insecurities to see where things could go. We talked until I had to leave to get my daughter.

He walked me to my car. When we got to his front door, his cousin walked in. His cousin was tall, skinny, and dark, and cousin had a woman behind him. Saw said, "This is Joss, and she will be coming around here."

I quickly said, "Hi!"

When we got to my car, Saw kissed me then told me to be careful.

Saw was trying to prove to me he could be trusted. I was feeling more and more comfortable about giving him another chance at a relationship. He had qualities about him I liked in a man. He was attentive to me in the past, and I'm confident that didn't change.

I realized he didn't make that strange "ha" noise as much when we were talking. I still didn't think he was aware he made the noise, but I was glad he didn't do it as much. I think he had a slight tic, causing him to involuntarily add the word. Saw's vibe was peaceful and relaxing, and I was sure that was all he wanted out of life.

The next morning Saw invited me to come over to his place again. When I got there, his cousin and the woman from yesterday were asleep in the living room. Saw ushered me to his room. He had a towel over the window, making the room dark. I understood what he was trying to do—blocking out the light because we were night owls. He told me to get comfortable, and I did. He wanted to take a nap, and I didn't mind.

I slept naked, and he remembered that from before. When he saw me get under the blanket with my sundress still on, he said, "So you're going to act like I never saw you naked? I told you to get comfortable, and I know you're not going to be comfortable in that dress. Go ahead and take it off."

I didn't say a word, and I knew what he was saying was true. Clothing suffocated me. I could only sleep one way, and that was naked. I wasn't going to get any sleep with my dress on.

Saw got into bed wearing his boxers and a wifebeater. He motioned for me to come closer to him to lie on his chest. While I lay on his chest, I started thinking of all the possibilities of having a man I could build a future with. It had been three days since Saw reentered my life, and he had me like putty in his arms already.

It wasn't long before Saw was on top of me pounding away. The bed was a bit worn, and he didn't have a headboard. Every time he thrust forward inside me, the bedrails hit the wall. The noise could be heard in the living room for sure. Saw didn't care about the noise. He said it was his house, and he didn't care. I tried so hard not to be loud, but Saw provoked my moans. He wanted to know he was doing a good job. He was doing just that. I could no longer stifle my moans. The folks in the living room had front row seats to the sounds coming from his bedroom. I was well pleased with everything Saw was giving me, with each thrust as well as each kiss. The walk of confidence was going to have me looking like a well-satisfied woman.

*****

Saw and I did the same thing every morning. The front door of his apartment would already be unlocked for me in the morning. Some days his cousin and the woman would be asleep, and other days they wouldn't be home. The actions were still the same. His bedroom gave sound to a perfect flick, with happy endings. I stopped caring about the loud moans that came from me. I was being pleased the right way, and I lost myself in Saw every time he gave his lovin' to me. We picked up right where we left off almost three months ago.

The seasons were changing, and everything was going well for Saw and I. We spent all our free time together. Our relationship was progressing, and we were rotating weekends at each other's house. My daughter was in her teen phase, so she was never at home. His cousin's girlfriend was getting on his nerve, and his neighbor played her music loud when he was trying to sleep. So, we exploited my home for our personal behavior on the weekends.

We wanted to go on a romantic trip to Virginia Beach for the Labor Day holiday. I had plenty of vacation time built up at work, and Saw had a good number of hours. We planned to stay for a week. We wanted a nice four-star hotel with our room on the top floor, with a jacuzzi in the room. We were going to go all out.

One Friday, Saw received a call from his cousin Greg. Greg told Saw his mom's house caught fire and the house was totaled. Saw loved his family, and he was close to his aunt (Greg's mom). He found out she was okay, but she needed some folks to come help clean up some of the debris from the fire in the morning. He immediately volunteered our service. I enjoyed being around his family, and I wanted to help.

We got up early the next morning and headed to his home county where all his older family members stayed. There was a handful of family members already there showing their support of his aunt. We cleaned, worked, and packaged items to be removed from the house.

Saw was with the men outside, and I was with the women inside. I was cleaning and packaging up the living room. One of Saw's older cousins worked beside me. She talked to me like she knew me all my life. We talked and laughed about life. When we got on to the subject of kids, she mentioned a name I recognized. She said, "You gotta know my daughter. My daughter knows everybody. Her name is Sade! Sade Strawberry!"

I had a cool relationship with a woman named Sade; she worked for me in the past at The Warehouse. She was someone I spoke to on the regular, and we had lunch a couple of times.

"Sade Strawberry is your daughter? OMG, this world is small. And you're Saw's cousin!"

She said, "Imma call her now!"

On the other end of her phone, Sade's voice said, "Hello, Mama!"

I was in good hands with my relationship with Saw because Sade would tell me everything I needed to know about her cousin if need be. Sade was my friend, and I was relieved in knowing they were all related.

Sade's mom was talking fast. "Your friend is over here."

She was popping off questions and comments all in the same sentence. Sade's mother then handed me the phone so I could speak to Sade myself.

"Hey, girl. I can't believe this beautiful woman I'm working beside is your mother. Better yet, I didn't know you were cousins with the dude I have been telling you I was involved with."

She said, "Is Saw the guy you've been hooking up with these past couple of months? The one you call the pounder? The funny one? Girl, bye." Her enthusiasm faded. "Yeah, that boy is my cousin."

I said, "Dang, Sade, do you know something I should know?"

"Nope, Saw is a good dude. You're in good hands. He's just a nut."

I laughed. "Okay now, don't make me have to make you a cousin short in this world. You know I'm crazy and I don't have time for no mess."

We both laughed.

I told Sade I would call her later; I handed the phone back to her mother, and they continued to talk. I felt a bit of peace knowing she knew about my past heartbreaks and personally knows the guy I was currently dating. Sade knew about Drew and how our relationship ended. I was sure she wouldn't let her family hurt me on that level. I mentioned to Saw I knew Sade and that we were pretty cool. Saw got excited and said, "Yeah, that's my cousin. How you know her?"

"I met her some years back at work. I was her trainer at the time, and she was one of my best workers."

He said, "I love my family. Ha."

A month had gone by. Saw worked, I worked. We were having sex every day, multiple times a day some days. We were spending most of our time at my house because we had more privacy there. His cousin and his girlfriend were always at his place, and with them constantly listening to us sexing, things were getting a little weird. Unofficially, Saw had practically moved in with me.

We had a healthy routine, and I was happy. Saw and my daughter got along with each other. They laughed and joked around with each other. My son was still at school and hadn't met Saw yet, but he knew about him from our texts and phone calls.

My job (now after my promotion) as a supervisor ensured me the privilege to recommend folks to come work for me during the busiest time of the season. I had my loyal folks that returned each year to work for me. One of those people happened to be my girl Sade.

Sade was a good worker, and we maintained a good friendship outside of work. I was glad she was coming back to work for me. I wanted to gossip with her about her cousin and to tell her about some of the good things about our relationship.

The following week, Sade and I were chatting it up on the production floor, laughing about current and past gossip. She surprised me by telling me she was getting married soon.

I was excited for her, and I picked on her for keeping her engagement a secret. She didn't want to jinx her marriage by telling negative people, and I understood how she felt. That same reason was why I kept Saw a secret in the beginning of our relationship. He was nobody's business but mine. "I'm lucky to have a guy like Saw."

She said, "Yeah, he's been through a lot. He is a really good guy. It's messed up how his wife did him though."

I instantly heard silence. It was a different kind of silence. It felt like I blacked out or something because Sade's mouth was still moving, but I didn't hear anything after the word "wife." "Hold up, hold up, hold up! Sade, did you say wife?"

She was surprised. "You didn't know about his wife? I thought you knew. Joss, I didn't know you didn't know."

I was annoyed, and I said, "Sade, I didn't know he was married. He never told me he was married. When we first met, he told me he had someone. We went about our business and caught up with each other three months ago after not speaking for a while. He told me he left whoever she was alone. No one in your family said anything to me about a wife, and we hang with your family almost every freakin' weekend." My voice got louder, and I was angry. "HELL NO, SADE, I DIDN'T KNOW HE WAS MARRIED!"

Sade grabbed me by my arm and guided me to my desk. While we walked, she said, "Calm down, Joss. I didn't know you didn't know. I know he's got a reason for not telling you, or maybe he is waiting for the right time to tell you. I know they not together. I know that much. His wife or ex-wife [she couldn't remember if they had gotten a divorce or not] put him out the house some time ago because he lost his job. She likes money, Joss, and her kids. I heard when Saw wasn't bringing in the money, she put him out. She put him out of the house a lot. Things got bad when he told her she had to pick him or the kids. I heard she went ballistic on him. She chose the kids over him. They aren't even kids, Joss, they are grown adults. And her son had two kids of his own."

Sade lowered her voice to a whisper. She said, "She works at my other job. She's a counselor's assistant, part-time, at the same clinic. That woman isn't right in the head, though. Sawyer would give her his whole paycheck to pay bills, and she spent it on the grandkids instead. When he was with her, he worked for nothing, Joss. No one in the family liked him being with her."

That to me only explained the reason he was stingy with his money. Sawyer forgot to inform me he was legally married.

I told her I needed to take a break. I didn't know how to feel. I wanted to call Saw to yell at him for lying to me or for not telling me the real truth about his somebody. I didn't want to confront him over the phone. I wanted to see his reaction when he finds out I know his secret, when I tell him I know he had a fucking wife. He needed to see the hurt in me this time around. I couldn't believe I was coming full circle as a volunteered mistress again.

The workday was almost over, and I couldn't wait to get home. I was going to get my answers today! I needed all this to be a dream. I was hoping Sade's information was wrong. Maybe I'd be surprised and he already had a divorce pending. Maybe all this would be a lie all in itself.

When I pulled into my yard, Saw's vehicle was nowhere in sight. He was normally home before me. I thought Sade warned him about the wrath that was coming his way. I knew Sade didn't do no such thing. I had time to calm down before he got there. I needed to calm down to ensure I got the answers I needed. I didn't want him to leave before I got my answers.

A few seconds later, Saw was pulling into the driveway. I could tell by his walk he didn't know I knew his secret. He was walking with a pep in his step. He was happy.

I stood in the kitchen pacing the floor. He stepped through the door, and I was facing the same door from the other side of the room. He said, "Hey, baby. What's wrong? Ha."

I shook my head at him as I yelled, "Why didn't you tell me you are married, Sawyer?"

Without saying a word, he looked up at me, turned around, and walked back out of the door. I went after him until I got to the door. I wasn't expecting him to walk away like he did. I hesitated on whether to follow him outside. I wanted to know what the hell was going on. I walked away from the door, and I sat up against the kitchen sink with my arms crossed silently, praying for clarity. It wasn't long before Saw walked back in the house. He said, "Who told you?"

"Why does it matter who told me, Saw? You weren't the one who told me. Sade accidentally told me. She was telling me how you deserved better than this wife of yours whom I knew nothing about. I can't believe you! Especially after I told you everything I went through with Drew. I don't mess around with married men, Sawyer. Everything we went through the first time we met…you were honest then. You could have told me you were married."

He started rubbing his head, anxiously. He was visibly agitated. He lowered his head. He lifted his head, and he was crying. I didn't know which way the situation was going to go.

"Joss, I didn't want to tell you because I knew you would leave me. I left her at the beginning of the year, sometime in February. We are going through our one-year separation, and it's up in February. I'm going to file for divorce the first chance I get. I swear because I want to marry you. I don't want her. After being with you, I realized I deserved so much better. I can stand here and admit to you my relationship with my wife was mentally abusive. She used me to take care of her and them kids, and it was 'fuck Saw' the whole time. She put me out. I got on my feet then got the apartment and a new job. I want you, Joss, and I'm sorry I didn't tell you I was married. Please believe me when I say I'm getting a divorce."

I wanted to be mad. I wanted to yell at him until I couldn't yell anymore, but Saw was standing in the middle of my kitchen trying. He didn't go anywhere, and he was always with me, so I knew he hadn't seen her. He and I were having sex every day, so I knew he wasn't fucking her. I hoped.

I asked, "When was the last time you saw her?"

He quickly said, "I haven't seen that woman since she brought the grandkids to see me. That March, right before I saw you at the park."

Out of frustration, I said, "Why couldn't you at least tell me you were separated? When were you going to tell me anyway? You told me I was going to be Mrs. Burnette all the while knowing that couldn't be the case until you got a divorce. I know you had to know I was eventually going to learn the truth."

Saw didn't hesitate to answer any of my questions. The more he told me, the more questions I had for him. My emotions were somewhere else, and I didn't know what to do. I wanted to leave him alone, at least until his divorce, but I knew his love for me was sincere. I was sure the divorce was going to happen after his separation period.

*****

A week after finding out Saw was, in fact, married, I noticed Saw's drinking increased. He was smoking more, and he wasn't acting like his normal self. He would come home from work with two beers and a new unopened pack of cigarettes in a bag. He'd sit on my front porch smoking and drinking, scrolling for cars on Craigslist all day and night. He started developing a depressing routine.

When his poisons were gone or empty, he would run back to the store to get two more beers and another pack of cigarettes. He would come in long enough to eat, and then he went back to drinking. Some days he would get so drunk he wouldn't make it out of his car. I didn't know what was going on with him, but I knew something was wrong, and I wasn't happy with his behavior. Saw had a happy-go-lucky attitude most of the time, and he wasn't laughing about much lately. He was distancing himself from me, and I gave him his space, whether it was time on the porch or in his car. I didn't know how to help him. He didn't want to go home, so that gave me a sense of relief.

One Saturday we were at Saw's house getting ready to visit his mother. She was heavy on his mind, and he wanted to physically make sure she was okay. Saw was in the bathroom getting ready, and I was in his bedroom adding last-minute details to my outfit when his phone began to ring. I thought it might have been his mom or someone else of importance.

I knocked on the door to tell him his phone was ringing. When I walked back into the bedroom, the phone stopped ringing, but it instantly started ringing again. I ignored the call until it stopped ringing once more. I started putting on my sandals when his phone rang again. I instantly became annoyed, contemplating answering his phone.

His phone never rang this much, and I assumed the call was important. He had the phone turned upside down with the screen facing down. I flipped the phone over, and the name that appeared on the phone screen caused me to drop the phone. While picking the phone up from the floor, Saw emerged from the bathroom.

Anger rose in me, and I wanted to know what the fuck was going on. It was instant déjà vu. I couldn't believe what just happened. Saw walked in the room smiling.

I loudly said, "Your phone has been ringing. I didn't go through it [he didn't have a lock on his phone], but I did see who was calling!"

I handed him his phone. He looked at his phone, and then he looked over at me.

He said, "Did you speak to her? Please tell me you didn't speak to her. I didn't want her to know about you because she is going to start harassing you. She has been trying to figure out a way to get alimony from me, and her knowing about you will just make her go after my pockets even more."

"Are you kidding me, Sawyer? Is that all you're concerned with, because I'm more concerned that the person you say you don't want to know about me is listed in your phone as Wifey!" I yelled. "What the fuck, Saw! It's ironic I learn of her, and now she's calling your phone. And apparently it's important, if she is repeatedly calling your phone."

I was fuming, and I knew there was more to this story. "Suddenly out of the blue, she starts calling you. There's a reason for her calls, Saw!"

He looked at me with a worried look on his face. He said, "Joss, you gotta let me explain. Ha. Whatever you think, I didn't lie to you! I swear! I got the apartment to get away from her so I can get a divorce and have a life. I want a divorce from her, and I am going to do everything in my power to make sure it happens. I really don't know why she's calling, Joss!"

I instantly called, "Bullshit!" Then I grabbed my things. "I'm going home!"

Saw became anxious. "C'mon, Joss. Can you at least wait until Carl gets here? Let him tell you everything if you're not trying to hear what I have to say. I don't know any other way to prove to you I'm telling you the truth. Please, please, please wait until he gets here to back me up before you leave. I'm not playing games with you, Joss. We are about to go see my mother. Doesn't that count for something?"

On the inside, I was crying. I didn't want him to see me cry. I didn't want him to know I was hurt, even though I was dying inside. I couldn't believe this crap was happening to me, finding out he was married and now her calling his phone. And to top it all off, he wanted me to act like a side chick by not answering his phone. Keeping me a secret from her. Sparing her emotions while trampling mine. Heat was rising through my body. I wanted to hit something. I wanted to go home.

As Saw pleaded for me not to leave, his cousin Carl walked in his apartment. Carl was taking the ride with us to see some people. Carl was always hyped and loud. I never saw him calm or sober. Carl was Saw's best friend, but he called him his cousin because they've known each other since elementary school. Carl had a different woman with him every time we saw him. And we saw him almost three times a week, hanging together on the weekend and coming to Saw's house after work for a drink or two. Carl thought he was an old-school Casanova, a pimp or something. He was proud he had a different woman with him every time he brought a woman around. He didn't hide who he was from me.

Carl walked in the bedroom, and he said, "What's going on, fam?"

Saw didn't hesitate to confirm with his witness. He said, "Man, that woman is at it again, and she's blowing my phone up. Can you please tell her [he pointed at me] how this woman is?"

Carl walked over to me and said, "Joss, this man is in love with you. I have never seen him act like he acts around you. That woman he is married to is a beast. Until you came along, Saw was never around. He was either locked up in the house or at work. He wasn't happy, he was miserable. You came and brightened up this man's world. He was planning on divorcing her before he even linked up with you."

Saw came over to me. He said, "Please believe me, baby! I can't lose you. I'm going to get a divorce as soon as this separation period is over. I have about six more months, Joss. I can file for a divorce then. Please believe me. I will do anything. You can come over here every day if you want. I will give you a copy of the keys to my crib. Just believe me when I say I want to be with you, baby."

Stupidly enough, I believed him. I felt betrayed and disappointed, but I believed him. "Saw, when I found out you were married, it broke my heart. I have faith you are going to do what you say you are going to do. That's the only reason I'm willing to see this mess through. I don't understand why she is calling your phone like she is. Or why you still have her listed in your phone as Wifey, like everything is still kosher between the two of you. I'm not trying to get hurt by you or anyone else. And I'm not scared of no one but God, so if she wants to start with me, she can."

Before I could say anything else, Saw said, "Joss, look, I'm not just a married man. I am a separated man, and I intend to get a divorce as soon as February gets here. I promise you I'm trying to get that woman behind me. I will prove whatever I need to prove to you to get you to believe me. If you leave me now, I know you will not be single in five months. You will move on without me. Please don't leave me, Joss, please!"

Against my better judgment, I told Saw I'd give him a chance to prove it all to me. I told him I wanted him to go to a lawyer's office as soon as possible to make sure he was following every protocol to make sure the separation was valid. "No more games or secrets, Sawyer! What ties do you have with her that may tie you to her after the divorce? Are any of the kids you speak about yours?"

"Nothing, no kids or anything. The grandkids were the only thing I felt bad about. I miss 'em, but those are her son's kids. After the altercation, I'm sure I can't see them anymore no ways."

Carl was going back and forth from the bedroom to the kitchen snacking on some chips. He said, "I hate to interrupt, but can we go already? I don't have time for you guys to sort out your relationship. I'm ready to go. I may have plans with a woman later, and you guys are holding everything up. Are we going or not?"

Saw looked over at me for approval, and I nodded my head as to say, "We can still go."

Things were awkward between us on the drive to see his mom. Carl was in the backseat talking to what I presumed to be the woman he was meeting up with later. Saw sat in the passenger seat anxiously directing me to his mom's house.

I needed a quick therapy moment to get my mind together. I kept Beyoncé's *Beyoncé* album on repeat in my car. I only switched it out to play Nicki Minaj's *The Pinkprint* album. But the way I was feeling, he was going to listen to all the songs they were going to sing or rap to my spirit for however long I decided was sufficient. I skipped "Drunk in Love," which was Saw's theme song for our relationship.

Every song that played resonated with my hurt. Their words helped me calm down. A few of the songs hit home for me. I needed my music therapy to get me through whatever this was I was going through. We listened to Beyoncé and Nicki Minaj the entire ride.

We visited his mom for a couple of hours. And she was happy to see him, and he was happy to see her. Saw loved his mother deeply, and it showed. His mother was almost seventy years old, and after he told her, everything that happened before we got to her, she said, "I never liked that woman, Sawyer. She was mean to you and you know it." Her comment backed what Saw told me earlier.

The rest of the visit went well, and Saw was ready to go so he could start drinking. Carl was also ready to go to get to his booty call. I just wanted to get home to process everything. I had more questions for Saw, but I also needed time to think.

When we got back in town, Saw and I headed to my place. When we got in the house and settled in, I said, "What did the message say?"

He replied, "What message?"

"The message 'Wifey' left you after calling your phone earlier. I heard your phone beep after one of those calls. The beep that indicated you had a message, I'm sure?"

Surprised, he said, "I didn't know she left a message."

He pulled his phone out, then he put the phone on speaker to play the message. She said, "I was just calling to say thank you!"

Saw's eyes met mine. My eyes said what my lips blurted out. "What is she thanking you for, Saw?"

Worried, Saw said, "OMG! Fuck! Joss! I forgot I let her borrow forty dollars like two weeks ago. She has to be thanking me for the money."

My blood began to boil. "Saw, why does this keep getting worse? I keep getting slapped in the face over and over because you constantly leave out information. First, I find out that you are married not from you but from your cousin. Then I find out your wife has been calling your phone, and the only reason I found that out is because I so happen to be present when she called. Now I'm finding out that you let her borrow some money two weeks ago. I'm pretty damn sure we were together at that point. And you told me you haven't seen her since February. Two weeks ago wasn't February, Saw! What else haven't you told me? What more is going to come crashing down on our relationship? Now I see why you are doing all this drinking. Your conscience is fucking you up! I don't know what to do or say, but I'm tired of it all!"

I got in bed. I didn't know what to think or do. I couldn't believe this was my life. I laid in the bed thinking about everything.

Saw was stingy with his money, and I assumed his wife was the reason. He confirmed it during one of my interrogation sessions with him. When it came time to dish out any kind of money, he did the bare minimum, until it was time to get drunk. I didn't understand why he was suddenly giving her money.

Saw went further into his depressing routine. He never brought a case of beer unless we were going to a family event, but once he was drunk, he would buy beer after beer as well as cigarette after cigarette. This was his daily routine, and he did it until it was time to go to sleep. He went through two to three packs of cigarettes every day. He lit up almost every ten minutes. I watched him smoke on occasion, and I noticed he only smoked half the cigarette. The other half would sit in between his fingers in the same hand as his beer. Saw was a heavy smoker, and if we weren't in a well-ventilated room, his cigarette smoke suffocated me. His smoking was out of control, just like his drinking.

Other than his personal routine, Saw and I settled into a couple's routine as well. We went to work, ate, and had sex. Free time with others came on the weekend.

Sex was important to Saw, and he was always ready for it. We had sex every day multiple times a day. More makeup sex than anything. We sexed to go to bed and sometimes before he went to work. He was addicted to my yoni, and he wanted to stay in it all the time. He was a few years older than me, but he had stamina for days. His desire for me every day was definitely a turn-on.

Our trip to the beach was approaching, and Saw was slowly returning to his normal self. I was glad his mood was changing because I wanted to have fun at the beach. I wanted to put the last month behind us. I desired to get back to us. I was secretly counting down the time until Saw was able to file for divorce. His one-year separation was up in February, and September was rounding the corner. I couldn't wait.

The day finally arrived for our beach trip, and we were finally going to get away from all the madness. We made the trip about us and us getting our spirit of love back. We allowed each other to make one phone call a day unless it was one of the kids. But no phones were allowed on our trip.

When we walked into our hotel room that was three floors from the rooftop, my thoughts read, *Sex, sex, and more sex!* Every surface in the room planted a quick image in my head as to the possibilities of sexual pleasure—from the balcony, the kitchen area, the table, sofa, the Jacuzzi, and the shower.

The shower was breathtaking. It was bright white glazed over marble stones. There was a solid stone bench that went alongside the longest wall of the shower. The shower had four walls and a door, and it was all encased in glass. There was a huge shower head that hung in the center of the shower. Each wall contained smaller showerheads that sprayed directly to the center of the shower floor. The wall with the knobs had the main showerhead and eight additional sprouts that sprayed into the center of the shower as well. It was beautiful, and I couldn't wait for us to use it. Saw had a lot of makeup sex to give to me, and I intend to cash in while on this trip.

We settled in, and we were both ready to explore. We decided to get some food before we went night fishing on the pier. We had time to waste until dark.

When we got back to the room, I figured it was no time like the present to play in the shower. I took my clothes off while Saw opened the patio doors to the balcony.

I caught his attention, and I said, "Meet me in the shower."

Saw looked at me, smiled, and followed me to the bathroom.

The water steamed the bathroom. Inside the shower, Saw and I were gently being sprayed with water across our bodies. Both of us were standing under the water, bodies touching. Water was pouring across our lips while we kissed.

Saw lowered to his knee, raising one of my legs and placing it on the shower bench. He grabbed me from behind, pushing me into him. He played with my yoni, some with his tongue and other times with his fingers. The water flowing down my body was gracefully being sucked off me by my lover. I closed my eyes, enjoying the moment.

I interrupted Saw while he basked in my love. "Sit on the bench."

He comfortably sat on the bench, and I slowly sat on his member. I rode him slowly while the hot water flowed down our bodies. Saw was entranced in my motions. He grabbed my ass, assisting my forward motions. He squeezed and gripped my ass. His grips were rough and aggressive, each squeeze making me bounce on him faster.

Saw softly bit on my nipples, alternating between light sucking. Every part of our bodies was moving, whether soft, light, fast, or hard. I wanted to catch my breath; I wanted to breathe. My body was giving him all my energy. My head fell forward with ecstasy, meeting his lips. Our lips barely touched as we exchanged breaths we each let out. I took in what he breathed into me. Moving together in a perfect rhythm, we became one. Saw wrapped his arms around my waist as he slowed my rhythm, and then I felt the throbbing of his release.

We both agreed we couldn't wait for round 2. We weren't ready to go after our week of bliss. Our vacation was everything we desired it to be. On the day of checkout, we didn't check out; we added two more days to our stay.

We came back from our trip refreshed. We had a fresh start on our relationship. Our trip put the focus back on each other. Before the trip, Saw knew I was over all the drama that came with him. I was about to give up on us. The trip was much needed, and on the trip, Saw showed me he loved me.

\*\*\*\*\*

Saw began to receive weird phone calls around six and seven every night. He said the calls were probably a bill collector for some auto loan. He would hit Ignore, then there would be a beep indicating a voicemail. He never hid his phone from me, and it was never an issue. Our phones were accessible to each other. I didn't think twice about the phone calls, but I was bothered the calls started out of nowhere.

A few days later, Saw came in the house from sitting in his car. He was drunk. He said, "Yo, I gotta tell you something."

Whatever it was, I knew with him it could go either way. Whatever it was, I needed to pay attention.

He said, "Man, that's her calling me every day. She found out my son was getting out, and she wants to see him. I told her that was between him and her, but she said the grandkids missed me too. I spoke to them on the phone, and I miss them, Joss. I want to see them. I don't give a fuck about her, but I do care about the kids."

My mouth opened, and the only thing I could say was his name: "Sawyer!" I started to raise my voice out of anger. "So, she has been calling your phone and you knew this the whole time? Then you cover it up with a lie. I can't believe we are doing this shit all over again, Saw! Why is it so hard for you to be honest with me? And you told me before you didn't care about what was going on over there, but now you miss the kids. Seems like a setup to me. Either you're trying to play me so you can go see your wife or she knows how to get you back into her house. What's next, Saw?"

"She invited me to Thanksgiving dinner."

"You blurted that out like I'm going to say, 'Okay, you should go'! Like I should freely let my boyfriend, who is supposed to be separated from his wife, who should be getting a divorce in a few months, go have a nice family Thanksgiving Day dinner with his other family. And I'm supposed to say what, Saw? I can't believe we are having this conversation right now."

"Joss, I need to see if she changed."

I instantly lost it. "What the hell do you mean you need to see if she changed? Who the hell do you think I am? You're supposed to be divorcing her, yet you want to find out if she changed. I can't believe my ears."

Before things got out of hand, I walked past him and went into the kitchen. I grabbed my keys and left. I got in my car and drove off. While driving, I listened to "Love and War," "I'm Cursed," and "Emotional Rollercoaster" on repeat. I was tired of this love thing.

I drove without a destination in mind. I listened to songs where women were singing about how to deal with a broken heart, songs dealing with the same crap I was dealing with. I was amazed at how many songs there were on being the other woman or songs where he promised to leave. Music was my way to survive the strongest drug in the world, which is love. I drove around for hours listening to love songs, praying, and crying. I cried even harder as I drove back home.

Saw's drinking was getting out of hand, and he was making stupid-ass decisions—decisions that were doing more harm to our relationship than good. This was the first time I began to doubt Saw and our relationship.

When I got home, Saw was sitting up waiting for me. I quickly told him I wasn't in the mood to talk to him about something he already knew the answer to. I went to bed emotionally drained.

Saw's wife continued to call every day until one day I had enough. He was in one of his drunken slumbers when his phone started to ring. I was over this woman at this point, and I wanted her to know I was around.

My intentions weren't to be ugly but to have a general conversation with the woman, especially since Saw told me she was older. In the past, I was never disrespectful when I spoke to the other women when my ex Marcus got caught up. I learned you get more information out of the other women being respectful. Saw's wife wasn't going to be any different. I decided to answer the phone.

When she heard my voice, she instantly started yelling, "Where is Sawyer? You do know you are messing with a married man, don't you? I want to talk to my husband, and you better leave him alone!"

I didn't know what to say to her words. She was aggressive and irate. It had been some time since she and Saw had been together, but this woman was on the other end of the phone acting like he had just left home. I instantly regretted the idea to try to talk to her. She was crazy just like I was told. I hung the phone up on her.

She called right back. I ignored it. She then started texting. "Bitch, you better leave my husband alone!"

I wasn't going to feed into her silliness, so I decided to ignore her texts as well. She continued to text throughout the night. I began to feel some kind of way about her behavior. I was getting frustrated with her texting, and I was ready to fire back. I wanted to set the record straight even if Saw wasn't going to.

Saw lay across my bed in la-la land while I was close to handling his soon-to-be ex-wife, something I wanted him to do. I wanted him to make it clear to her things were over between the two of them. He had his chance to do whatever it was he needed to do to set her straight, but he failed.

I turned his phone on vibrate, and I let her text away, occasionally looking at the messages. She said, "I will take you to court, bitch! You're messing with a married man. I can take you to court and sue you. I'm going to get you, bitch! Watch and see! You will be getting served this week, boo! Watch and see! You're no woman, sleeping with another woman's man."

Saw woke up to twenty-five messages from his dear old wife. He was shocked. "You spoke to her? Please tell me you didn't! She's not going to stop calling now that she knows there is another woman in my life."

He looked at the phone. He began reading the messages. "Joss, she is talking about suing you for alienation of affection. This shit is going too far, man!"

I yelled, "You created this problem, Saw, and now you want to say that it's getting out of hand? If you're getting a divorce, she shouldn't be calling you and harassing you. Who cares if she found out about me? She was going to eventually find out from friends or family. Why the hell are you protecting her feelings? You're definitely not protecting mine. Is it because she is still in the picture, Saw? And as far as her trying to sue me, I wasn't the reason your marriage broke up. That's between you and her. You already had your apartment when I came around. She may be getting me confused with some other chick, but she needs to get her stories straight too."

He said, "You don't understand. She is going to try to use you to get alimony from me. That's why I didn't want her to know about you. I don't want to pay her alimony."

My anger multiplied. I went from zero to one thousand real quick. I said, "Fuck you, the alimony, and her!" I walked away from him. I turned back around, and I said, "This is why I don't fuck with married men!"

Things were changing between Saw and I rapidly. The atmosphere was different, and it was mostly on my part. I was beginning to wonder if Saw was worth all the drama. This woman had control over him, and it wasn't healthy. Deep down, I knew we weren't going to make it.

That Saturday, Saw and I decided to get a little dressy and go for a ride. We didn't have any plans. We were just trying to look good outside of our normal work clothes. Saw's phone rang as soon as we got in his truck. He said, "Hello!" Then he added, "Man, I ain't fucking with you today!" He looked over at me, and then he said, "Okay. That was Carl. He wants us to come by his place for a little bit."

I was shocked. "What? The way he stays in the streets? With all the women we see him with? I didn't think he had a home!"

Saw looked over at me and laughed. "Girl you're crazy."

"No, I'm serious."

He quickly said, "Oh, shoot, that reminds me. Carl lives with his wife."

I looked over at Saw in even more shock. Angrily I said, "So, this must be a family thing! I find what ya do disrespectful as hell. Both of ya have women you're involved with as well as wives. Whether you're happy at home or not, it's not right. I don't feel comfortable going over there and meeting his wife when I know the truth. We still have your drama and wife to contend with."

We continued with our plans to go for a ride.

*****

One night at work, I got a phone call from my daughter. Getting a phone call from my daughter at three in the morning instantly made me worried. When I answered, she started whispering.

I said, "Why are you whispering?"

"Can you come home?"

"Why, Nila? You know I'm at work."

"Mommy, Saw just walked in the house with a bunch of guys. I'm in my room. I heard him when he came in the house. I thought he was by himself until I heard them all laugh. I called you as soon as I shut my door."

I heard silence again. "He did what?"

She said it sounded like a lot of guys and she didn't feel comfortable. I quickly told her I was on my way. I went to my desk, grabbed my keys, and headed to my car. I dialed Saw's phone as I headed out of the building. The phone rang until his voicemail picked up. I left him a message to call me as soon as he heard my message. I hung the phone up and instantly hit redial. I continued to call his phone until I pulled into my driveway. I was surprised to only see Saw's vehicle in the yard. I assumed everyone left already. I was tired of Saw's drunken behavior. He was getting worse, and he didn't even know it. I knew he was drunk.

I went to put my key in my front door, and the door slowly opened. My heart instantly sank into my stomach. I prayed as I ran in my front door to check for my daughter. Carl looked up at me from my living room couch and said, "Hey, Joss! What's good?"

My fear subsided seeing Carl. Other than Carl cheating on his wife, he was a pretty decent guy. He was older, and he had some dignity about himself. Everything had to be okay if he was here at my house.

My eyes panned the rest of my living room. My couch was filled with sleeping drunk men. There was another guy asleep on my floor, and there was another asleep at my desk. I was about to lose it.

I went to my daughter's room. She still had her door locked, and while on the phone, she said she barricaded it with her dresser. I knocked on the door while calling her name, letting her know I was home and everything was okay. She opened the door, gave me a hug, and told me she loved me. She went back in her room, shutting her door behind her.

I walked to my bedroom where I assumed Saw was. The bedroom TV was on, giving me enough light to see Saw was passed out on the bed, drunk as usual. That explained why he didn't answer any of my calls.

I yelled his name. "Sawyer!"

He didn't move or react to me calling his name. I yelled his name again. "Saw!" He still didn't flinch.

I got closer to him and yelled dead in his face, "Saw!"

He shifted and said, "Huh?"

I snapped. "What in the hell do you mean HUH? Get the hell up!"

I looked at him, and no matter how much I told myself I wasn't going to belittle him in front of whoever those guys were camped out in my living room, I couldn't help it. I exploded. "I'm tired of your reckless behavior, Saw. I'm tired of your drinking. You're too damn old to not be able to hold your liquor. I'm tired of you getting pissy damn drunk and not remembering anything the next day. You're drinking is out of control."

He sat up while steering at me. His face contained a stupid look that made me want to slap the shit out of him. I cut on the bedroom light to get a better look at him. Saw was sitting up straight, but he wasn't comprehending a damn thing I was saying to him.

My fury multiplied. Nothing I said or did was going to be remembered in the morning. I was going to make damn sure I repeated myself as soon as he was coherent. As soon as he was alert, I was going to tell him to get his shit together or I was done with him.

I waited patiently for three long hours for Saw to gather himself. No matter how much he drank, he never had a hangover. He was a well-functioned drunk. By the look he gave me, I could tell he knew I was pissed.

He said, "Hey, baby. I fucked up this time, didn't I?"

I exploded on him, "I have five dudes in my living room that you didn't ask permission to bring to my house. All of ya being drunk. Then you were drinking and driving! My daughter was here in the next room scared. Anything could have happened, Saw! Your disrespect is unreal. You owe my daughter an apology, and I want them guys in my living room out of my house. Now, Sawyer!"

Saw knew how I felt about guys being around my daughter, let alone guys in my house. He knew about my experiences with men in the past. He knew all this, and he still did the dumbest thing he could have done to make me want to end our relationship on the spot. He risked the security of my home and scared my daughter.

He saddened his face. "I'm sorry, Joss!"

I said, "Sorry isn't going to cut it, Saw! I'm really getting tired of your shit, and that includes your drinking."

Saw had my mind all over the place. He was a good dude with bad tendencies, and he wasn't mature enough to take responsibility for his behavior.

*****

One Sunday evening, I took Saw to meet my Mama Jess (my great-grandmother). When she saw him, she instantly told him she knew him. Mama Jess had a good memory for her to be ninety-seven years old. She remembered everything. She knew everyone's family lineage and which child belonged to what family.

Saw said he didn't recall meeting her, but he wasn't saying she was wrong. When we were leaving, Mama Jess whispered to me, "Only time will tell if he is the one for you, Joss! I think he is a good enough man to be the one for you."

Saw heard her and chimed in, saying, "I'm going to marry this woman soon, ma'am. Watch!"

I was still keeping his secret, that he was married, to myself. I didn't want anyone to know the truth about his situation until the divorce was final. Even though I knew his divorce was going to happen, I was still involved with a married man going through his separation phase. The whole notion of knowing that much didn't sit right with me.

I was fighting a battle with myself every day, wishing time away until February. I was questioning everything. I kept trying to convince myself Saw's situation was different because he was going to get a divorce. And that was the only hope I had left to hang on to.

That Wednesday Sean (Saw's son) showed up at his apartment. At this time, Saw was practically at my house every day, but this day he went to his apartment to greet his son.

Sean made prior arrangements to stay with his girlfriend when he got out. Saw didn't agree with his decision because he felt the girl was trying to trap his son. Saw didn't think his son was mature enough to have a live-in girlfriend. So Saw offered his room at his apartment to his son instead. His son declined.

Three weeks later, Saw was asking me if it would be okay if his son stayed at my house for a while. I didn't think about it long before I told him it was fine. His son had been through a lot, and a lot of it was because of dumb childish ideas.

Sean was seventeen years old. He had been in and out of the detention center since he was fourteen. He needed guidance. He needed his father around. I loved Saw, so I loved his son. I expected Saw to accept my kids and treat them like his own as well. Letting his son stay at my house was another way of me showing Saw I had his back.

His son arrived at the house on Friday. His son caught hold of his excessive drinking and his nasty language. They started bumping heads by Sunday.

I was in the kitchen cooking a giant Sunday breakfast for everyone when I heard Sean yelling at Saw. Sean walked past me and went straight out of the house. I went to check on him knowing it had to be Saw that said something wrong. I knew he still had some alcohol in him from the night before. Sean looked like a lost little boy while he tried to light his cigarette.

Out of concern, I said, "What's wrong, Sean?"

Almost crying, he said, "He doesn't know how to be a father to me. I wanted to give him a chance, but he doesn't know how. It's hard not to take the things he says seriously when he is drunk. He told me he didn't want me here, Joss. He told me this was his time in life. And he didn't have time to deal with me begging. All because I asked for a cigarette. He said I needed to get a job and be a man. I'm not staying here anymore. I've called my mom already, and I'm going to stay with her for a while."

I didn't know what to say to Sean. It had only been two short days, and Saw's drinking was already affecting his son. I didn't expect their relationship to take this kind of a turn. I felt bad for Sean, and I was glad he was going to go stay with his mom. He didn't seem happy being around his dad any longer.

I said, "Sean, I'm sorry you're having to see this side of your father. When you were away, all he talked about was trying to have a relationship with you. He is a different person when he drinks, but he doesn't see it himself. Maybe you guys should ease into a relationship. I'll take you to your mom's house after breakfast."

Sean thanked me, and I went back in the house to check on Saw and the food. When I walked in my bedroom, Saw was sitting on the end of the bed with his cigarette in his hand. There was a beer on the nightstand that I didn't know he had. If he had one, then there had to be another, or he already drank it. I was sure it was the latter. He was quiet for a moment while I stood there looking at him.

He said, "This boy doesn't do shit. He thinks I'm supposed to get him everything he wants, like I owe him something. He smokes all my cigarettes, man, asking for a cigarette every five minutes. He wants a beer when I get a beer. Then he wants me to give him money because that girl thinks she is pregnant."

I said, "Saw, what kind of example are you setting for him? All the stuff you said you wanted to do with him because you have the opportunity, but you're quick to let him go. You need to look at yourself too."

I left the room to finish cooking.

While we ate breakfast, the subject of Sean's mother came up. Sean was excited about staying with his mom.

I asked, "Where does your mom stay, Sean?"

He said, "I think she stays around the corner from you here. She lives with my grandmother off Freshwater Road."

Excitedly, I asked, "What do you know about Freshwater Road?"

"My nana has lived on that road her whole life."

"Who's your nana?"

"Mrs. Queenie Shaw. People call her Queenie."

I laughed and said, "I think we are related. Your nana is my great-grandmother's [Mama Jess] sister. Freshwater Road is the family road. Majority of the folks that live on that road is family."

I couldn't wait to tell my mother. I called her immediately. When I told her everything Sean told me, she confirmed that we were indeed related. Sean and I both agreed that it was a small world. Mama Jess was sure she knew Saw from somewhere, and she was right.

*****

That Thanksgiving morning, I got up early to cook. Saw said he was going to see his mom and dad, and then we were going to spend the rest of the holiday together. My kids were spending the holidays with their father, so it was just him and I.

I was in the kitchen finishing up Thanksgiving dinner when Saw left to go see his parents. Some time had gone by when I realized I achieved a lot in what I thought was a short amount of time. Last time I looked at the clock, it was eleven thirty in the morning. My eyes went straight to the clock on the stove, and I realized it had been four hours since I last looked at a clock. Suddenly, I realized Saw had been gone since ten o'clock that morning.

I grabbed my phone to see if I had somehow missed a call from him. No missed calls or texts. I called his phone. Saw's phone went straight to voicemail. I called again. This time I left a message for him to call me.

I was hoping he was safe and nothing happened. I was really hoping he wasn't drinking and driving. I heard nothing from him for hours, and that wasn't like him. I assumed he got caught up seeing some other family members. I didn't get too bent out of shape over his absence, but I was wondering why he wasn't answering my calls.

Three hours later, Saw pulled into the driveway. It was late in the evening, and the holiday was practically over. I went to the porch to watch him watch me watch him.

He got out of his car and proceeded to walk up to me with his arms out for a hug, wrapping his arms around me. "What's wrong, baby?"

I pulled away from his hug to looked at him. "Really, Saw? Where the hell have you been? I spent the day by myself, and you come back like you haven't been gone all day. You didn't bother to call or text."

Saw put his head down. His face quickly changed. I knew from his facial expression I was about to hear some bullshit.

Sadly, he said, "Joss, don't be mad at me."

I anxiously said, "What the hell did you do, Saw?"

"I had to know, baby, please understand."

My head spun quickly toward his direction to look him straight in his eyes. "I know you didn't go to the home of your soon-to-be ex-wife's house? Please tell me you didn't do that, Saw? I know you didn't chance the terms of your separation to go see if she changed? You couldn't wait two months, Saw?"

"It's not like that though, Joss. She wanted me to come over to spend time with the grandkids."

"Saw, you have got to be the biggest sucker there is! She used them kids to get you to step your foot back in that house. Now she can have them kids say you were there on Thanksgiving, hence making the separation void and the whole year starting over. You were dumb enough to fall for her trick. She got to you using them kids."

"What do you expect me to do?"

"I expect you to realize what she is doing to you and for you to grow a pair and stand up to her. I want you to tell me that you love me and promise me you're not going to give up on us, especially for something you already know isn't going to work. I expect to be the one you're with."

Saw walked around the house drinking and smoking. His drinking put me in a mood. Almost everything about him was irritating me. His annoyance was starting to get to me, from how I heard the moisture in his mouth while he chewed to his smoking. Even his voice was pissing me off.

I wanted him to leave. I wanted him to go back to his wife. Our relationship was damaged. Saw somehow thought I was an option. He assumed I was going to sit around and let him decide whether or not he was going to leave me and go back home to his wife or stay with me until the one-year anniversary of his separation.

I wanted him to go back to his wife. I was ready to be rid of him. He didn't know how to stand up for himself just because she threatened his pockets. He couldn't see manipulation staring him in his face. He was never going to face the truth.

Two days later, Saw sat in his car doing his after-work routine. I knew he was in his car drinking, so I didn't bother him. When he came in the house, he spoke to me, went to the bathroom, and then went back outside. I heard his car crank up, knowing he was heading back to the store for another round of cigarettes and beer.

I lay in my bed watching a movie while he sat outside getting drunk. I heard him come back in a couple more times to use the bathroom. I heard him leave a few more times as well. The third time he left, I got up to go talk to him. By this time, I knew he was way past the threshold to drive, and I didn't want him drinking and driving anymore.

I grabbed my robe, and I went out to his car. To my surprise, he had relocated to his van. It was dark out, so all I could see when I got into the van was his phone screen lighting up his face. I assumed he was searching for or looking at cars.

I asked, "What's wrong with you, Saw? You haven't spent any time with me today, and you have been to the store at least three times already."

He mumbled, "Man, nothing is wrong. Ha."

I hadn't heard that "ha" in a long time, and I was wondering why it suddenly reappeared. The mood inside of the van didn't feel right.

He said, "Can you carry me to the store? I need another beer."

Out of concern, I said, "Saw, you don't need any more alcohol. You have been drinking all day. Clearly something is wrong with you. And instead of you talking to me about it, you'd rather sit out here drinking until you think you have drunk your problem away. But tomorrow, you will still have to deal with the problem."

Saw turned up the can of beer he had in his hand to finish it. When he was done, he said, "Can you carry me to the store? Please!"

"Fine!"

Saw didn't want to hear nothing I had to say. I got out of the van, slamming the door, and went into the house to grab my car keys. Saw was torn-up, out-the-frame drunk. I didn't feel like there was anything I could do if he wasn't going to talk to me.

I drove him to the store. He knew I was pissed at his behavior because he returned to the car with one beer, a pack of cigarettes, and some crossword scratch-offs. He handed me the tickets and said, "These are for you, beautiful. I love you."

When we got back to the house, we sat in the driveway. I asked him again, "What's wrong with you, Saw?"

He quickly said, "Huh?"

I shook my head while saying, "Never mind!"

I was about to get out of the car when his phone started to ring. It rang once, and then there was a beep, indicating he had a text message. He didn't attempt to answer the phone, the call, or the text message. Saw didn't flinch.

I was curious as to who was calling his phone. "Sawyer, can I please see your phone? You can easily say no, but I will find out who the hell just called and texted you before you walk your ass back in my house."

I had to put my foot down, and now seemed like the perfect time to start. I was sick and tired of being used by someone's dusty-ass son. I wanted to mush his face into the car window and take his phone, but I wanted to be civilized. But this sent my blood boiling. Saw didn't budge. I turned toward him, and I snatched the phone out of his hand. Saw didn't try to stop me.

I looked at the phone and then over at Saw. He had twenty-five missed calls from the wifey. Adrenaline started flowing through my body. I went to the last message he received. There was her name again. I clicked on the message, and up popped a picture of her yoni staring at me in the face. I looked at the phone and then at Saw.

In the calmest tone I could muster, I said, "Oh, so this is what we're doing? This shit is really getting old! You're sitting here getting drunk, texting your wife? And she is sending you yoni pictures too. What are we doing, Saw?"

"I told you she was crazy. She does this type of shit to get me to come back. I don't know what to do, Joss. I know I'm probably going to lose you for sure."

"You got that shit right."

"You don't understand. She keeps telling me she has changed and the grandkids missed me. I know you're not going to allow me to be around the kids because she always has them. I just don't know what to do anymore."

I was losing my composure. I wanted to smack some sense into him, but I said, "What do you mean you don't know what to do? You know what, Saw? Go ahead and grab your shit and go back to your wife, since you're so torn by your decision to stay or go. You created this monster, and you either tame her or go on your way. As a matter of fact, I'm not doing this with you anymore! With you being a miserable drunk and her butting in our relationship, I'd rather be alone. You fooled me into thinking you were going to get a divorce, wasting months of my time. Go back to your wife, Sawyer Burnette. Go home!"

I got out of the car and went in my house to start getting his crap together. I wanted him gone. I didn't want to think about the time we shared. I didn't want to think about anything but getting him out of my way.

He came in the bedroom an hour later. "She has some kind of hold on me, and I can't explain it, Joss. I don't want to leave. I want to be right here with you, where I belong. I texted her and told her to stop calling me and that I was in a relationship. I told her I wasn't coming back home."

I wanted to believe him, but this was the second time I saw how weak he was. In his mind, he was trying to convince himself he was strong enough to walk away from her. But he wasn't. They danced this dance before, and he wasn't the lead; she was. I knew our time together was over. I wasn't going to play second fiddle to some bullshit that wasn't worth fighting for. Saw was weak. I didn't want to control him, but because I'm an alpha woman, I was going to. I needed a king, and sadly Saw wasn't him.

I looked at him and said, "Saw, we have crossed way too many bridges when it comes to this part of your life. You have told me you wanted to be with me. We went on a trip and had a beautiful time. Hell, our whole relationship has been beautiful other than this mess you call a wife. That continues to pop up. I don't know how to make us work from here."

He quickly said, "I want to be with you, Joss. No one else, especially not her."

"I don't want to talk about it anymore, Saw. You're drunk, and you're not going to remember most of this conversation anyways."

This was the first day in eight months Saw and I didn't have sex. I went to bed. The next morning, when Saw was coherent, I told him we needed to have a serious conversation. He agreed, and we went on the porch to talk.

I said, "You know I love you, right?"

He grunted slightly. "Oh boy! I know where this is going."

I laughed a little. "Oh no, you really don't. Saw, you have one decision to make today. You need to decide today if it's going to be me or your wife. I'm not going to keep going through unnecessary drama with you and her. I've already started packing your stuff last night, so if you choose to leave, then that part is already done. I'll give you all day to think about it, but by midnight, I need your answer. Yes, I will be hurt if you go, but I'd rather see you happy. If I'm not the person to do that for you, then I'm okay with that. But from this point forward, I'm taking what I want to take, and no one is going to tell me to deal with it or force me into something I don't want to be in."

He looked at me with a surprised look on his face. I didn't know what he was thinking, but he said, "Okay, let me think about it."

He didn't even realize he had just made his decision. If I was who he wanted to be with, he wouldn't have needed the time to think about anything. With him telling me he had to think about his decision told me he already thought about the possibilities of her. I wasn't even surprised when he came in the room around 6:00 p.m. and said, "I have made my decision. I'm going to go back home to my wife. I talked to her and told her what you asked me to do. She told me that things were going to be different. And she reassured me she had changed. She wants me back, Joss!"

Hearing the words come from his lips pierced my heart. I loved him, and I knew he was making the wrong decision. I was all for marriage, but mental abuse was real, and I experienced it firsthand from my relationship with my ex Marcus. Saw didn't realize he was being controlled, and everyone around him saw it but him.

I said, "Once you walk out of my door and step foot into her house, this, us, is all over! Your year separation starts over from that exact moment. She is going to make sure of it."

"I know it, but can I ask you a question? Can I have some yoni one last time?"

I laughed. "I'm not that desperate to give you one last fuck. When you get home, ask your wife for some and see if that changed. Please don't play with my emotions any further."

"I might as well leave now then since you won't give me none!"

I quickly said, "Bye!" I pointed to his laundry basket of stuff. "I wish you a happy life, and please tell your wife she won and congrats."

I walked him to my front door, shutting it right behind him. I told myself to be strong for the next couple of days. I didn't want to get in my feelings or think about taking him back. Plus, knowing him, he was going to reach out first.

When Saw left me to return to his wife, I was fine. He was a headache I was glad was gone. I had feelings for him, of course, but he was no longer my responsibility. He chose to return to a dead marriage. And I survived being in love.

Saw wasn't gone two days before he started popping up at my house, pleading with me, telling me he made a mistake. He professed his love for me repeatedly, begging for us to get back together.

I shut him down instantly, reminding him how close he was to divorce. I told him we could have been together, but he threw it all away when he went back home to his wife.

I told him she wanted him back because he found someone and he was happy. She screwed with his head. She didn't want him; she wanted him to be miserable, and he fell for it. He chose not to listen to love but stayed in misery because of fear.

Sawyer (Saw) and I were in love for eight months while he was going through his separation. I stuck it out with him because he said he loved me, and he promised to get his divorce when it came due. I knew he loved me, but I guess his wife knew what strings to pull.

Saw was no player. He wasn't a man to have multiple women. He was confused. Naive, even. But I was the dumb one to think that I could compete with a woman who had been married to him for years, who shared his space and time for over a decade. He didn't trust himself without her. She controlled him and the relationship, and he didn't know how to be free. When he decided to leave a year ago, it wasn't his decision. It was hers.

I laughed to myself as I walked in my room to open the windows to let the smell of stale cigarettes out so fresh air could come in.

# Dear Future Wife

"Dear future wife" was the comment I read under my social media post. Earlier in the day, I made a "dear future husband" post in a group I was a part of. On the post, I was putting it out there to my future husband, whoever he may be, that I was waiting for him to arrive in my life, and I was patiently waiting.

The comment was from someone named Micah. I didn't know him, but he was a part of the same group. I thought nothing more of the comment as I hit the Like button and moved on to the other comments under my post. I was just about to get off the book when I received a direct message from Micah. It said, "I wasn't playing about being your future husband. I already love you, and you don't even know it yet."

I laughed to myself. This dude had to be one of those chronic online "Tinder, swipe left, always in someone's inbox" kind of a dude. I hit the Like button again, and then I logged off. Getting back on later that night, I was looking for a little entertainment. It was a Saturday night in late July, and I of course didn't have any plans.

I chose to be single for a while after my breakup with Sawyer eight months ago. I was tired of the lames in my area and all the drama surrounding them. So, I gave myself a break from the dating game. I wanted to try something different, so I started doing a lot of online dating. While surfing profiles, I received another message from Micah. He said, "Good evening, my future wife."

I shook my head. This dude wasn't going to go away easily. I was online for some fun, so I decided to respond. I said, "Hey! What makes you think you will be my future husband?"

Micah wasn't bad-looking at all. He was light-skinned with a fair complexion. He had a beautiful smile I knew made the women melt. He was tall as far I could tell from his profile pictures. He was rocking a low fade haircut, and you could see the river of waves on his scalp. And he was young. He was twenty-seven years young.

He quickly responded with a whole paragraph answering my previous question. The response was quick, as if the paragraph already existed.

In the paragraph, he explained how he felt about me being his future wife. He stated he grew up fast to help his mom and dad. He didn't have time to waste in life because he dreamed of having the same kind of relationship his parents have. He wanted a marriage that was going to last over fifty-plus years. And he wanted to start early, and he was ready for his wife. He told me how mature he was for his age and how he knew what he wanted out of life. He had two kids by two different women, and he didn't want a girlfriend. He wanted a wife.

His words seemed genuine. I felt truth in his words, but in the back of my mind, something felt off. It felt like there was more to his story.

Micah lived almost six hundred miles away in Connecticut. With the distance alone, I knew he wasn't right for me. There were too many miles between us. Long-distance dating wasn't for me, and I heard people say long-distance relationships didn't work out in the long run. I wanted long-term love. Not a hope and a prayer, long-distance relationship. I didn't put any more thought into a relationship with Micah further than us chatting on Messenger.

As I finished my thought, I received another message from Micah. He was asking for my telephone number because he wanted to talk on the phone. I told him I didn't give my number out to people I didn't know. I told him we could talk on Messenger for a while, and I would think about giving him my number later.

Micah and I messaged back and forth all night until the sun came up. I felt like I knew his whole life story in just a couple of short hours. We talked about almost everything, down to our religious beliefs. He had two boys, the youngest one was a junior (Micah

Guess Jr.) and the other one (his oldest) he didn't see as often because he and that child's mother didn't get along.

He told me he was on good terms with his youngest son's mother. They were actually best friends in school, and they ended up hooking up during prom and ended up with a kid. He was active in his son's life as much as he possibly could be. His mom and dad lived in another county, almost fifty miles away from him. He said he moved to a different county to get a better job and to make more money for his future.

At work that night, I thought about how mature Micah presented himself. After our conversation, I realized he left an impression on me. I still wasn't sure about the long-distance thing or the part where he wanted to marry me, but he was interesting enough for me to highly anticipate our next conversation. I couldn't wait to talk to him again.

He worked the night shift at an extended stay hotel as night security. He had nightly duties that lasted the first two hours of his shift, then he made rounds every hour until his shift was over.

He enjoyed the perks of his job. He had two phones, one his job provided and his personal phone. He was also given a suite, where he lived for the time being until he saved his money to buy a house for his future wife and kids. He got paid to live there, so he was comfortable with his life. The setup sounded convenient. But the two phones sounded suspect to me.

He punched out an hour before my shift ended. By the time I walked in my house, Micah was already in my inbox saying, "Good morning, my future wife." The feeling inside felt good. I was excited to talk to him.

Micah was eager to pursue me, and he wasn't afraid to show it. The words he typed proved how dedicated he was in convincing me I was going to be his future wife.

I had nine long months after Sawyer to think about what I wanted in my life as far as a man was concerned. I was over Drew and Saw emotionally. I still saw Drew at The Warehouse, and Saw called on the regular, making it impossible to forget him. He became an annoyance, causing the love I once had for him to fade. Sadly, he was still at home with his wife, trying to find his way back into my bed.

My great-grandmother Mama Jess told me it was time for me to get back on the playing field to get me a husband, especially after Drew and Sawyer. She would say, "You're not getting any younger, you know?" She wanted to see my mother and I find someone that was right for us. She didn't shy away from making that known every time I saw her.

Micah and I texted in the morning after work until we both fell asleep. If one of us got up before the other, we'd call on Messenger to wake the other person up. We texted most of the day until we had to go to work. While we worked, we texted off and on.

We continued that way of communicating for about a week. We chatted so much the distance didn't even matter. We talked like we knew each other for years and like we were down the street from one another. I didn't think we were going to get married, but I wanted to see where our relationship was going to go.

Friday morning, when I walked through the door of my house, my Messenger notification went off, and I knew it was Micah. Without fail, the message read, "Good morning, my future wife."

I got excited reading the message. I wanted to surprise Micah later by giving him my real telephone number. I felt comfortable enough to share my number with him. I finished winding down from work, and I messaged Micah back. "Hey, would you like to move to the next step in our relationship?"

His response was immediate. He asked, "Did you quit your job? Because the next phase in our relationship is you coming to Connecticut so we can get married immediately."

I laughed at his response. "No, crazy. I'm talking about us exchanging numbers."

Before Micah could respond, I was already hitting the Send button on the message, including my number. My phone vibrated instantly, notifying me that I had an incoming message. I knew it was Micah.

He said, "This is Micah. I got you saved in my phone, beautiful."

I said, "And this is Joss. Same here."

Micah called my phone a few seconds later. I answered the phone with a schoolgirl tone. "Hello."

A deep, smooth voice said, "Hello back at you."

Micah's voice didn't match his face. He had a fresh young face, but his voice said, "I'm all man over here!"

My body got chills listening to him talk. I think he knew his voice was mesmerizing because he continued talking as I lay across my bed, kicking my feet in the air. I didn't hear anything he was saying. I was stuck admiring his voice. He asked a question that required me to answer, which shifted me out of my trance.

He said, "Are you taking me seriously about you being my future wife?"

I laughed. "You don't even know me, but you assume you are going to marry me. We have too many things going against us for us to have a future together. You are younger than me, and the distance alone is going to be a problem."

"Age don't mean a thing, and I can move closer to you. I'm not going to let the opportunity pass me by for you to be my wife. And before you think of anything else to go against our pending relationship, I'm going to go ahead and send you the number of my other phone. I want to make sure we don't have any secrets. I want you to have all access to me. I don't have anything to hide from you."

With him offering to give me the other phone's number brought another sense of relief and security. I didn't even have to ask for it.

I was stunned by his persistence. Everything in me couldn't help but wonder if this guy was really supposed to be my future husband. I wondered what this young man saw in me that he couldn't get from a young tender yoni in his own state. In the week and a half that we texted, Micah was consistent in what he wanted from me, and he didn't give me a reason to second-guess him. We were constantly on the phone. Sometimes talking longer than we should because one of us, if not both of us, had to go to work. We enjoyed each other's conversations, day and night.

Micah was adamant I was going to be his wife. He had no objections about anything. It was scary to think someone knew exactly what they wanted and wasn't scared of coming on too strong, especially after the guys I was previously involved with. It was refreshing to be dealing with something different.

In one of our phone conversations, Micah told me he was going to make our relationship the best relationship he ever had. He'd been through a lot in life, and he didn't have time to waste on things that weren't going to last. All he wanted to do was love and to be loved.

With the relationship developing over the phone, it was time we made plans to see each other. I had vacation time available, so I decided to be the one to travel to him. We made plans for me to visit Connecticut in mid-October—six long weeks away.

By the time of the visit, we would have hit a three-month milestone in our relationship—enough time for me to get over the fear he could be a serial killer and could possibly be leading me to my death.

I told Micah about the guys I dated in the past who broke my heart because they couldn't be true to themselves. I told him the guys in my past caused so much pain, and I didn't want to be involved with anyone who would rather lie to me to be with me, manipulating love to work in their favor.

Micah said he loved me and told me all he did was think about me every minute, every second, every day, and every night. He promised to never keep secrets from me. He told me he would love me forever.

I didn't doubt his affection for me because his actions were persistent. He told me a thousand times a day he loved me and I was going to be his wife. He started telling me he loved me within a week of us talking over the phone.

I constantly questioned what he could possibly want from me. Was he looking for a sugar momma? Did he think I had money and I was going to support him? So many times we would hang up the phone and I would question what he was getting out of stringing me on, if that were in fact what he was doing.

Micah and I video chatted and talked on the phone daily. We did everything to make sure distance wasn't an issue for our relationship.

*****

My cousin Roxanne and I previously planned a night out in the big city for her birthday. We were going to a giant R and B reunion tour concert, and the lineup was amazing. It featured a handful of male R & B artists. I wanted Micah to be there. The musical genius from each artist was going to have every woman at the concert in the mood for lovin' by the end of the show. I wanted to be able to go home to him and ride him the same way I was riding the flow of the music.

I wanted to take the warmth of my loins to him. To seduce him. To give off the scent I was hot, horny, and ready to go. I wanted to trace his chest with my tongue, biting each nipple as I made my way downtown toward his growing member, taking him in my hands as he continued to swell with excitement. I wanted him to take me and break up all the sexual tension he created over these past few months. His member would slide through my wetness, arriving at the spot that would make me gasp for air. The part of my body and mind there was no coming back from. The part of the body that gives the sexual exchange meaning. I wanted him available to make love to me after being foreplayed by the musicians on stage.

The following two weeks after the concert were unbearable. I already had made up my mind; three months was enough of a waiting period to allow Micah to sex me. I needed sex, and I definitely wanted it after all the sexting and teasing we had done to each other over the phone. Plus, I wasn't going to drive over six hundred miles out of the way and not get laid.

Some of the songs the artists sang that night had me genuinely thinking about him; I would call to video chat him so he could hear the songs also. My cousin Roxanne thought it was a bit much by the facial expression she had on her face. She was happy for me. She always loved when I was happy and smiling. She even told me so after the concert. She said, "Things seemed to be going well with you and this guy. I'm glad to see you happy, but be careful and mind your heart."

She was referencing the other guys I loved and let invaded my heart. My cousin always had my back and always wanted the best for me.

A week before our pending visit, Micah got sick. He had a cough that was taking his breath away. His voice was changing over the phone. He was feeling bad. We didn't talk much while he was sick. I would text him, and his responses were sometimes delayed. When I called, he always sounded asleep. I accepted the lack of communication because he was sick. I felt bad because I wasn't there to help him through it, but I let him have his space to heal.

I thought maybe Micah was trying to stall me from coming to Connecticut. My negative thought didn't last long because the day Micah got better, everything went back to the way it was beforehand. We were back to polishing off our plans to see each other in a few days.

The day finally arrived for me to go meet my future husband. He told me he was going to call me every hour on the hour until he got off work. It was five in the morning, and I was scared and anxious at the same time. I was taking the journey on my own. I was going on an adventure and to meet a man who could possibly be the man of my dreams. The rush made me feel alive. I didn't know what I was headed to, but I wanted to see what happiness had in store for my life. Micah was a breath of fresh air I needed in my life, removing all the stale air life was suffocating me with. I welcomed the journey, and I was preparing myself for the consequences, praying for the consequences to be rewarding.

I hopped in the rental I rented just the day before, turned my music on medium, and headed toward the highway. I was on my way to the next adventure in my life. Micah called every hour on the hour like he said he would. Once he was done with work, he called, and we talked on the phone for a little while. We agreed he needed to get some sleep before I got there. He told me he was going to need his rest, and I didn't disagree.

I sat back in the car and enjoyed the scenery while I drove to see my man. I was coming from the countryside, driving up north, enjoying every bit of the view. I watched the trees disappear and the buildings getting bigger. It was breathtaking to see this part of the world. And I was doing it on my own, something I didn't think I'd ever do.

I wanted to call Micah to tell him about the journey, but I wanted to wait until I was closer to call him. As I got closer and closer to him, I held off on calling him. I wanted to reach him before he woke up or before he called to see where I was.

My GPS said I was fifteen minutes away. I couldn't believe I was so close to him after talking to him on the phone for three months. I was going to touch him for the first time. I was about to see the man who promised to make me his wife these past three months.

I pulled over to call my daughter, who was back home having a sleepover with my mother. I wanted her to know I made it to Connecticut safely. My mother didn't want to talk to me because she didn't know Micah. She thought I was putting my life on the line for a man. She was mad, but I didn't want to miss an opportunity to be happy because of what someone else thought. After the phone call, I got back on the road to head toward Micah's spot.

When I pulled into the neighborhood, I was amazed. The extended stay was in a nicely developed neighborhood. There was a waterpark within walking distance of his job. There was also a handful of executive offices neighboring a small college campus. There was a waterfall statue in the middle of a giant field. You had to go around the fountain to get to where the extended stay was located. I called Micah to tell him I was around the corner.

He didn't answer. I called again, and he still didn't answer. My chest dropped. So many thoughts took over my mind. I didn't want to think he could be that mean. I was praying he didn't have me drive all the way up to Connecticut to stand me up. I was about to flip the hell out. I picked up my phone and went to his social media page. It said he was active. As I stared at the active button on top of his picture, I felt my temperature rising.

I waited another few minutes, then I dialed Micah's number once again. I waited to hear his voice on the other end. My heart stopped as soon as I heard his voice. I told myself to stay calm. I needed to stay calm. I was too far from home to show my crazy.

In a soft tone, he said, "Hello, lovely."

I paused before I responded to get my tone under control. I said, "I'm around the corner. I tried calling you before I got this close, but you didn't answer."

He said, "I'm sorry, baby, I just got out of the shower when I heard my phone ring. This is the first time I heard it. Let me grab my jacket, and I'll be outside in a second."

I was relieved to not hear him say, "Sucker!" I waited a few more seconds to see him. I parked along the side of the entrance. I wanted to spot him before he made it to my car. I wanted the opportunity to pull off if I felt like I was being catfished. But to my surprise, an even taller yet younger-looking Micah walked toward my car. It was him but with an even cuter baby face. I sat, shocked the past three months hadn't been in vain.

I got out of the car as he got closer. As he got closer to me, I was able to notice he had something in his hand. He was trying to hide it behind his back. This dude was causing my blood pressure to rise trying to figure out what he was hiding behind him. I didn't think he was crazy enough to kill me in broad daylight.

I moved closer to the car anticipating I might have to make a quick dash. I was measuring his body structure, and it looked as though I could take him in a fight if need be. My mind was going a hundred miles per hour wondering what he had behind his back and if I was going to have to defend myself.

Micah walked across the front of the car and stretched his arms toward me, holding a stuffed puppy with its tongue sticking out with a heart that said, "I love you." I smiled from ear to ear as he handed the stuffed animal to me. He walked around the door and hugged me tighter than any man has ever hugged me. I hugged him back without hesitation. Micah let me go as he took a few steps back. He looked me over and said, "Girl, you look good."

I quickly responded, "And you look like a baby."

"Don't do me like that."

I laughed. "It might take a while."

We both laughed. Micah told me to leave everything in the car. He said he would get everything from the car later. I didn't argue. I was relieved he looked like his pictures, and he was happy to see me.

We went into the building, and Micah pointed out a couple of things around the building that he would reference while we talked on the phone. He also spoke to a couple of people on the way to his room. The more people that saw me with him, the more comfortable I felt. The more witnesses, the better.

The extended stay had two floors, and it was spacious. Micah's room was on the first floor next to the security office. I walked in the room, taking a quick glimpse around. His hand touched my arm. He turned me around slowly. Micah kissed me and then kissed on me. Micah pulled me away from him as he stared at me.

He said, "I can't believe you are here."

I stood in front of him staring at him. I looked at his baby face, admiring his smile.

"What's the matter, baby?"

I looked him in the eyes. "I can't believe I'm here either. I can't believe you want to be with me. What is it about me that makes you want me?"

"Why wouldn't I want you, Joss?"

I pointed at him. "Look at you, Micah! You're young, with a job, and you look good as hell."

He laughed, but his laugh turned serious. "Can we let God figure everything out? Can we accept what is real and enjoy the fact we are standing in front of each other instead of on a telephone screen? You are going to be my wife one day. And when I say one day, I mean soon."

Micah called his mom and dad before it got too late. As soon as she answered, he told her I made it to Connecticut. Micah told his parents about me the very same day I gave him my telephone number. He said that was how confident he was we were going to get married. He told me his mom and dad were happy for him.

Micah gave me the phone so I could speak with her. His mother was more excited for us and our relationship than we were. She ended our conversation with "I can't wait to meet you for myself, Joss, and take care of my boy." I passed the phone back over to Micah. He said bye and hung up.

He walked over to the side of the bed where he apparently slept, opened the nightstand drawer, and placed his phone inside. His room had a laidback feel, but you could tell it had a hotel layout. He had a tiny kitchen table in the center of the kitchen floor. A table TV sat on top of a dresser with the two kitchen chairs in front it, the bed, and the bathroom.

The bed was positioned evenly between the wall. A regular-size dresser was pushed up against another wall. He had decorations and pictures on the wall around his side of the bed. His closet was full of hanging clothes. Micah really tried to make his room home.

Micah and I laid across the bed talking. We were both still in shock we were in the same room with each other. We were video chatting every chance we could as well as sexting like crazy. We were finally in front of each other.

He told me our previous plans had to be tweaked a little because he had to work. He said we were probably going to make it to the mall, but we weren't going to make it to see his family. I didn't care what we did as long as we spent time with each other.

Anxiety started building within me as it grew closer to us calling it a night. We were comfortable with each other, and we laughed and talked nonstop. I was tired from the drive, and it was getting late. I didn't want the night to end because that meant another day would be subtracted from the time I had with Micah.

I excused myself and headed to the bathroom for a shower. I wanted to shower before we headed to bed. The shower eased my anxiety. I imagined what the rest of the night was going to bring as I rubbed soap across my breast. I was anxious to be touched by him.

I walked out of the bathroom wearing a shimmering black nightie and a smile. I placed oil drops of Black Woman (my favorite fragrance oil) behind my ears and behind my kneecaps. I was ready for whatever. I wanted him to ravish me the moment he saw me step out of the bathroom, but I was also fighting sleep.

When I stepped out of the bathroom, Micah was on his phone again. I heard him say, "Goodnight, and I love you too!"

The way he said it, I could tell he was talking to his younger son. He looked up at me and smiled as he hung up his phone. Before

I could say anything, he shook the phone a little and said, "My youngest son."

Micah placed his phone back in the top drawer and proceeded to take his clothes off, down to his boxers. He folded every garment and put everything in its specific location. I thought his anal behavior was cute. Micah lifted the blanket and slid in the bed. I hopped in bed and scooted closer to him to give him a seductive kiss. Micah kissed me back. His hands guided me closer to him. He held me close. My head rested on his chest. As I lay there, he said, "Get some rest. We don't have to do anything tonight."

We had been sexting and teasing each other for over three months. I was surprised by his gesture. I knew he wasn't like the other guys I knew or had been with because they would have already been on fourth base, possibly heading to home base by now. My anxiety went away as I fell asleep.

The next morning, I awoke to Micah's phone ringing. It was the phone he placed in the drawer earlier. It was incredibly early in the morning, and the caller was persistent in being heard. The phone rang three times in a row, and then the other phone began to ring. I knew whoever was calling him had to know him.

I said to myself, "Let the bullshit begin!"

Micah didn't budge to the ringing noise. He was fast asleep. After a couple more rings, his phones went silent. I closed my eyes and eventually fell back asleep. The silence was interrupted by the phone in the drawer again. I became annoyed instantly. I rubbed Micah's chest to let him know his phone was ringing. "Your phone is ringing. Whoever it is has been calling both phones."

Micah reached over to grab the phone out of the drawer. He didn't look to see who was calling; he just answered it. "Hello!"

I rolled over to my side of the bed while he spoke.

He said, "Why are you calling my phone? If it isn't about my son, then you shouldn't be calling."

I instantly assumed it was his baby mama. Without saying bye, Micah hung the phone up. He looked over at me as he got out of the bed. "Good morning, beautiful!"

I said, "Good morning to you too! What were the wake-up calls this morning all about?"

"My son's mother is trying to use my son as an excuse to call about irrelevant stuff. She calls at least once a week to start some non-son related topic that ends in me getting pissed off. She wants me back. It frustrates me because I don't want my relationship with my son to be impacted by her acting stupid. She is one of the reasons I don't care about relocating with you."

His words were stern and sincere. I didn't bother to ask him anything else.

Micah hopped in the shower while I made us a quick breakfast. Breakfast was finished, and I was waiting for him to emerge from the bathroom. I scanned the room, taking in the suite I was going to be staying in for the next few days.

The room needed a woman's touch, but he had things nice and taken care of. The room had those ugly bulky hotel curtains hanging over the windows. He arranged everything to look like a miniature-size apartment. He had a spot on the floor where a green-colored disc caught the ashes from the incense he burned. Next to the TV was a red ashtray that contained a half-smoked cigarette. I didn't recall Micah telling me he was a smoker. Sawyer's smoking regime was enough to make smoking a turnoff for me.

The bathroom door opened, and Micah came out with a towel wrapped around his waist. I couldn't help but stare. His yellowish toned body was semiwet. Water beads sat atop his hair waves. He looked good. Almost edible good. I imagined what he tasted like.

With a little smile, I asked, "Did you tell me you smoked and I forgot?"

Without hesitation, he replied, "I smoke occasionally. It's nothing serious, that's why I didn't bring it up. This place is a smoke-free facility and has a strict policy on smoking in the building. I burn incense to kill the smell sometimes. Everyone needs a smoke every now and again."

While we ate, Micah talked about all the places he wanted to take me. Every few sentences he brought up he needed a haircut. His hair was well-groomed and wavy, from what I could tell. I sensed he was obsessed with looking good. He talked about his barber and getting a perfect hairline. He said he wanted to get a haircut before the day was over. He walked over to the tall dresser and grabbed his brush. He started brushing his hair nice and slow. The top toward the front and the sides he brushed downward.

He said, "I only sit in one barber chair. If Joe isn't working, I don't get my haircut. He's been out sick, so I've been waiting for him to get my head cut. I want to try to make an appointment for later today."

I stood in front of the bed, playing with my hair as he talked. He stopped brushing his hair and turned toward me. He gave me one of his pretty grins as he walked over to me. He reached his hands out toward my hips as he grabbed me and brought me close to him. He lowered his head to me as I looked up slightly toward him. Our eyes made contact as our lips met to kiss. We started kissing softly and passionately. The heat of love was slowly rising through my body. After kissing and hugging to the point I couldn't take it anymore, I softly pulled away from him.

I sat on the bed in front of him, staring at him as he looked down on me. Our eyes were seducing each other, showing the other person what the other was desiring. I made the next move by slowly backing up onto the bed. I backed up far enough for my nightie to reveal my thighs and a slight glimpse of my yoni.

Micah just stood there watching me. His anticipation was growing quickly. He stood naked, tall, and strong while looking at me lying seductively on his bed. I opened my legs and place my fingers on my yoni, slowly massaging myself, giving him the okay to engage me.

Micah came closer to the bed and lowered himself to the floor. He reached under my knees, wrapping his arms around my thighs. Using a gentle but strong grip on my thighs, he pulled my yoni slowly into his face. His lips met my yoni's lips. He sucked and licked me softly. He didn't leave any part of me go untouched. I rubbed on the waves in his hair as he played between my legs.

Micah slowly eased his way from between my legs and greeted my breasts, kissing them and cupping them, aggressively and gently.

I stopped him. I said, "We are going to need a towel."

He laughed and said, "What happens, happens."

Micah came face-to-face with me. His member was hard and strong. As he kissed my lips, I felt him enter me. He didn't need his hands to guide himself inside of me. His body relaxed on top of me as he filled my insides. He slowly made love to me.

He watched me while he moved inside of me, being attentive to my moans and groans. He went fast and slow at all the right times. He loved me down for over an hour as if it were our wedding night. He was good at making love.

When we were done making love, Micah reached into the side drawer and pulled out a pack of cigarettes. He lay in the bed for the next few minutes smoking his cigarette. He didn't look like your average cigarette smoker to me. He got out of the bed and headed toward the tall dresser. He grabbed his brush and resumed brushing his hair. While he brushed his hair, he gathered the clothes he was going to wear for the day.

He laid out a pair of crisp khakis with a red button-up short-sleeved shirt. He pulled out his all-white Nikes from the closet floor and a black durag from the dresser drawer.

We took some time getting ourselves together. It was longer than we both expected. It was late afternoon when we headed out. We hoped in the rental to start out on our adventure together. We had things to do and places to go.

Micah told me he wanted to show me a few places he enjoyed going to. We drove forty-five minutes until we reached a soccer park. We sat at the park for a few minutes. He told me he loved watching the kids play, and coming to the park was peaceful for him. We hopped back in the car. It was getting late, so I said, "Where to now?"

He said, "Well, we are close to the barbershop I go to. Maybe we can stop by there before we go anywhere else? Especially if he doesn't have anyone in his chair."

I realized Micah had a deep obsession with his hair.

We drove another fifteen minutes before we came to a run-down shopping center. The center contained four different office businesses, one of which was his barbershop. Micah got out of the car, walked over to my side of the car, looked into my halfway rolled-down window, and told me he would be right back. I watched as he headed to the entrance of the barbershop and disappeared inside. He emerged a few minutes later with a smile on his face. Whatever he was smiling about, to him it was good news.

Happily, he said, "Dude said he can get me in today. He has four other people ahead of me, though, but if I wait, I can get my haircut today."

I could tell he really wanted to get his haircut more than anything. I said, "I guess we can wait."

After my response, I thought Micah was going to get in the car with me to wait for his time in the chair. Instead, Micah opened the passenger side door, reached in, and grabbed his phone. He said, "No women are allowed in the barbershop. You'll have to wait out here. The neighborhood is a bit rough, so stay in the car. I'll come out and check on you when I can."

Micah shut the door and headed back into the building. I was shocked he was going to leave me in the car by myself, especially after telling me about the neighborhood. He knew I didn't know the area. It was almost four in the afternoon, and I still had a decent amount of daylight time left. I rolled my windows up and decided to listen to music.

Forty minutes went by, and Micah hadn't come out of the building to check on me. I tried to remain as calm as I could, but I wasn't okay with him not checking on me. It was a happy time for me, and I wanted it to remain that way.

To ease my mind, I went for a ride. I cranked the car up and headed into the direction of the park Micah recently took me to. It was the only place I could think of going without going too far from the barbershop.

I called Micah to tell him where I had gone just in case he was looking for me. By his response, I could tell he didn't know I was even gone, and that meant he never came out of the building to check on me.

He said, "'Ight! Dude has one more person ahead of me. Take your time."

I said, "Time? We are running out of time. It's been an hour and a half and you're still not in the chair! Just call me if you get done before I get back."

He said, "I'll make it up to you, baby! I promise!"

His response calmed me just a bit, but it was getting late, and nothing that we set out to do was looking as if we were going to be able to do. At the park, I thought about how the trip was going so far.

I was enjoying myself, but there were some things that didn't sit right with me about Micah. I didn't like that he smoked and he didn't tell me. His pretty-boy hair fetish was becoming annoying, and based on the phone conversation this morning with his baby mama, he had a temper that got out of control sometimes.

On the other hand, he adored me, at least he acted like he did. He was an experienced lovemaker. He loved me and wanted to marry me. I came out of my trance and headed back to the barbershop.

When I got there, I waited another thirty minutes before Micah came out. It was almost dark. I was hungry and annoyed. Micah got into the car, smiling and bragging about his hair, as if we didn't waste three hours of our time together on his hair.

He said, "What's next?"

Annoyed, I said, "You tell me? At this point, I'm ready to get something to eat."

"I know the perfect spot."

Micah gave me directions to an all-you-can-eat Chinese buffet. When we got inside the restaurant, I was amazed at the assortment of food. They had a little bit of everything that I liked. I got enough food to eat for now and later. Micah did the same. We took our plates to go so we could be in our own private space together.

We arrived at the register, and Micah said hello to the cashier. The woman recognized him, so I knew he was a regular there. The cashier rang up our food and gave us our total. I was expecting Micah to say he had it, but he said nothing. I noticed he didn't even bother to pull out his wallet, let alone reach into his pocket. I pulled my wallet out then handed the woman my debit card.

On the way back to his suite, Micah asked me to stop by the store. I pulled into a gas station near the extended stay. I got out of the car to go inside with Micah. I wanted to get some snacks for later. I didn't think we were going to make it back out once we were back in the room.

We grabbed what we needed and headed to the register. Micah spoke to the dude checking us out. He was a frequent customer there as well. The guy rang our stuff up together, and I assumed Micah was going to pay this time. Micah looked over at me and repeated the total to me. I was wrong again. He continued to talk to the clerk as I handed the guy the balance for our stuff.

Micah grabbed the bag of snacks as I started walking toward the exit. I paused as I heard Micah ask the clerk for a pack of cigarettes. I looked back as he pulled his cash from his pocket to pay for the cigarettes.

When we arrived back at the room, I started preparing the food for us to eat. Micah's shift was starting soon. He wanted us to eat without any interruptions. We ate and talked about the future. He changed into his uniform as soon as we finished our meal.

He said, "Make yourself at home. I'll come check on you every chance I can between rounds."

He kissed me, grabbed his two phones, and headed out the door. While he worked, I looked around the room some more. I checked the drawer he kept his personal phone in. I looked in his medicine cabinet. I looked in spots I deemed secret spots. He didn't have anything lying around that seem suspicious, easing my curiosity.

I took a shower, then I put on something red and sexy. I waited for him to come back to the room on his break. I kept myself busy by searching the book, playing games on my phone, as well as making a couple of phone calls while he worked. I was going to stay up until he clocked out in the morning. He came to check on me during all his breaks. He called me on the phone to talk when he had the chance. Each time Micah entered the room, he would smoke two cigarettes. He blamed it on the residence.

Micah walked in the room as soon as his shift was over. He removed his uniform and walked his naked body across the room, straight into the bathroom. He kept the door open while he showered. He shouted from behind the curtain. "Hey, future wife!"

I said, "Good morning, baby! How was work?"

He grabbed his towel as he walked to the bed where I lay ready and waiting for him. He dried off, and then he got into bed. He said, "I'm glad I'm off and here with you."

As he lay down, I pulled the covers back gently, exposing his body. His member laid limp across his leg. I looked him in his eyes as I proceeded to take it into my hands. It began to swell in my hands. I was amazed at the immediate response. I gripped it firmly in my hands as I slowly moved my hands up and down, arousing him to his peak. His eyes closed as he enjoyed the pleasure I was giving him with my hands.

I kissed his lips and then lowered my body until I was face-to-face with his member. I licked my lips as I proceeded to let him feel the warmth of my mouth. I made sure his shaft was nice and wet. I caressed him repeatedly, increasing his excitement. I massaged his member with my mouth. Slow then fast. Firm then soft. My rhythm was grooving to his moans.

His fingers played with my hair as I pleasured him. He massaged my neck off and on when the pleasure wasn't consuming him. Each gesture was making me hornier and hornier. I moaned lightly while pleasing him. I was extremely turned on with his interaction with me while sucking on him. I didn't want him to cum. I wanted his excitement to build up. I wanted him inside of me. I sat up from my position and positioned myself on top of him.

I gasped as I slowly sat on top of him and his member entered me. The feeling was making me breathless. I reached for the headboard in front of me as I lifted my body up and down on him. Heat rose inside of me as my yoni clenched and gripped him with each motion. He hugged my waist with his arms, his movements thrusting up inside me. His breathing was hurried while I tried to regain my breath between motions. I was ready to cum, and I could tell he was too.

He grabbed my hips, gripping hard and firm. He gave a hard thrust inside of me, and I released a mellow moan. I fell forward toward his face. Lip to lip, nose to nose, we breathed into each other, exchanging intimate energy. I fell over to my side of the bed. I couldn't believe sex could be this good. It was beautiful and amazing.

Micah's schedule remained the same the rest of the trip. He worked as I played wifey. We didn't go to any of the places he said we were going to visit. When we did go out for something or to a store, I paid for everything. We had such a good time I didn't care about the money. I just made sure I had enough money to get home.

Our time together was coming to an end. We had less than twenty-four hours together before we had to return to reality. We talked about our life together as a married couple. He wanted to move to North Carolina to live with me. He wanted me to help him find a job, and he wanted to go back to school. He also had plans to bring his son once he was situated. He said, "I need a do-over in life, and I am willing to relocate to do it. You make me so happy. I couldn't ask for anything better. Get ready to be Mrs. Guess very soon."

I never had a man that was so sure of his wants and dreams. We spent every minute we could together. He took a few extra breaks from his work duties to come in the room to play around. I wasn't ready to leave him. I wanted to stay longer, but I had to get back to my life in North Carolina.

On one of Micah's visits to the room, I asked him about the girl from Florida who always commented on all his posts. She was something I wanted to ask him about. She was always on his posts and in his comments.

I asked, "Do you know the Floridian girl that's always commenting and posting on your page personally?"

He quickly said, "Nah, I don't know her like that at all. She was a super fan in another group we are in together. We talked on the phone a couple of times about the game and stuff. We talked about linking up in the past, but she didn't want to come up here, and at the time I couldn't go to Florida."

"I don't want to start questioning you because of Facebook like the book tends to do to relationships. Just don't let the conversations get out of hand, or I'm going to have to hurt some feelings."

We laughed.

The mood was bittersweet. I didn't want to leave. I thought of a million excuses to call in to work. I wanted to stay one more night. I knew I was just being extra. I needed to take my butt to work and return to my normal life until Micah could join me in North Carolina.

I was leaving at five in the morning. While Micah was working, I was sleeping. Or at least I was trying to sleep. The time to leave came quickly. He made it a point to take his break a little early so he could see me off. He walked in the room as I finished gathering my stuff. He walked up to me, reaching out for me. He was coming for a hug, but I handed him one of my bags instead. He was surprised by my actions. I said, "I don't want the mood to get sad and sappy. I need to get out of here before things get emotional."

We walked out to the rental together. I placed the stuffed puppy he gave me in the passenger seat. We placed all the other bags in the backseat. We hugged, and he gave me a long, hard kiss. And without words, I got in the car and drove away.

Micah called my phone as soon as we were out of sight of each other. "I love you! Be careful, my love."

I said, "I love you too! Now get some sleep."

I thought about everything on the ride home. My visit gave me hope for love—something I desired in my life. I wanted to be married. I wanted to be someone's wife.

The long-distance part was new for me, but I felt like was worth it. He had some questionable behaviors, but nothing that made me want to go a different way. He could be my future husband. He for damn sure knew how to make love. I was excited for us, for our relationship.

I was excited for the next trip out to see him, which we agreed would be in a couple of weeks, sometime around the 2016 election. I drove all the way home thinking about my happiness, listening to and singing love songs from my favorite artists, Mary J. Blige and Debra Cox, to name a few.

I couldn't wait to tell my kids and my mom about my adventure to find love, even my work family, who were always concerned for my love life.

Ms. Sandra and Ms. G (the older women out of the bunch); T Mack, Riah, Drika, and Ney (the younger ones); and a few others at work treated me like family, and they were praying hard for me to find love. They witnessed my heartache when it came to love. They were going to be excited to hear about my adventure. Some of them (the younger ones) were going to be more concerned about the sex part more than anything else. I couldn't wait to get back home to tell them how well things went.

I was happy when I arrived home. I was happy I got to spent time with Micah, but it was also nothing like home.

*****

Micah and I went right back to our regularly scheduled program. We talked on the phone and video chatted. The phone sex was better now, since we knew exactly what set the other person off sexually.

The two weeks we had to wait for our next visit was taking forever to arrive. My funds weren't where I needed them to be to take the trip the same as before. This time I was going to have to drive my own vehicle, and I could only stay three days. I had just enough money to make the round trip and nothing more.

Because of the way things went the first time I went to Connecticut, I decided to make all the plans. I didn't expect us to leave the room the second time around either. So I planned for us to have a nice romantic dinner with candles. We were going to play drunk Uno, and the rest was going to be spontaneous.

I had most of the stuff at my house to make the dinner special. I put a box together with all the things I needed. I brought a set of wine glasses and a plate set. I had candles and had steaks in the freezer. The only thing that was left to do was wait for the day to arrive for me to leave.

Every day, Micah expressed how much he missed me and how he couldn't wait for us to be together again. He told me how much he yearned for me and how he was ready to marry me, making me his queen. I was ready. Maybe too ready.

The day before I was supposed to leave, Micah and I went over the details of the trip—the time in which I was leaving North Carolina, which route I was going to take, and how long I was staying. We agreed everything was in place for a safe and rewarding trip.

That morning I spoke to Micah was the same as every other morning. He said he was tired from work, and I needed to get some rest as well for my trip later. Before lying down, I set my alarm to go off around 10:00 p.m. I planned to leave around midnight to avoid traffic. The car was already packed, fueled, and ready to go.

When my alarm went off, I was surprised I hadn't heard from Micah. I called his phones. My calls went straight to voicemail. I called him a handful of times on each phone, and I continued to get his voicemail. I went on Messenger to see if he was active, and it showed he was recently online. I left him a message on Messenger telling him I was leaving out and for him to call me when he received my message.

I continued to get ready for my trip. Realizing I never received a call or text back from Micah, I was beginning to worry. It wasn't like him to not respond to any of my communication attempts. I sent him a message letting him know I was on the way.

I drove to Virginia, calling and texting Micah along the way. He didn't respond to me at all. I went on his Messenger to see if he was active since I left the house. It showed he was online. I quickly messaged him to see if he was okay. I was relieved when he messaged me back telling me he was going to call me after he finished making his rounds.

I continued to drive, and Micah never called. I had driven halfway. I wanted to get to him to find out what was going on with him. Micah knew I was on the way. I told myself not to worry and I'd get the full story once I was in Connecticut. I finally received a call from Micah.

I said, "What is wrong with you, and why does it seem like you're being distant? You have been acting weird tonight. And you knew I was coming for two weeks now. If you don't want me to come, just say so."

My inner gut was telling me something was going on with him. I wanted to know what changed. Why was he being distant and acting strange toward me suddenly? I finally shut up long enough for Micah to talk.

He said, "Calm down, Joss, you're tripping for no reason. I got some bad news, and I don't know how to tell you."

I instantly felt the blood boiling inside me. I knew he was about to tell me some messed-up shit. He was about to tell me something I didn't want to hear after driving six hours toward him.

He said, "I'm not at the building in Connecticut. You can't come see me right now. I was assigned to another site at the last minute."

I got angry. "Bullshit. You knew I was coming tonight. We confirmed plans less than twelve hours ago, Micah. We even spoke before we took a nap. You didn't say anything about having to work at another site."

His voice changed, and I could tell he was getting angry. He said, "This is why I didn't want to tell you, why I have been avoiding you. I knew you were going to think it was something else. I didn't want you to go down that road of you not trusting me. Now I'm mad!" Then he hung up.

I swiftly shook my head in disbelief trying to figure out how things went so wrong so quickly. This was not how I imagined my trip going. I was supposed to be on my way to enjoy the company of a man who insisted he was going to be my future husband.

Instead, I sat in my car in an empty parking lot in the middle of God knows where six hours from home and four hours from him. I felt guilty even though I knew I didn't do anything wrong. I wanted to call him to fix things. I wanted to know if we were okay, if it was even okay to continue my trip to see him.

My feelings went into overload, and I began to cry. I questioned myself on why I even tried to be in a relationship with someone younger than me living hundreds of miles away from me. I didn't understand why I kept putting my all into relationships that I just knew couldn't work just to be disappointed in the long run.

I gathered myself together and decided to give Micah another call. I wanted to know if he still wanted me to come see him. I wanted to know if he calmed down. I dialed his number, but I got no answer. I put my phone down, looked around the parking lot, started my car, and headed toward the highway home. I wasn't going to sweat him. I wasn't going to chase him either. I turned my music up and headed home, confident it was his loss and not the other way around.

As I got closer to home, I stopped to get a cup of coffee. I wanted a break from driving as well as a break to clear my mind from thinking about what went wrong. Micah hadn't called me back yet, so I decided I'd give him a call once I stopped.

It was early in the morning, and the sun was barely crossing the horizon. I pulled into a gas station that didn't look like it had customers since the third shift cashier took her post. I knew the coffee wasn't going to be any good. I started on my way to continue my journey home.

I made a U-turn to return the way I came. My eyes caught sight of an older woman lying on a bench. I looked around the area to see if someone else was around or with her. It was cold outside, and looking at the woman's situation, I wanted to help her.

The woman appeared to be homeless, cold, and in her late fifties. She was frail-looking also. She wore a thick cotton hat on top of her head, and she had a long coat and a blanket covering her body. She had a small stack of bags piled next to her. I wanted to help her. I rolled the window down to see if she was okay.

She said she was fine. She was waiting for the bus so she could get to work. She said she had to catch the first bus (which came at 8:00 a.m.) in order to get to work on time. She got off her second job late and arrived at the bus stop late, so she had to stay at the bus stop to catch the first bus back out. She didn't have any other way to get to work. She had been sitting on the bench for the past six hours, waiting for the buses to run so she can get to work across town.

I could tell she was cold, and I didn't want to leave her lying on the bench in the cold. I said a quick prayer to the Lord for guidance. I wanted to help, but I also didn't want to get killed for doing a kind gesture. I said, "Ma'am, please get in the car and out of the cold."

She looked at me in shock. She said, "I'll be okay, don't you worry about me."

I said, "Ma'am, please! I'm going to stay with you until the bus arrived."

When she got in the car, I turned the heat up for her so she could get warm. I liked to help people. Doing so always made my heart warm on the inside. The whole situation kept my mind off Micah.

I asked her, "Where do you work? I'm going to take you to work. That way you don't have to wait for the bus."

I wanted to do something nice for someone while I was going through my storm. There was a reason the Lord put this woman in my way. I was a true believer everything happens for a reason. The woman's job was farther away than I thought. It was out of the way from my destination home, but I was okay with that, because I needed the distraction.

As we drove around, I questioned if she was actually giving me directions to her job. The woman talked the whole ride, sometimes making sense and other times sounding incoherent. She told me her life story. She was proud she was drug-free for over a year. She had a daughter who was pregnant, and she was trying to get her life together for her. She told me she got a second chance with her daughter, and she wanted to keep doing right by her. She worked two jobs to keep her mind busy, focusing on her future instead of her past.

She asked, "What are you doing out this early in the morning, sweetie?"

I replied, "I was going out of town to see a guy who claimed he loved me."

She laughed. "Honey, it seems to me you are going a long way to be with someone. You need to love yourself before giving yourself to a man. The same energy you are using to go see him you should be using on yourself."

I knew she was right, but she didn't know the complete story. After driving for forty minutes in a direction I was unsure about, we arrived at a hospital parking lot. I truly thought the old woman was crazy. She made no mention that she worked at a hospital.

I asked, "Why are we here at a hospital?

She happily said, "This is where I work. My other job. I can't get a job in my area, so I ride the bus every day to work at the hospital."

She grabbed her belongings and got out of my car. She said, "God bless you." As she disappeared into the lobby of the building, I drove off thinking about what the woman said. I didn't catch the woman's name during our ride, but I truly felt like she was an angel in disguise.

When I got home, I grabbed the steaks and put them back in the freezer. I headed to my bedroom. I was surprised I hadn't heard from Micah as I lay in my bed. I eased my emotions by admitting to myself I dodged another love bullet. It was better for him to hurt me now rather than later, I assured myself. I went to sleep with mixed feelings for Micah. I awoke later that afternoon feeling conflicted about what was happening between Micah and I. I went on about my day as if I didn't have previous plans to be out of town.

Around four in the afternoon, my phone rang, and it was Micah. I looked at my phone and contemplated whether to answer it or not. I decided not to. Micah called my phone seven times. He even messaged me on Messenger. I ignored them all. I wanted him to feel ignored like he made me feel.

I called my cousin Roxanne to see if she thought I should talk to him. After everything I told her, she told me to leave him alone. She told me she didn't want to see me go down another downward spiral of hurt and pain caused by another man.

I wanted to agree with her. I wanted to be strong enough to not care about understanding why Micah decided to play games with me for four months. Despite her advice and my better judgment, I wanted to hear his side of the story.

I didn't tell Roxanne, but the next time my phone displayed Micah's picture on my phone, I was going to answer his call. I was going to ask him why he did me the way he did, especially having me drive six hours out of the way only to return home disappointed. I was going to get an answer. My anticipation didn't last long because Micah called within minutes of my thought. I answered the phone calmly. "Hello."

"Hey, future wife."

I sucked my teeth loud enough for him to hear.

"I know you're mad at me, but I need to explain. Please let me explain. Joss, I want you here with me. Better yet, I'd rather be in North Carolina with you. Work got in the way, and I didn't know how to tell you that I couldn't tell my job no."

I interrupted him. "You had plenty of time to tell me you weren't going to be at the building. You could have told me what was going on instead of having me drive six hours out of the way, especially knowing I didn't have money to waste. Every extra dime I had was planned for this trip. Micah, you are wrong for not telling me. You told me you would never hurt me, but I beg to differ. If there is someone else in the picture, just tell me. Or if something else is going on, just let me know."

Agitated, he said, "There you go always thinking someone is messing with someone or cheating on you. I love you, and I always will. I want to marry you. I want us to be together forever. And I mean it! Get in your car and come to me."

Confused, I said, "I just drove twelve hours just to end up back at my house. I'm not about to get back on the road. You messed that up. What you did last night was wrong on so many levels. You don't deserve to see me anymore, let alone call me your wife. I don't believe you know what love is. You're just in love with the thought of me, Micah."

"You still have two and a half days left off work, Joss. You know you want to come see me because you don't believe what you just said."

Micah begged and begged for me to come see him. He told me we were wasting time talking about it on the phone when we could be having makeup sex. He said if I came to him, he would make it up to me.

After an hour of begging, he wore me down. Everything was still in my car except for the steaks. Against my better judgment, I grabbed my keys and headed to Connecticut anyways.

Micah called me nonstop on the ride. His behavior now was totally different from the behavior he had a few hours ago. He was the Micah I knew, the Micah I was falling in love with. I was anxious to get to him. I was beyond frustrated, but I so desperately wanted to see his face and be in his presence. The mood felt different—the ride, my feelings, the anxiety that was building in me, as well as whether I trusted him or not.

When I arrived at the extended stay, I went straight to Micah's room. I didn't take any of my stuff out of the car. I didn't know if I was going to be staying.

Micah welcomed me in the room. My eyes panned the room to see if anything looked out of the norm. His room wasn't as organized as it was before. He had stuff everywhere, and the room smelled like pure cigarette smoke. From what the room looked like, he wasn't ready for me to visit.

Micah wore the same khakis he wore the last time I was there. He had on a white tank top, some black-and-white sneakers, and a black durag on his head. He didn't look like the vibrant Micah I saw the last time I was there. He looked antsy, as if he was worried or ashamed about something.

I walked into the room and sat on the bed. I didn't make a sound. I wanted Micah to do all the talking, since everything that happened was his fault. He approached me. He said, "Please forgive me, baby! I'm sorry! Next time I'll just tell you what's going on instead of ignoring you and shutting you out."

His words were convincing enough for me.

We talked for an hour straight. He updated me on everything that happened. And he apologized for hurting me, again. I was tired from my trip. I asked him to get the stuff from the car. I updated him on the plans for later that evening. I got in his bed to get some sleep. I was tired and ready to put everything behind us. I wasn't going to give him any of my yoni. At least not at the moment.

Micah didn't sleep when I slept. I woke up a few times, and he was busy playing his video game. I woke up another time and found him watching me sleep. He smiled at me and whispered he was sorry for hurting me.

That night, things went on as if the hiccup we experienced earlier didn't happen. I didn't want to keep holding the situation against him, and his apologies every minute helped eased the emotional part of the pain. I went on to making the room romantic while preparing our steak dinner. Our trip was cut short, so we didn't have any time to waste.

Admiring my cooking, he said, "It's been a long time since I had a home-cooked meal. You cooking all this food is really special."

We made love right after we ate. He was slow and gentle. His loving made me forget about the night before. I enjoyed having him inside of me. We made love, and he dick-matized me until I came.

Micah appeared to be back to his regular self for the remainder of the trip. Our time together went by quickly, and the day came for me to get back on the road home. Right before I planned to leave, Micah asked me to take him to the store.

We headed to the store, and I sat in the car as he went in. I didn't want to spend any unnecessary money if I didn't have to. Plus, I felt like if he wanted something, he was for damn sure going to pay for it himself.

When Micah returned to the car, he asked me to take him to the Chinese place around the corner from the store. Micah went in the restaurant to order his food. He didn't ask me if I wanted anything. He went in, and a few seconds later, he came back out. He walked over to my side of the car. He said, "Do you have ten bucks so I can get something to eat?"

I couldn't believe he was asking me for some money to get him some food. He knew I had to make the journey back home, knowing I didn't have any extra money to blow. I'd wasted most of it on a drive that resulted in me going back home. I assumed I was missing something, and he was trippin'.

I quickly said, "I don't have the money to waste, Micah. I barely have enough money to get back home. I can't spare any money right now!"

Micah gave me a look as he walked off. I could tell he had an attitude. He disappeared inside the restaurant. I assumed that was to cancel his order, but he returned with a bag of food. He got in the car and didn't say a word. Apparently, he had enough money.

When we got back to the extended stay, he began to eat his food without asking me if I wanted any. He instantly started acting like I was a complete stranger. I gathered my things while he ate. He still didn't say a word to me. I said, "I'm ready to go!"

Micah walked me to my car. The mood was nothing like the last time. His demeanor was cold and distant. He pecked me on the lips, told me to be careful, then walked away.

I knew at that moment that was going to be the last time I saw Micah. Things were good until they weren't. I didn't know what happened, but I do know something happened. Micah was never going to be my future husband.

I drove away in silence. Between the distance and his attitude, he wasn't enough for me to hold on to. I thought about the strange old lady I had given a ride to a couple of days ago. There was a reason she and I met. The interaction wasn't an accident. She was there to tell me to put more energy into myself, to put myself first. Her purpose was made clear as I drove back home to North Carolina.

I arrived home in a record eight-hour time. I was afraid to stop other than for gas because I didn't have any more money to put in my gas tank. When I pulled into my driveway, I thanked God for the experience and for getting me home on little to no gas. I didn't call Micah to let him know I arrived home. Micah didn't call me to see if I made it either.

The next couple of days went by with no communications from Micah. I missed him. I missed our conversations, but I wasn't going to chase him. He professed he loved me every day, multiple times a day, and somehow it took a matter of days for him to switch up on me. All the pleading for me to give him a chance to prove he was different and serious about love meant nothing.

When I got bored, I checked his profile online. I wanted to see if he was still active, but mostly to make sure he was alive. I gave in one day and called his phone. I called both phones multiple times, and my calls went straight to voicemail. I hung the phone up and went on about myself. I made a random post on my page about not living in your mistakes. It was a repost, but it made sense for my life at the moment, and I wanted to record the memory.

I received an inbox message from Micah immediately after the post was on my page. I thought my eyes were playing tricks on me. I was interested in what he possibly had to say.

He said, "Hey, wifey! I haven't heard from you in a while. I figured you were mad at me about something. I have been keeping my distance, and I miss you!"

I laughed at the message. Thinking to myself, he had to be bipolar. I waited a few before I responded. I was still in shock he had the nerve to message me out of the blue, let alone say he missed me. I responded with a simple "Hey."

He said, "Your response seems dry!"

I messaged him back, and I let loose. I didn't care about his response. "Something happened, Micah. I don't know what happened, but something happened. You haven't acknowledged the fact I drove more than halfway to you and ended up back at my house. I drove well over a thousand miles to see you, only for you to act like you didn't want me to be there. You ignore my phone calls. You haven't called or texted. You didn't even bother to check to make sure I made it back to North Carolina safely. And now, days later, you want to message me like none of this shit happened. I told you not to hurt me, Micah, but you are for damn sure headed in the right direction."

"I know you think I purposely tried to hurt you, and I'm sorry for that. I have a lot going on in my head, and I truly don't know how to talk to you about any of it. I took my feelings out on you, and I didn't mean to. I didn't mean it at all. I didn't do any of it the right way. I should have talked to you about it all. I should have done a lot of things differently. I'm sorry. I hope you understand I love you and I want you to be my wife. I want to spend the rest of my life with you."

I quickly fired back, "You talk and make love like a grown man, but your mind is immature. Someone that can't communicate with someone they claim they love is not mature. As a mature adult, you talk about your feelings or find a healthy way to release them. You did it all in the worst way, and now you expect me to forgive you because you ask. This relationship is too new to me for me to stay in something I already see the ending to."

"I understand it all, baby. I'm sorry for all that it's worth. Can we please start over?"

"I'll give you an answer in two days."

I don't know why I said two days. It worked for Drew, but Micah sent a laughing emoji, and so did I. We chatted through Messenger for a little while until he had to leave to get his son.

During our chat, he said he was ready to move to North Carolina with me, but he was scared his youngest son's mother was probably going to try to keep him from his son. He didn't want that for his son. We talked about other things during our chat, but nothing came up as far as the next time we were going to try to see each other. I knew I wasn't going to make the trip again any time soon.

\*\*\*\*\*

Micah and I went on as if the hiccups didn't affect us. It was still in the back of my mind, but I wasn't going to hold it against him. He had a lot more to prove to me than I previously thought, and he still wanted to marry me.

His loving behavior lasted three days. He professed his love, called, texted, and wrote me beautiful messages. On the fourth day, Micah stopped responding to my messages. I'd message him at our normal time, and he wouldn't respond. Phone calls went unanswered and straight to voicemail. His Messenger always showed him as active. He was even making posts about his favorite sports team.

Before I went to sleep for work, I sent Micah a long text message letting him know how I felt about him. I wanted him to know I cared about him and I wanted a future with him. I told him I could see the pain in him that his past created and I only wanted to help him heal. I pressed Send and went to bed. I assumed I'd have a reply by the time I woke up to go to work, but I woke up to no response at all. I checked his page and noticed he made five posts since I messaged him. I continued to get ready for work, confused over his actions.

My workday went by slow. I constantly looked at my phone to check for a reply from Micah. I knew he was at work. I knew he had the two phones. I knew he was shutting me out. No response from him meant he was ignoring me, again.

I continued with my morning tasks without hearing a word from Micah. I decided to send him a message telling him I loved him before I headed to bed. I wanted him to know I cared, even though it was hurting me to be ignored. I woke up to a message from him the next morning. It simply said, "Hey."

I messaged him back. "You have been quiet, and I think we need to talk."

"I can't talk on the phone at the moment, but I can text."

"I need to get some things off my mind, and I need to say them to you while you're responding."

He quickly replied, "You're being a smart-ass, Joss, bringing up the fact I'm not texting you back. You're throwing everything I'm doing wrong in my face. Something doesn't feel right. Maybe you're the one that changed. Maybe you should find someone in North Carolina to be with until I can come be with you. Maybe that's what you need. Look at you, you're beautiful, and I know you have other men you can be with. You're too damn beautiful to not have other men want to be with you. I know I'm not the only one. I can't be."

I was shocked by his ranting response, and I could tell he was getting irritated, but I needed to tell him how he was making me feel while I had him going. "Micah, we are at the point where nothing seems right anymore. I'm being woman enough to tell you how I feel about things. I'm being honest with you, about not being able to trust you and your actions. You're doing the same thing one of my exes did, never answering the phone when I call or text. I'm not stuck in the past, but my eyes are open to shit that I'm not trying to repeat. You should understand where I'm coming from. We constantly talked about trust and not getting hurt on both of our parts, but you act like my words are new to you. And being beautiful doesn't mean shit. Me having a bunch of dudes lined up is bullshit. I know my worth, and I don't have to be with a man to validate me."

He didn't respond at all. A few minutes later I sent him a message, "So, I guess it's easy to ignore someone when they aren't in front of you!"

He responded immediately. "I don't know what to say to you right now, Joss."

Before work, I decided to send Micah a text. I wanted to make my words clear to him. I wrote,

> Micah, I wanted to talk to you before I went into work to get some things out, but like always, I can never call you. A lot of things you're doing has me thinking. I'm not trying to argue with you, nor do I want to continuously bring up certain situations, but I *do* want to try to let you know where my thoughts are at.
>
> Before I came to Connecticut, you were in my inbox calling and messaging me like I was all you could think about, like I was your whole entire life. Once I returned home, all that changed. We barely have a decent conversation now. I've sent you messages on Tuesday that you still to this day have not answered.
>
> Please help me understand why I can't freakin' call you or why I always go to voicemail when I call. I haven't changed, especially how I feel about you! Or what I want. I care about you more than you know. I would not have made the trips to see you. You told me you were going to climb the wall I built around myself and one day destroy it, but yet you're quick to tell me to go be with someone else here in North Carolina when I'm trying to be with you.
>
> You not once tried to figure out why I feel the way I do or work with me on easing my emotions—the emotions you created. Then you want to throw it back on me. I didn't want to do this through text, but I wanted my voice to be heard. Plus, you're not answering my calls. You don't

know how it is to have feelings for someone and not be able to express them.

Yes, I mentioned my past because I refuse to fall for another man's bullshit again. I've seen some things I wanted to address early on in our relationship, but I didn't want to ruin what we had because of past insecurities. Things like your phone. You kept your phone on vibrate most of the time I was around you. On the first day, you hid it in the drawer. That's a relationship issue for me. That's why I kept my phone out in the open. I wanted you to see I was an open book.

On our last visit together, I heard an interesting ringtone. A romantic-sounding ringtone. You told me it was nothing. It was a notification. It was more than just a notification. Every time it would go off, you texted someone, especially when you were in my car. I'm just trying to let you know why I'm having these feelings.

Now, you can choose to respond or not, but I'm being honest with you and myself. Honesty is key especially if we are going to move ahead, but I'm sure you probably don't want to because I'm sure you're going to insist I'm wrong about it all. You told me you wouldn't hurt me, but it seems like once you had me, you thought you didn't have to do anything else to keep me.

I feel ignored by you, and you can't say I'm wrong especially when I can't call you. I hoped love was finally knocking on my door. Then I came to see you this last time. Then you showed your true colors. I feel like we talk when we talk. Text when we text. I don't feel special to you at all anymore. I feel like another woman on another man's hit list.

You haven't been talking to me. I called you and sent you a long-ass text message, and you decided not to acknowledge that either. How do you propose we make this right; how do you propose we get back to smiling and being happy? To communicating?

I don't know if I said everything I needed to say, but I'm sure this is not all. But hey, I'm not trying to be a bitter bitch or say I don't care, but I want forever with pure honesty and no doubts. And for the record, I don't want anybody else.

Later that day Micah sent me a message. "Hello. Why are you making nothing into something? Us not communicating every day is not that serious. You're making our relationship difficult, Joss."

Angrily, I texted back, "What am I making so difficult? Especially since we no longer communicate! Do you expect me to go with the flow and not say anything and then let things fall the way they fall? Good or bad? I have gotten my feelings attached to you, and all of a sudden, I'm not supposed to care how you treat me. I love hard, and I swear I don't say I'm a good woman just to be saying I'm a good woman. I know with every fiber in me I'm loyal way down to a fault. I'm honest and sure as hell faithful to whoever I'm with. My heart is big, and when I give myself to someone, they have my attention. This is me, and I mean a lot to myself. If I'm guarded, then so be it. I need security, and I need to know you are there for me and not to hurt me. Is there someone else in the picture on your end, Micah?"

His response was fast. "No! Why do you think that?"

I replied, "So, what is the big deal then? You say I'm making a big deal out of nothing, but you're for damn sure acting like a totally different person from the first time we started talking up until now. What's up? If I'm not what you want or if you're not interested in me anymore, just say so. If you're on to the next person, just say so. I sit here waiting all day to see if you are going to call or text, and you do nothing."

A few seconds later, Micah sent me a song dedication. He said, "I dedicate these words to you!"

The song was by Gerald Levert, "Made to Love Ya." I understood what he meant.

For thirty minutes, Micah sent one text after the other with song dedications, each telling me in its own lyrics how he felt for me, telling a story for him through song.

Admittedly it made me weak for him all over again. I didn't want him to know I was weak for him. I didn't want him to think that his music dedications excused what he had been doing to me. The music didn't take away from the pain he caused. It just soothed the ache.

The next day I didn't hear from Micah at all. The following day the same. I thought about Micah day in and day out, but I didn't want to be the one to break. Micah was hardening my heart for him, and I wanted him to know. Against my better judgment, I texted him anyway.

I texted, "I guess out of sight means out of mind! Was this all just a game for you? I really gave a damn about you. If you were going to end up just doing you and you didn't want to be bothered with me anymore, you should have just said so. I'm in my feelings right now, but I don't expect you to care."

He replied instantly, "What are you talking about?"

I said, "Micah, you can't keep ignoring me and think I'm happy. A simple text back would do, but I'm done talking. If you text back, you text back, but I don't care if you don't anymore."

Micah didn't respond.

Hours later, I texted his name to both phones and his online messenger. I didn't get a response. By this time, I was hurting—hurting because I did nothing to deserve the behavior he was giving me. I quickly reminded myself to woman up and straighten my crown. It was his loss and not mine.

Midshift, I received a message from Micah. I was shocked because I didn't intend to ever hear from him again. I let his silence mean something to me, and that was that we were over.

In his message, he said, "I'm hurt you feel the way you do about me. I never thought you would give up on us that easily."

My fingers moved swiftly across the phone. I didn't care about the spelling or proper sentencing. I had to say what was on my mind, as quick as possible.

I typed, "I was always making future plans for us. You are the first guy in a long time I actually wanted to be with. I've read over our text messages from when we first started talking. How you were so interested in me and how you expressed your wants and desires for us. One thing was never changing how we communicated with each other, and we both agreed in order to make our relationship work we had to do at least that much. There would be days I'd text you a message, and you wouldn't answer either one of your phones, in which they pretty much stay on you 24-7. Why don't you answer them? I got excited when I received a message from you, but now each message is a disappointment. What's the deal now. Why can't I call you now, Micah? I feel a lack of interest on your part. You're the one that told me you loved me first. If I'm wrong, I'm wrong, but I'm going to tell you how you're making me feel one way or another. I'm tired of giving you everything a man needs because it's not enough for you. We had a short amount of time together, but I'm already tired, Micah. I have been in constant thinking mode since my last visit. There is something about me that always believe in love. You were one of those things. I don't believe you ever loved me, and you never will. In some ways I feel as though I was just a Band-Aid for whatever wound you needed healed. I don't feel any love from you. I'm hurting. I have failed yet again and I acknowledge that, but I will survive every relationship after you until I am finally with someone that will love and respect me. I hope you as a man get what you deserve in life."

Micah didn't respond, and I went back to work. A couple of days later, a text came to my phone from Micah. It said, "Call me when you have time. It's important, plus I miss your voice."

I waited most of the day to text him back. I texted, "Hey."

He replied, "I'm in the hospital."

Hearing him say that made my heart sink. A million reasons popped up in my head for why he was in the hospital. Why was he texting me after two days? Why didn't he text me earlier? Was he dying, or did he have an STD and he had to inform me because I might have contracted it too? I finally said, "Why, Micah? Why are you in the hospital?"

He replied, "I'm sick. Sick with food poisoning."

I sighed out loud. I thought he was dying, but he called me out of blue to tell me he had food poisoning. I was already over the text conversation. I continued to text to see where the conversation was going to lead. I asked, "Where did you get food poisoning from? If it's really bad, you're going to need someone to look after you. To take care of you."

I was being sarcastic with my response. He didn't realize he had someone, but he lost her—that someone being me.

He sadly said, "I don't have anyone, baby."

I said, "Baby! I don't know what we are anymore, but I don't think I'm your baby."

I didn't hear from Micah again the rest of the day. I wasn't one bit surprised. His behavior was becoming more and more comical. I didn't bother to put any more effort into his words. Micah was a self-absorbed fool of a man playing childish games. And from past experience, there was a reason for his behavior.

I texted Micah a few times after that day to see if he was all right. I didn't expect anything from him. I didn't want anything from him either. I just wanted to make sure he was doing okay. All my messages went unanswered, no matter which platform I messaged him on. He didn't respond. I shrugged it off for what it was and went on about my life.

Pop-up conversations took place between Micah and I for a couple of weeks. In the span of two weeks, we texted four times. The texts on my part were concern for his health and the lack of communication. On his part, he sent poems, song dedications, and "I love yous." Our conversations were always short.

One day, Micah texted me, "I'm running out of money!"

I didn't know what to think of the text, so I responded with "What are you talking about?"

He said, "Joss, I'm out of money. What I saved I had to spend on my son, and now I don't have anything to last me until payday. I have bills to pay. My mom needs me to send her some money too. I'm almost out of cash, and there is this game I want as well."

He lost me at "game." I knew this dude wasn't calling me asking me for money. I know he didn't think I was going to send him money, especially not for a video game. Micah broke my attention when he said my name.

He said, "Joss, this is serious for me. I have things to take care of including my bills. I don't know what to do, but I know you can help me. Can you send me some money?"

My mind was blown. The nerve he had texting me to send him some money. He didn't even have the nerve to call me to ask me. I laughed to myself as I texted back, "I don't think that is a good idea on my part. I don't have money to waste on a game, let alone a game for you."

He replied, "Dang, Joss!"

And my phone went silent. He stopped texting as always.

I went a week until I couldn't take it anymore. I told myself I had to be crazy to continue going through the back and forth with Micah. I had to delete him from my life for good.

I went on the 'book and unfriended him. I went through my phone and deleted all his text messages. I went into my contacts to start deleting his telephone numbers. I deleted his work number first, but when I got to his personal cell number, I decided to call him to leave a nice, sweet goodbye. I knew he wasn't going to answer. He texted a week ago telling me his phone would be off for a while. I knew the call would go straight to his voicemail.

While the phone rang, I prepared my voice to sound sexy but stern, letting him know I meant every word I was about to say. On the third ring, someone picked up.

I said, "Hello."

There was a pause.

I said, "Hello! Micah, just say something. You said your phone was off, and apparently it isn't. Just speak."

The voice on the other end caught my whole world off guard. It was a female's voice.

Again, a thousand thoughts filled my head. Maybe I dialed the wrong number. Maybe it was a family member or someone stole his phone. But deep down, I felt I was calling at the right time. Micah didn't expect me to call because he told me his phone was off. All I knew for certain was there was a woman answering what I knew to be my man's phone.

The woman on the other end said, "Excuse me!"

I said, "Maybe I have the wrong number. I'm looking for Micah."

She politely said, "He's not here. Can I help you?"

I politely asked, "Can I ask whom I'm speaking with?"

In an innocent and polite manner, she said, "Lisa, Lisa Guess. I'm Micah's wife. I can pass on your message if you like."

There was a pause on both ends of the phone. Apparently, she was trying to put two and two together, and I was shocked to hear the word *wife*!

My voice turned serious, and I said, "Excuse me, Lisa, my name is Joss. Your husband has been lying to both of us for the past five months. Your husband and I have been in a relationship. He has not once mentioned he was married. I never knew you existed. He never mentioned anyone named Lisa. He told me about his two baby mamas—Marisol and Kay, but he never mentioned a Lisa."

Her tone changed. "My whole name is Lisa Kay Guess. And I'm no one's baby mama! I knew he was up to something. For six months he's been acting strange, not wanting me or his son around on the weekends and at night anymore. He claimed he had to work at other job sites, so he would send us back home to New Haven. I should have known something was up when he cleaned this junky-ass room."

I was shocked to hear her words. I couldn't believe I was going through this crap again. I calmly said, "Lisa, can I ask you some questions? I'm not mad at you, and I hope you're not mad at me, because we both got played. But can you tell me about your husband? How you choose to deal with him is on you, but you will never have to worry about me after today for sure."

She hesitated for a while. Then she told me everything.

She was the same age as Micah. They went to high school together and became high school sweethearts. They were best friends (at least he didn't lie about that part). They eloped after they graduated from high school when they found out she was pregnant with their son. His family didn't know anything about the marriage because he didn't want them to know. They never broke up, and they were still together, trying to make their marriage work for their son.

She sent me pictures of Micah and their son together at her family's get-together a couple of days ago. She told me he got a job outside of New Haven because there were no good jobs in the area where they lived. He knew if he went out of the county, he could make better money. He went home to New Haven where his wife and son lived once a month, but she and their son would come visit and stay with him every other weekend.

She never called him while he was at work because she knew he couldn't be on his phone. He always called her instead. She said sometimes he would get mad at her for calling, especially if he was asleep. I witnessed that part for myself.

Earlier in the year, she said, she caught him messing with another girl from Florida. Micah told her he was sorry, and it would never happen again. He started cheating with females out of states to keep her from knowing, especially because the women had to go back home.

She broke it off with him for a couple of weeks, and that was when he started begging her for them to get back together. He promised her a better future, even suggesting therapy. He begged her for sex, and she wouldn't have sex with him all the time. He stopped asking her for sex, and that was when she knew he was getting it from somewhere. She said she caught on to the subtle changes he was making around the room. One Friday a few weeks ago, she popped up on him. She didn't call or text him to let him know she was coming. Her plan was to catch him off guard to see if he was cheating. She knew something was out of the ordinary; she just didn't know what it was.

I thought to myself, *That was the reason for the delay on the last trip. He wasn't off-site.*

She said she stopped trusting him months ago when she found out about some girl in Florida.

*Hmm*, I thought. Lisa gave me clues and details on other things Micah did and didn't do. I was amazed. One phone call changed my life yet again.

Micah and I were in a long-distance relationship for five months. For three of those months, we talked nonstop over the phone. We video chatted, we talked all hours of the night, and we were on each other's social media pages daily. He commented under my post, and I did the same to his. I went to visit him at his room twice.

The other two months Micah spent trying to figure out a way to live both of his lives happily. Instead, Micah only succeeded in pushing me away. In his pushing me away, his lies began to unravel, leading to the end of something that should not have begun.

When I went to visit him, there were no strange phone calls to question his faithfulness. No one showed up at his room. Nothing was said out the way on his post other than the girl from Florida.

After speaking with Lisa for twenty minutes, I heard everything I needed to hear. I wanted revenge, but Micah wasn't worth the energy or time to get back at. He was in another state far, far away from me. I would never have to worry about seeing him ever again. No one really knew about him except the ladies at work and a couple of other family members. And I was glad.

I was hurt but not destroyed. I was going to learn from this mistake and move on.

# Hey, Beautiful...

I was still new to the online dating thing. I was constantly getting inbox messages from random guys. I was taking to the 'book to vent some of my frustrations about relationships and love. I found myself commenting under posts and memes expressing my feelings.

My breakup (if you want to call it that) from Micah was still fresh. A month with no lies was refreshing in itself. I was still hurting from falling down a love pitfall once again, but I was looking forward to a positive future. All the deceit taught me love was going to be hard to find. The battle was going to be a struggle going forward because so-called men were now acting like boys, and they weren't loyal. I was in no rush for love. I wanted someone to love but not at the expense of my values.

I still only went to work and home. I was not getting much out of Facebook, but it was a good place for venting subliminally. I questioned being able to meet anyone from my bedroom. Since social media was popping, online dating seemed to be on the rise. I was cautious after Micah, and I intended to stay local with whomever I got involved with.

"Hey, beautiful" was the message that popped up on my phone along with the message bubble from Messenger. The guy's name was Jaxxon, and apparently it was his second time saying, "Hey, beautiful!" I assumed his hello was a harmless one. I wasn't in a relationship, and I wasn't really looking for anyone, so I didn't think speaking back would hurt either of us.

I chatted back and forth with him continually through Messenger, with him constantly asking me for my number. I refused to give him my number because I wasn't sure where our communications were going to lead. I didn't want a repeat of Micah, so I decided to hold off passing my number to him. After about a week, I finally gave in and gave him my number. Jaxxon appeared to be mature and more my type than Micah; he also intrigued me.

By this time, I learned he was from another state. He had a son who didn't live with him, which meant of course he had a baby mama. He stayed with his cousin, had a job, and was single. Jaxxon insisted he was ready for that everlasting relationship. He was looking for his forever woman, someone to love him for him.

We talked on the phone day in and day out, kind of like we were high schoolers. He kept trying to get me to meet him at his house or at his cousins' house if I didn't want to meet him alone. I didn't want to get caught up again, so I kept feeding him excuses. Plus I didn't know him. I was over relationship drama, so keeping him at a safe distance worked for me.

After three weeks of talking and texting, I agreed to meet him at his house. I wanted to see what Jaxxon was all about. I couldn't lie; he had me feeling all kinds of ways mentally, physically, and emotionally, especially when he promised to do so many sweet things to my body when he finally laid eyes on me.

It was a Friday night, and I wasn't trying to stay out late. My weekend started that morning, and I wanted to have a relaxing weekend. I pulled up to his house and instantly became nervous. I froze, not knowing what to expect while sitting in his driveway. I wanted to leave, but I was no chicken. I made it this far, plus I wanted to know more about Jaxxon. I got out of the car and went to knock on the door.

Jaxxon's body filled the door frame. He was six feet, five inches' worth of tall. He was brown-skinned, and he was medium built, just how I liked 'em. He was cute in the face with a full mustache and beard. He also had a bald head. He looked good to be in his forties.

Jaxxon grabbed me and hugged. He pulled me back from him to stare at me. After our introduction, he led me to his room. His nephew had company in the living room. I assumed we went in his bedroom for privacy.

I felt comfortable with Jaxxon as soon as he put his arms around me. We started talking and laughing as soon as we hit his room. We talked about what we wanted in a relationship, our past relationships, our children, our jobs, and especially our future. Four hours passed before we knew it. It was one in the morning, and I needed to get home. I promised him I'd come back over later in the day when he got off work.

He kissed me on my lips as I stood in front of him gathering my things to leave. I was surprised at his approach, but I kissed him back anyways. I was turned on by how much of a gentleman he was. He walked me to my car, we hugged, he kissed me again, and I left.

I was excited and anxious the whole day. It was Saturday, and I knew I was going to see Jaxxon later that evening. I didn't know what our plans were going to be like for the rest of the night, but I was happy I had something like a date.

I arrived at Jaxxon's house around seven o'clock in the evening. He was already outside waiting for me. As soon as he was close enough to me, he hugged me just like the night before, warm and inviting. His arms wrapped completely around me.

Jaxxon already had music playing from his phone and some candles burning on the dresser. The room smelled like warmed mulberries. He offered me something to drink from his mini fridge he had in his room. I sat down on his bed, which was pushed against a wall with a window. Other than another dresser with a TV on it and a chair, that was the equivalent of his bedroom.

We started talking and ended up picking up right where we left off earlier that morning. He was sitting in his chair directly across from his bed while we talked. My back was up against the wall facing him. He got up for a moment to cut the lights down and to get us a drink.

Jaxxon came back to the chair. He reached out for my feet. He never stopped talking as he continued to massage my feet. His massage moved upward from my feet to my calves. He took his time. His big hands engulfed my calf as he moved his hands up and down my legs, like he was trying to remember every inch of me. I was getting lost in the massage. I never had someone massage me like he was massaging me. He was amazing with his hands, and I had no intentions to stop him.

The massage got more intense as he reached my thighs. He backtracked back down to my calves then back up to my thighs again. He grabbed my ass with both his hands. A cheek filled each hand. He rubbed and massaged me, slowly applying pressure as he moved up and down the curve of my ass, gripping and rubbing at the right moments. I didn't want things to go too far, but I also didn't want him to stop. His hands were warm, and it felt good.

Jaxxon continued massaging my body. He rubbed my lower back, still gradually going back and forth over my ass. He made his way up to my shoulders but never went too far away from my curves. He gripped my body like I was a toy in his hands. He rubbed with precision, touching me like he knew me for years and I had previously given him the rights to my body. He asked me to turn over, and I did. He asked me to remove my shirt, and I did.

As I lay on my back, thoughts flooded my mind. I didn't know him. Where were we going to go from here? Did he do this with other women? Should I sleep with him? Should I leave? I couldn't stop thinking. He was making my body feel so damn good, and whatever negative vibe I had was soothed away with each rub.

He started massaging my breasts while kissing on my stomach. His hands never left my body. He lifted my legs, and he placed my feet on his chest. One at a time he sucked on my toes. It instantly sent chills down my spine. My back arched as he went from one toe to the next.

He kissed his way from my toes up until he was between my legs. His lips were parallel to my yoni lips. He didn't know me like that, but he pleased me as if he knew me for a lifetime. He kissed my yoni lips, tasting me, sucking on my flavor. He licked and kissed me like that was the way to getting to know me. He licked with the rhythm of the music playing in the backroom. His whole mouth was on my lips. He massaged my yoni lips with his tongue and his lips as he just did with his hands across my body. Jaxxon created an orgasmic flow I couldn't hold back. I came as he continued to taste me.

His finger replaced his tongue as he climbed on top of me. He slid his fingers inside of me, through all my wetness. I heard him exhale, and then I exhaled. What he was doing to me was much needed. His body was feeding my body with pleasure I couldn't deny.

*****

It was the second week in December when Jaxxon and I hooked up. I was working six days a week, so the only time I could spend with him was on Saturday nights and all day Sunday. We talked and texted on the phone every day. I didn't know where he came from, but he was like a dream come true, as well as too good to be true.

Jaxxon was from South Carolina. He didn't know anyone in our area but his cousins. He didn't know the area very well either. He went to work and came home. He was a homebody, and I liked that about him. When I called, he answered. I was invited to his house every weekend. He sometimes wanted me at his house in his bed waiting for him before he got off work.

We talked about making our relationship serious. I wanted to get to know Jaxxon, and I found no fault in him. I was okay with seeing where things may lead between the two of us, and he was on the same page.

Before Jaxxon came along I already had prior plans to go out of town for Christmas vacation. Jaxxon and I made plans to spend the New Year's holiday together since we couldn't spend Christmas together. We were a new couple trying to make memories already.

I didn't want to go out of town. I didn't want to leave Jaxxon. I figured it was too soon to leave him. But we needed to build trust. I was going to miss him for the week I would be gone.

Every chance Jaxxon and I got to be together, we hooked up. He was always feeding me and making sure I ate. He brought me a leather jacket and gave me money. He texted me, and he called. He acted like a man who had a woman. I felt like a woman who had a real man. I was happy, and I had no complaints.

Before my trip, I spent the night with Jaxxon, and we made love. We talked about our plans for the New Year. We were together for three weeks, but it felt like a lifetime. He said, "I'm still going to call you every day. Nothing is changing because you're going out of town." Hearing his words made me feel good inside.

It was hard to get in touch with Jaxxon the first day I was gone. I would text him, and he wouldn't respond for hours. His responses were short, nothing like our normal text conversations. I knew he still had to work, so it wasn't a big fuss. I was growing antsy when almost the whole day had gone by and I hadn't heard much from him. It was late in the evening when Jaxxon finally called.

He said, "Joss, baby, I saw your text. I was busy working. I'm tired as well. We can talk more tomorrow?"

As soon as I said okay, Jaxxon hung up the phone.

I didn't get to say anything; he said what he had to say and then he hung up. There wasn't shit I could do until I got home, but I wasn't going to fall for another man's bullshit. I wasn't about to be treated any kind of way by another man anymore. I wasn't going to entertain his actions while I was out of town. I was going to stay calm and deal with it once I returned home.

Jaxxon had me distracted from my vacation with family and friends. We were still new to each other, but I didn't understand why he switched up on me so quickly.

While I was away, Jaxxon and I talked on and off, but nothing like we did when I was home. He blocked me from his page on the 'book, which made me suspicious of his behavior. When I asked him about it, he told me something was wrong with his page and he got locked out of his account. Something wasn't right, and I didn't know if we had much to pursue once I got back home.

I was ready to go home, ready to be by myself. I was mad at myself for opening myself up to love again, only to be disappointed yet again.

The day I got home, I was expecting to hear from Jaxxon. He knew when I was returning from my trip. Our conversations were short, and we made plans to see each other, but I wasn't getting my hopes up, and I really wasn't sure if I cared. Jaxxon acted like he didn't want to have anything to do with me while I was away. I didn't think his attitude changed just because I was home.

It was the day before New Year's Eve. The day came and went, and of course, I didn't see Jaxxon. On New Year's Eve, I sat around the house like it was a regular day. I was debating on what to do that night. My prior plans weren't going to pan out, so I was going to make new ones.

My kids were old enough to have their own plans for the night, and they had already made their way out. I was home alone watching movies. Jaxxon and I exchanged texts earlier in the day, but as evening struck, he went silent.

I didn't care anymore, so I stopped thinking about him. I was disappointed, but he wasn't about to know it. I watched my movies, and I had my wine. I was going to bring in the New Year by myself, and I was okay with it. I fell asleep before the ball dropped, until my phone rang. It was Jaxxon.

"Joss, my cousin got shot tonight. I'm headed out of town right now. I'm about to handle some fools for hurting my cousin."

I was in shock a bit. Scared for him maybe. I said, "Are you okay?

"I got caught up because of this mess. I really wanted to spend New Year's with you. I got a jacked-up past, and I'm not sure how you are going to handle all the details about me. I don't want you to see me in this state. I promise I will call you tomorrow, and you will get your New Year's hug and kiss when I get back."

We said good night to each other. It was 11:21 p.m. on New Year's Eve, and I went back to sleep.

The next day Jaxxon texted me. He was on his way to work. I thought he was still out of town. He called me off and on while he was at work. Things seemed to be back to normal, as if I never went out of town. His demeanor was normal, and he made no mention of his cousin.

My day went on as normal, until Jaxxon called me and asked me to meet him at his house. I was anxious, but I wanted to see him. I hadn't seen him since the night before my trip. I wanted to confront him about his behavior. I wanted to know what the hell was going on with him. And I wanted to know what happened with his cousin.

When I arrived at Jaxxon's house, it looked as though he was just arriving himself. He was outside in the driveway standing next to his truck. His cousin was there as well, and they were in the middle of a conversation.

When I got out of my car, he introduced me to his cousin Shawn. Shawn was the cousin he worked with. Apparently, they were just getting off work and recapping the day. Jaxxon's demeanor didn't appear anything like he gave off the night before when he called to tell me about the shooting.

Jaxxon hugged me and held my hand while he continued to talk with his cousin. He made a comment to his cousin that stayed with me. He said, "This one right here, she is different." I wanted to ask him what he meant by the statement, but I didn't bother. Once they were done talking, we went inside.

Jaxxon acted as if he was excited to see me. He kissed me and rubbed up and down my body as he hugged me. His warming grip had me in a trance, and I welcomed all his touches. I wanted more.

We didn't do much talking. Clothes quickly came off. The room turned hot. Jaxxon picked me up and placed me on the bed, his lips never leaving mine. My head hit the pillow, and he slowly went for my neck, biting with just enough pressure to start the waterworks down below. His fingers were already making their way between my thighs to feel my heat. He was surprised at what he found. I was already ready. Ready for him to enter me. Ready for him to penetrate my hot spot so I could show him how much I really missed him.

Jaxxon wasn't ready for penetration. He gave me pleasure in all the ways he knew how. His trip down on me was sheet-grabbing, leg-trembling, hair-pulling, don't-know-whether-to-scream-cuss-or-cum moment. A deep wave was about to take over my body. The heat was rising and flowing straight to my yoni. I held his head close to my yoni, gyrating my hips while he licked and sucked, speeding up my movements as I reached my peak. I couldn't hold back any longer, and I finally gave him what he was down there for.

After I came, Jaxxon slowly entered me. He sent chills throughout my body as he filled me. Jaxxon made me cum multiple times. I didn't know my body could do the things he was doing to my body.

Jaxxon made love to me like he missed me, like he loved me. As we wrapped up the first round of lovemaking up, he closed it with "I love you, Joss."

I didn't doubt him after the pleasure he just gave me. He catered to me and my needs. He asked me if I wanted something to drink or eat. He even brought me a washcloth to place on my yoni. I was falling for his ass too. We continued to make love. I had to work the next day, but I figured I may end up taking a sick day.

A pretty bad winter storm was on the map for our state. I received a call from my job saying we were shut down for the night. I was excited. I wanted to spend every minute I could with Jaxxon. And the way he looked at me, I could tell he wanted the same.

We got up and went to the store to get some things just in case we ended up getting snowed in. Neither one of us had plans to leave his room for a while once we returned from the store.

For almost a week, we were snowed in together. We left the room only to shower and to cook. We made love every single day almost all day. Each session was even more intense than the one before it.

We spent our downtime from sexing talking about stuff that mattered and stuff that just came to mind. We had a lot in common, and we wanted some of the same things out of life. Jaxxon was a giant teddy bear. He had a hard-looking exterior, but he just wanted to be loved. I wanted to be the one to love him and to show him what love was about.

The remnants of the storm had passed, and the roads were clear. We had one more night together before we had to return to reality.

Jaxxon was in the shower as I was lying on the bed watching TV. His phone rang. I wouldn't have thought anything of the call except the caller was a female named Liz. It was 11:47 p.m., and she called three times, back-to-back. My mind started racing. My heart started beating. I contemplated with myself as to whether I should say anything to Jaxxon about the call or just wait for him to say something about it when he noticed the call. With the history I endured when it came to cell phones, I was going to address his phone situation one way or another.

By the time Jaxxon got out of the shower and came in the room, I decided I was going to say something right then. I said, "Your phone rang earlier, and it was a woman named Liz. She called three times in a row."

He said, "Yeah, that's my sister. I'll call her back later. She should still be up."

I didn't know his people yet, but I knew he had a sister. I didn't think anything about the call after that night, even though my gut told me otherwise.

From the first time I arrived at Jaxxon's house, I started watching him put his password in his phone. I knew his code to unlock his phone. The phone call tonight tempted me to use the information I have.

Soon after his shower, we made love. I made sure to push him a little harder round for round. When he was done, I got on top, and I started us off again. The session lasted a while, but I wanted to make sure I put him to sleep. A good sleep.

As Jaxxon slept, I unlocked his phone, and all I wanted to do was throw up. I instantly felt like a dumbass, questioning how I could have been so blind. Jaxxon's phone revealed he had been talking to multiple women.

Question after question entered my mind. Anger then pity. Then anger again. I was falling apart in a matter of minutes. I wondered when he had the time. All I know is he had me messed up.

After reading some of the messages, I found out Liz wasn't his sister. She was a woman he met around the same time he met me on the 'book. They met the same way. In the text, she was wondering what was up with his lack of communication the past couple of days. Reading on, apparently Jaxxon would text her all day, but at night he would always went ghost on her, and she wanted to know why. She also replied to him not answering the phone just a couple of hours before.

She said, "I assume you're tired from work. I haven't heard from you today. I miss u, baby. Call me." I knew why he was ghosting her, and it was because he was with me at night.

Trina was another name that showed up on his message log. As far as I could tell, he was doing her off and on. In the text, he was complaining she wasn't tight enough for him, and to him, that meant she was doing other dudes and he didn't want that. In the message, she was reminding him about their agreement. Her yoni was all his when he was in town, but when he was away, she could do what she pleased.

Melissa was another one that stood out. I saw so many "I love you," "I miss you," and "you're the only one" texts, as well as "I will see you soon" texts between them. One caught my attention, and it said, "I moved here to start our life together. Once I get everything together, I'm going to come for you." I was so damn confused.

There was another chick he was telling he couldn't wait to taste her. I didn't catch her name because I had already seen enough. I was already seeing red. And my anger was about to get the best of me.

And then there was Zoe. Zoe's messages really sent me for a loop. This one I read and read. Throughout their message thread were pictures. And those pictures were mine. All the pictures I sent Jaxxon. He forwarded them to this Zoe person. He told her in one of the picture attachments of me he found another one. He was telling her he could get women to do anything he wanted. Then he asked her how she thought I looked, if I was pretty. He told her about me helping him get a tire for his truck.

While we were snowed in, his truck tire went flat. He had twenty-two-inch rims. He didn't have the money to get another tire, and I told him I was going to help him so he could still get back and forth to work. We had planned to take care of the tire situation later in the week. But he was bragging about it all to this Zoe person about using me.

I read enough. I wanted to take something and beat him upside his head while he slept, but I realized quickly he wasn't worth it. I quickly grabbed my stuff and his phone as I was about to walk out. I unlocked it while calling his name loud enough so he could hear me. He looked at me surprised. He saw my stuff in my hand.

He said, "What's up?"

I didn't say a thing. I took his phone and threw it at his face and walked out. My ride back to my place was slow and long. There was still ice and snow on the road. It was two thirty in the morning, and I was in my feelings. I wanted to go back and cuss him and slap out. I felt dumb and used all over again. I kept going over the text messages over and over in my head on my drive. Who were these women? Why did I even care? I had all the evidence I needed to just put this dude behind me. I regretted not forwarding myself the messages for evidence.

I pulled into my yard, and my phone began to ring. It was the ringtone I set for Jaxxon. I ignored his call. He called right back. This time I answered. For some reason, I was expecting him to be mad because I went through his phone, but he didn't sound mad at all. His tone was soft, and he was calm. He said, "Why are you not in my bed right now?"

I shouted, "REALLY?"

He repeated himself. "Why are you not in my bed right now?"

"Jaxxon, do you not realize why I left? Do you even care? I'm not the only woman you are talking to. I don't like liars! And you wonder why I'm not in your bed. This seems to be a game for you. I'm not going to sit back and be any man's side chick or other woman. Then you call me and ask why I'm not in your bed. Whatever."

In a nonchalant and soft voice, he said, "Come back to my bed, and we can talk about it in the morning like normal people. All the questions you have, Joss, I'll answer in the morning. Your choice."

I sat in my car wondering how and why he was so calm. I had to admit he was handling this a whole lot differently than I thought. I wanted more with Jaxxon, and I wanted answers. I was scared to go back. I imagined he was going to beat my ass as soon as I walked back in his house. My dumb ass reversed out of my driveway and drove back to his house. The whole ride I questioned my stupidity. I grew even more afraid once I was outside Jaxxon's front door.

I opened the front door, passed through the living room, and headed to his bedroom. He never moved from the position he fell asleep in. Music was still playing low. He knew I was there because without saying a word, he pulled the blankets back. I got undressed and climbed in bed next to him. Once in the bed, he wrapped his arms around me and held me until I fell to sleep. Surprisingly, I slept well.

I awoke to Jaxxon sitting in the chair across from his bed staring at me. He always stared at me with an astonishing look on his face, like I was amazing to look at. I never had anyone stare at me like he did—like I was truly special.

Concerned, he asked, "Are you hungry or anything?"

I was lying in his bed after everything I read only hours before, feeling stupid. I wondered how he planned to do damage control.

"Joss, those women mean nothing. You are the one who is here every night. I will stop talking to them all just to prove you are all that matters."

He proceeded to tell me he wasn't sure where he thought we were going to go as far as our relationship was concerned.

He said he met Liz the same time he met me, and he talked to her for a while. He stopped talking to her months ago, but she won't leave him alone.

Tina was his baby mama, and she always wanted him back. The only time he saw her was when he went home to see his son, and he only spoke to her to keep her appeased because she was a vindictive baby mama.

Melissa was his ex, whom he admitted having feelings for, but he said they could never be together because she was a whore. She slept with one of his homeboys, and he had a deep obsession for wanting to get revenge on her for hurting him.

Zoe was his best friend whom he supposedly told everything to. The pictures of me to her was his way of trying to get her approval as far as my looks. He said the statements he made had nothing to do with me, as far as getting women to do whatever he wanted.

The other random woman whom he said he wanted to taste he claimed was just entertainment.

"Jaxxon, am I not enough entertainment? Why do you need to find entertainment from all these other women?"

I used this as my chance to ask him why I was blocked from his page on the 'book for the tenth time.

He said, "As of this moment, you won't be anymore."

*****

Jaxxon did a total 360 after the incident. He went to work and came straight home. He called and texted while he was at work and every free chance he could. I felt important to him, and he wasn't doing anything that made him look suspicious.

His job sometimes required him to go out of town. When he was away, he made sure we communicated. He kept me in the loop and left no room in my mind to wonder about any of his misdeeds, if he had any.

Jaxxon was very convincing. He wanted to prove to me I was special to him and our relationship was no game for him. He suggested I travel home with him to his hometown to introduce me to some of his family, most importantly his son. I was excited and ready. We turned over a new leaf in our relationship.

It was last minute, but we took a weekend trip to his hometown. Jaxxon was excited to be home and for me to meet his people. I met a handful of his family and friends, and I also met his best friend, Zoe.

Zoe was very entertaining, not what I thought based on the text message. She was a short young lady in her twenties. She had her own place, and she appeared to have her shit together. That seemed odd because Jaxxon was in his forties and didn't appear to know what he wanted in life, and it became more and more apparent the longer I kept dealing with him. They were an odd pair of friends.

Zoe seemed like someone I'd hang with, so I was cool with staying at her crib when Jaxxon insisted we stay with her.

My emotions were all over the place the next morning. I was going to meet the little one. Jaxxon's son. His pride and joy. The whole reason I came out of town with Jaxxon. I could sense nervousness in Jaxxon as well over me meeting his son. He kept looking at his phone supposedly waiting for Trina to call to tell him it was time for him to come get his boy.

Jaxxon stayed in his phone, mostly texting. His phone rang on and off, but he never answered it, growing suspicion on my part. He was preparing to get his son soon.

Jaxxon already mentioned to me beforehand he had to ride an hour and a half to go get him. He didn't think it was wise if I came with him because he didn't want his baby mama to not let him see his son because she might get jealous of me. I didn't want to be the reason for him not seeing his son, so I agreed to stay back and wait for him to come back with his son.

He said, "I'm excited for you to meet him."

As Jaxxon prepared to leave, Zoe was getting ready to go to work as well. She let Jaxxon know she was going to cook later, and she threatened him, telling him to make sure he kept her house straight while she was gone. He promised her the house was in good hands. "Joss, will you be okay while I'm gone? Do you need anything?"

I said, "I'm fine, baby. I'll be okay. I might need some chips or some snacks to go with my Paul Massan though."

Jaxxon left, ran to the closest store, and returned with my favorite snacks. In a matter of minutes, I was alone in Zoe's house with a whole bottle of alcohol and a bag full of snacks, waiting for Jaxxon to come back with his son, who I was going to meet for the first time.

I watched one of Zoe's movies. Most movies last about an hour and a half. I knew once I finished the first movie I should be hearing from Jaxxon. And he should be on his way back. After the first movie, I received no word from Jaxxon. I was texting and calling his phone, and I was being sent straight to voicemail. My texts were going unanswered. For a while I was worried, but then my worrying just turned to anger.

I started drinking. I needed to calm down. I was out of town with this man, and I didn't want to get out of character. I knew he was going to have a crazy excuse. I was in an unknown town, sitting in a stranger's trailer all by myself. He wasn't answering my calls or anything. I realized he could easily leave me stranded. I continued to drink, and I continued to get angry.

After two and a half hours, I finally received a text from Jaxxon. He said, "HEY, BABY. THIS WOMAN SENT MY SON OUT OF TOWN KNOW-

ING I WAS COMING TO SEE HIM. SHE KNEW YOU WERE GOING TO BE MEETING HIM, AND SHE DIDN'T WANT THAT. SO, YEAH, SHE SENT HIM AWAY. HER MOTHER IS SITTING HERE LECTURING ME ABOUT BEING A BETTER DAD WHILE I WAIT FOR HIM TO GET BACK."

I texted him back asking him if his son wasn't there, why was he still there. Why was he just hitting me up two and a half hours later telling me about this, and why the hell was he not answering my calls? Jaxxon never texted me back.

I continued to finish off the bottle of alcohol I had. I was getting sick, and I knew it. The room was spinning. I was drunk. I drunk a whole pint of brandy in less than four hours to conceal my pain.

After another two and a half hours, Zoe walked in. She saw me, and she knew I was drunk. She said, "Where's Jaxxon? Have you been here by yourself the whole day?"

I said, "I've been sitting here waiting for him to return. He texted earlier and told me some stuff went down. But after that, I haven't heard from him. I've been sitting here drinking my alcohol and eating my snacks all day."

She sensed the anger in my voice because she instantly tried calling Jaxxon. She got his voicemail just like I had, and she left him a message.

Zoe and I chatted while she cooked. I tried to have a sobering conversation, but it wasn't in me. I drank too much. She kept bringing me food to put in my stomach to help sober me up.

The more time that went by, the angrier I got. I wanted to go home. I was over the whole trip. It had to be Jaxxon's idea to have Zoe babysit me while he did whatever dirt he came back home to do.

Jaxxon strolled into Zoe's house after being gone for six hours. His son wasn't with him. He acted natural and as if nothing were wrong. He sat down next to me on the couch. And he didn't say much to me at all. Zoe said what I wanted to say. She said, "Why you leave this girl here by herself?"

With no concern, he said, "She's all right."

I shook my head. I didn't want to cuss him out while we were out of town. I didn't know anyone that would come this far to get me if I didn't get a ride back with this idiot, so I kept my cool. I looked at Jaxxon and told him I was hungry. He used me being hungry as his doorway to soften the mood between us as always.

He said, "I'll take you to get something to eat on the way to meet my sisters." I didn't care about meeting any more of his people. I wanted to go home.

Jaxxon told Zoe what our next set of moves were going to be, and we would be back at her house after we went to see a few more folks. Deep down I was anxious inside. I knew Jaxxon was up to no good. I was so drunk I was afraid I had alcohol poisoning. Jaxxon didn't realize any of it. He didn't notice I had drunk the whole bottle of brandy we brought with us.

I knew Jaxxon had someone in the truck as soon as I got in it. My stuff wasn't where I had it. It was hidden in the farthest seat toward the back of his truck with stuff covering it up. My heels and shoes were thrown in the trunk instead of in the seat like I had them. My lip gloss and earrings that were on the center console weren't there anymore either. All things pertaining to me were gone or hidden. While buckling my seatbelt, the smell of cotton candy perfume hit my nose. Between that smell and the alcohol, I instantly became nauseous.

I was angry. I yelled, "Where's my shit? And who the fuck was sitting here? I know it was a bitch because her perfume stinks! This is some bullshit, Jaxxon. I came out of town with you for you to be on some shady shit."

When I looked in the backseat, he had a takeout tray from some restaurant, and he had the nerve to say he brought his scraps for me. I was over the trip. And I was over him.

He said, "You're tripping. Everything is going well, and you're trying to find something wrong so we can argue. My homeboy was smoking weed in the front seat, and he wanted to kill the smell. He sprayed something on the seatbelt for the smell. I didn't answer your calls because I was upset with my baby mama because she wouldn't let me take my son and needed time to think."

I got a detailed excuse for a whole day's worth of events. We made it to his sister's house, and the alcohol in my system kicked in full force by then. I wanted to throw up, but I couldn't. I was dry heaving. I was ready to go home.

I kept hearing Jaxxon tell his sister and Zoe he planned on coming back to town the following weekend. He already knew he was coming back home, and I was wondering when he was going to mention it to me. By this point, I didn't care. I wanted to hit the road and get home. I wasn't myself with all the alcohol in my system.

Jaxxon said bye to his sister as she walked us to his truck. I was waiting for his lying ass to get in the truck so he could take me home. He finally got in the truck and tried to crank it. It stalled. He tried again. It stalled again. His damn truck died on us. We got out of the truck and went back in his sister's apartment. I was frustrated. Jaxxon acted as if his trunk not cranking was nothing, and he just sat on the couch.

He said, "We are going to have to stay here tonight."

I just shook my head. This trip was beginning to be the death of me. I never wanted to go home so badly in my life. Jaxxon was asleep in a matter of seconds. I went through the night drunk and tripping. I was up and down all night, trying to get through the rough symptoms of alcohol poisoning. I was back and forth to the bathroom trying to throw up. My stomach wouldn't stop hurting. I couldn't sleep in a complete stranger's house. Plus, I really wanted to do my boyfriend harm.

There was a lot of movement in the apartment that morning. Everyone was getting ready for school and work. By the time Jaxxon got up, I was already in the bathroom freshening up. We were the only ones in the apartment by then.

I said, "What's the plan? Did you notice how drunk I was yesterday and that I drank the whole bottle of brandy we bought with us? Why did you bring me out of town with you only to be on some grimy shit, Jaxxon?"

He said, "You don't know what you are talking about. I was just trying to see my son, and that's it. Things didn't go as I planned."

I wasn't buying his bullshit. I had to wait for the right time to find out the truth.

Jaxxon called Zoe to come get us from his sister's apartment. Zoe took us around to find a battery for his truck. Once we got the battery, we were back on the road home.

It was late when we got home, so we went straight to bed. The trip had me not trusting Jaxxon even more. He was sneaky, and he was always up to no good. While he slept, I went through his phone. He had a lot of passwords on his phone, and he changed them a lot because he knew I knew them all. He assumed I'd go through his phone again, and he was correct in his assumption.

I unlocked his phone and went through his messages. What I didn't understand was if he was going to do some dirty shit, why didn't he erase the messages? Why keep the evidence in his phone for me to find? He never seemed to disappoint in this area. He kept all his messages. And sure enough, he had messages from his baby mama Trina. I was about to read to get my answers.

She knew we were coming, but she had no idea of me. She asked him about going out on a date. Of course, his ass told her yes. There was also a text about her thanking him for a good time. This text came after he got back to Zoe's house. The one thing he didn't lie about was not getting to see his son because his baby mama mentioned him being out of town.

I was heated. I really didn't know what to do or what my next move should be. I figured if I confronted Jaxxon, he would probably go ballistic on me because I went through his phone again. I also felt this situation could be the end of us. I had my evidence, and my only thought was taking a few steps back from our relationship. I wasn't going to give my all to the relationship anymore. If he was going to play games, so was I.

Dealing with all these deceitful men created a savage spirit in me. I wanted to treat men to the same energy as they gave me. I wasn't going to just take their crap any longer. I was going to exact my revenge and sit back and watch it play out, all in an attempt to guard my feelings. Two wrongs didn't make things right, but I wasn't going to let another man hurt me and he not walk away with a scar.

The week following the trip was a long and drawn-out week. Jaxxon and I spoke and did our normal thing, but nothing came about the information I found. By Thursday, Jaxxon was making me aware he was going back out of town to do his cousin Shawn a favor. I wanted to believe his trip had something to do with his cousin Shawn, but since I already overheard him tell others he was coming back, he had something else planned.

Friday morning, Jaxxon and I made love. Afterward, I watched him gather his stuff so he could leave. He said, "I'm going and coming right back. I got to pick something up for Shawn because he can't go do it. I told him I'd do it for him. He also needs it done ASAP. I'll keep in touch with you the whole time I'm gone."

My gut feeling was telling me Jaxxon was going to test our relationship with this trip. He didn't text or call that day or night. I texted and called him repeatedly. I was angry. In less than twenty-four hours, he had already forfeited on his word. I wasn't sure if he made it safely or if he was in jail or dead. My anger quickly changed to worry.

The next morning, I continued to text and call without hearing a word from Jaxxon. I received a video chat from Jaxxon later that afternoon. I started going in on him as soon as I accepted the video. Worried, I said, "You are so full of shit, and you had me worried about you! You got to stop doing dumb shit!"

He quickly said, "Sorry, baby."

I noticed he was video chatting from Zoe's house. She was currently at work. We talked for a little while. He told me what was going on and why he couldn't get the stuff he was supposed to get for Shawn. He had to wait for Shawn's daughter to get off work to help get everything completed. That wouldn't be until later that evening. He was letting me know he wouldn't be home tonight either. He was going to let me know once he got everything completed and when he would be on his way home.

Honestly, I was over his excuses. They all had excuses. Nothing about Jaxxon was ever straightforward. He was bullshitting, and he was stringing me along so he could be out of town all weekend. It was Saturday at three o'clock in the afternoon when Jaxxon went missing.

Jaxxon texted me around three that afternoon to let me know he was getting on the road around five o'clock that evening. With him being about three hours away and me giving him room for his procrastination, I estimated he would be home about nine that night. Jaxxon was supposed to call me once he got on the road. Five o'clock came, and I never received a phone call.

I went on about my day as normal. I had to work that night, but it seemed like I was doing something to check on Jaxxon almost every thirty minutes. I was calling his phone, sending him text messages, sending him messages on the 'book, tagging him in posts on his page. I was constantly checking the last time he was active, checking to see if he was making posts. There was no activity. Jaxxon was gone.

After three days, I started thinking the worst. Every day I made an attempt to reach out to Jaxxon. I thought he had gotten into a car accident or maybe something worse. I thought he had gotten himself arrested. Hell, I assumed he might have even broken up with me and just didn't want to face me. I thought the worst, and I had no way of knowing anything otherwise.

On the fourth day of Jaxxon's disappearance, I started thinking about Drew and how he used to go MIA on me. I instantly got on the internet and began googling Jaxxon's name. I was checking for any and everything. His mugshot and police record from some years ago came up. He had a record, and I wasn't surprised. He told me he had a past. I was beginning to wonder what else I didn't know about him. His police record just showed mediocre crimes; nothing major stood out, except the fact that Jaxxon's license was revoked. He was riding around without a license for over four years.

I wanted to be pissed, but I was worried and concerned how a whole human being could just up and disappear without a trace. There really wasn't much I could do. I knew if I hadn't heard from him by Friday, I was going to try to ride out of town and trace our steps when he took me to his hometown. Then it hit me.

I remembered his cousin Shawn. I rushed to inbox his cousin. I asked him if he heard from Jaxxon. I told Shawn the last time I spoke to Jaxxon and what his plans were as far as coming home that day.

Shawn hadn't heard from Jaxxon either. He knew the same things I did. He was calling and texting Jaxxon as well. I asked Shawn if he thought it was strange for Jaxxon to go missing and not reach out.

Shawn's level of concern changed due to my concern. He said he was going to start making some phone calls. I gave Shawn my phone number and told him to call me as soon as he found out anything. I told him about my plans to drive out of town on Friday to go looking for Jaxxon. I invited him to ride with me. Since Shawn didn't know anything about Jaxxon being missing, my level of concern heightened.

Shawn was having no luck finding Jaxxon. Some family members said they saw Jaxxon's truck around town, so we knew he wasn't lost or stuck somewhere. I didn't bother to go look for him on Friday. But by Saturday, I was done stressing over him. He was alive and didn't want to be found. He was on some stupid shit.

My mind wouldn't let me be still. I kept thinking about what the hell could be going on in Jaxxon's head. Why did he do the shit he did? Was this normal for him? Was this an indirect attempt to end our relationship? I was racking my brain trying to figure out the whats and the whys.

Sunday night I received a message from Shawn. He said he spoke to Jaxxon, and he was okay. He was going to send Jaxxon some money and he would be home in a couple of days. I asked Shawn if he told Jaxxon I was worried about him. I also asked him why Jaxxon didn't call me. Shawn said he didn't know what Jaxxon was thinking. He warned me if and when Jaxxon called me not to ask too many questions.

*What kind of shit is that?* I thought.

I knew I would sound like a crazy woman yelling at his cousin, so I just thanked him and hung up. Jaxxon came home two days later. He called me as soon as he got to his house. I went to see him. I had questions, and I wanted answers.

Jaxxon greeted me as he always did, with a big kiss and hug. He seemed as though he missed me, but I sensed he didn't know what to expect from me. I didn't wait for him to say anything I started in with my interrogation.

I was getting mad while standing in front of him. "What the hell, Jaxxon? Do you not know how to pick up a phone and call someone to let them know you're okay? Where the hell have you been?"

He said, "I messed up and had to go into hiding. Nothing was done intentionally, Joss."

He kept rubbing me while repeating how he was glad he was home and happy to have me in his life. I could tell Jaxxon wasn't trying to answer any of my questions. He wasn't trying to tell me why he was missing for over seven days. Jaxxon was going after what he wanted the most. He was rubbing his way into my pants.

I had to admit Jaxxon knew how to distract me. He had a knack for placing my mind on other things. And in this case, it had been a week, and he was going to make sure my mind was distracted by what he was going to do to me and my body.

Jaxxon stood in front of me. His hands were rubbing up and down my hips. I was mad, but I didn't want him to stop either. He removed my shirt while kissing my neck in all the right places. That sent vibes down to my yoni. While he was kissing and biting, his hands caressed and groped my breasts. He bought my breasts together and started licking them, gently, playfully biting my nipples.

I felt the heat rising between my legs, and I was ready for him. All the anger I had for Jaxxon was gone in that short moment.

He stopped kissing and caressing me long enough to take his clothes off until he was totally naked. I laid back on the bed and removed the rest of my clothes as he watched. Jaxxon opened my legs, kissing up my thighs until he was sipping on my love. He licked, kissed, and sucked as I exhaled and tried to keep my breath. Every lick caused my body to twitch. While he licked me, I rubbed his head, clenching my thighs. I moaned while calling him names of pleasure. My body and mind wanted more of what he was giving.

Jaxxon rolled me over onto my side. He lay behind me. He lifted my leg over his and entered me from behind. As soon as he entered me, I came. He grabbed my hips as he began to grind inside me. With every other stroke I continued to cum. Waterfalls left my body, and I had no control. Jaxxon was running this show, and he was in full control. Every touch, every stroke was his way of manipulating and controlling me. He found a weakness I didn't know I had. That weakness was sex.

The next day, Jaxxon went to work, and things went back to the way they were. He never answered my questions as to who, what, where, when, and why on those seven days. I was going to play phone detective to get my own answers soon enough.

One thing Jaxxon and I made clear was he wasn't allowed to go out of town anymore unless I was able to get in touch with him the whole time or if I was going with him. I didn't trust him to go out of town by himself anymore.

Over time things got better for us. There were still some things he did that didn't sit right with me. I didn't want to ruin what we had going on, so I ignored most of it since I knew who he was coming home to every night.

Jaxxon and I had a routine. He worked in the mornings, and I worked the overnight shift. I had his keys to his house. I came and went as I pleased. Some days we went out to eat, and other days I'd cook. Some nights we made love, and I would be able to nap happily before work. On the weekends, we stayed closed up in his room watching TV and making love, only leaving the room to shower and to get something to eat. That was our routine, and neither of us had any complaints. We grew closer each day. I knew he loved me because he expressed it every day, but I knew Jaxxon was still up to no good.

On Valentine's Day, I used his key to let myself in his house. I had red and white balloons along with a bunch of balloons that said "I Love You!" I made a red velvet cake the night before to add to his surprise. I brought him a jacket and a massager for his back and a bunch of his favorite snacks. I had a card and rose petals strewn around his bedroom.

I went through Jaxxon's room and decorated it romantically. I placed all his gifts evenly around the bed and made a heart with some of the rose pedals, placing the card in the center. I cut the lights off and lit a candle while I waited for Jaxxon to get off work.

I had a little time, so I took a quick shower. I oiled my body down and made sure I smelled good in all the right places. I put on a black lingerie outfit and waited for him to come home.

I was so caught up in surprising Jaxxon I realized I never received a "Happy Valentine's Day" text from him all day. While I was thinking, I heard Jaxxon enter the front door. I met him at his bedroom door. I stood on my tippy toes and kissed him.

I grinned from ear to ear as I said, "Happy Valentine's Day, baby!"

When I looked up at Jaxxon in his face, I realized he was crying. I didn't know what to think. "What's wrong?"

"Joss, no one has ever done anything like this for me."

He was excited, and I was excited for him. I was happy I did something special enough to make him cry, and I was happy he finally saw how serious I was about him. I sat in his chair across from the bed as he checked out all his gifts and read his card. Jaxxon pulled out his phone and took pictures of the room and of me.

He said, "I got to tell Zoe about this!"

I was happy he was happy.

*****

A few weeks after Valentine's Day, Jaxxon came to me and said he needed to go back out of town. He knew I wasn't having it, so he insisted we go together. He needed to handle some personal business, and it was only going to be a day trip. I was happy he was including me in his dealings and not shutting me out.

I was excited for the trip because we were at a good point in our relationship. We weren't arguing as much, and the sex was amazing. He was making an effort to do right by our relationship.

The next day, we were on our way out of town. We had a three-hour ride, so we had plenty of time to talk, laugh, and play around. He was going for business, so we needed to get to the location spot before the business closed. We got to our destination, and Jaxxon went inside to handle whatever it was he came for.

He came back to the car in a hurry. He said, "Can you help me forge some documents?"

All I could do was shake my head. I knew it had to be something crazy. Nothing was ever simple when it came to him.

He said, "You don't have to do anything bad. I'm just trying to get this money, and I need you to sign your name saying I work for you.

Amused with his request, I said, "Well, whatever you got going on, I'm not going to be able to help you this time around."

He didn't seem upset with my response. We left the place, and we went riding around his hometown. I met a couple of new family members and visited some of the others. We were having a good time just making a day out of the trip. We ended up at Zoe's house.

Jaxxon and I were sitting on Zoe's love seat together when his phone started to vibrate. I recognized the sound, so I knew it was a text message. He knew I was watching him, especially since I told him I didn't trust him when he was out of town. He started replying to the message. He didn't cover up the message like he normally did in the past.

I asked, "Who are you texting?"

He said, "Slim. He's just a street boy I know."

A few minutes passed and we were back in the car, ready to head home.

I was memorizing everywhere we drove and places we visited, just in case I needed to make a trip for Jaxxon in any way, shape, form, or fashion.

Before we got on the highway, Jaxxon made a bunch of random stops in areas we never visited before. He was texting and calling someone between the stops. I assumed it was the Slim guy he mentioned before. He was agitated about something, and he was looking for something the way he was pulling up on places, jumping out, and jumping back into the truck.

Confused, I asked, "What's up with you? And why do we keep stopping at all these random-ass places?"

He said, "It's nothing you need to worry about. Stop trippin'. I'm just trying to find something to smoke. One more spot and we can head home."

Since I knew why we were making all these crazy stops, when we got to the last spot he wanted to check out, I started watching and paying attention to everything. I wasn't paranoid, but I was going to make sure I was 100 percent aware of my surroundings.

We pulled up along the backside of an apartment building. Jaxxon parked his truck next to a dumpster right underneath a light. The road in front of the truck was empty except for the dumpster and the light. The road behind the truck was dark. I could see more apartments, but that was it. Nothing else but darkness.

He hurriedly said, "I'll be just a minute." He jumped out of the truck and disappeared into the darkness behind me. Jaxxon was gone for a good minute. Finally reappearing, he quickly jumped inside the truck.

He was a bit out of breath. His bald head was full of sweat beads. His baby-blue shirt was soaked with sweat. He was sweating a lot, practically dripping wet. I was sure something happened. "Jaxxon, what happened?"

He looked at me and said nothing. "I'm still high and drunk from earlier. Are you ready to hit the road?"

He didn't want me to know something had happened. I said yes before I sat back in my seat, examining Jaxxon's behavior. We had the music playing on low. Jaxxon was sipping on a bottle of brown liquor.

Feeling a little freaky, I asked, "Can you play with my yoni while you drive?"

"Baby, I'm a little too drunk and distracted to fool around with you right now."

"Well, I'm going to going to please myself, you can just listen."

I had my bullet vibrator in the bag I bought with me. I removed my pants and placed my legs on the dashboard of his truck, spreading my legs wide open. I took the vibrator out of the bag and placed it on my yoni. I moved it across my most sensitive spots—the spots that were going to increase my climax.

I moved the bullet around. Moaning with excitement, I rubbed my breasts. My body heated up as I became aroused, as my moans became louder. Jaxxon reached over with his hand and began to rub on my breasts, pinching my nipples. His rubs added to what I was doing to myself. The twitching began inside my yoni. My breathing increased. Jaxxon knew by my moans I was close to orgasm.

He reached his fingers between my legs and began massaging my yoni with his fingers. I moaned out loud as I came. My yoni twitched with satisfaction. Jaxxon's fingers continued to move with my bullet until my climax was over. Once I regained myself, I sat back in my seat and enjoyed the aftermath of my release. I knew he couldn't help but join in.

My pleasure was interrupted by my phone making a noise. It was the noise of my Messenger. I saw the familiar name on the message, and adrenaline went rushing through my body. It was Melissa from Jaxxon's text messages and posts.

It said, "PLEASE CALL ME 919-555-4367!"

I didn't know if I wanted to answer her. I didn't want Jaxxon to know she messaged me. I messaged her back telling her I would call her as soon as I got the chance.

I asked, "Why do I have to call you? Do you know me?"

She replied, "Are you dating Jaxxon right now?"

I quickly typed, "Yes, why?"

She said, "Your man just left my house. Did you know that? He told me you guys were just friends with benefits. You know he asked me to sleep with him while he was just here?"

I questioned her statement because Jaxxon had been with me all day. I thought back to when Jaxxon told me she was a liar and she wanted to destroy him because she was jealous of him. She had to be telling a lie. I asked, "Who are you to him, and when did you see him for him to ask you this?"

She said, "CALL ME!"

Even though I knew who she was, I still asked. "Who are you again? And did you fuck him, and when did he come to your house?"

She said her name loud and clear, "I'm Melissa, his ex."

I looked over at Jaxxon, and I started fuming. I didn't want him to see that I was upset. I have learned from past situations I went off before finding out what I wanted to know. I wanted to hear his side of the story.

I didn't know this woman named Melissa, and I needed to get to the root of why the hell she was calling my phone. I was calling her the first chance I got. With an attitude, I said, "I got to pee. Can you stop at the store at our halfway point?"

By the look Jaxxon gave me, he knew something was up. We pulled into the gas station, and I jumped out of the truck. I ran straight to the bathroom. I was nervous as hell, but I wanted to know what this woman was about to tell me about Jaxxon.

The phone rang once. She instantly asked me the same questions she asked in text. "Are you Jaxxon's girlfriend? Or are you guys friends with benefits? He and I have been texting all day."

He was with me all day, so I didn't believe a word she said.

She said he wanted to come over to her house earlier and have sex with her, but she told him she was entertaining another dude.

She said, "Girl, he got upset with me and told me he was still going to come to my place anyways." Melissa proceeded to tell me what happened almost two hours ago. Jaxxon busted into her apartment and tried to fight the dude she was entertaining.

She added, "Jaxxon and I got into an argument, and I made him leave my house."

I stood in the gas station bathroom emotionally confused. I didn't know what to believe. I instantly remembered Jaxxon returning to the truck after the last stop we made sweating out of control. Her story was becoming believable. I didn't want to believe her. I didn't want to believe Jaxxon had the balls to bring me to his ex-girlfriend's house to have sex with her while I sat in the truck waiting. I didn't want to believe Jaxxon was that guy.

She asked, "Are you still there? Are you okay?" She continued to tell me about conversations she and Jaxxon had about me. She knew so much about me. She knew my name and that I worked nights. She knew I was keeping him in line, washing his clothes and cooking his meals.

She said, "He's calling me now while we are on the phone."

My heart skipped a whole lot of beats. I didn't want to believe this fool was calling her while I was in the bathroom. I was ready to confront him and go upside on his head. I started to exit the bathroom.

She said, "Let me do a three-way so you can hear how he talks to me. So you can hear with your own ears he was just at my house."

I didn't decline. Melissa attempted to get Jaxxon on the line as I placed my phone on mute. We connected on one try. Their conversation seemed normal until she bought me up. She asked him about me and our relationship. Jaxxon didn't let me down. From his mouth to my ears, he said, "We just fucking."

I couldn't take it anymore. I took my phone off mute and was ready to go off. As soon as I was about to blast Jaxxon, the phone disconnected on his part. Melissa tried to get Jaxxon on the line a couple more times with no success. We were never able to restart what was started.

I realize I was in the bathroom way too long, and I needed to get back to the truck. I was ready to go in on Jaxxon. Melissa called me right before I exited the bathroom. I told her I heard everything I needed to hear, and I hung up.

As soon as I sat down in the truck, I asked Jaxxon the nice way I knew how to see his phone. He instantly became defensive. "There is nothing in my phone that you need to see."

I snapped. "So, are you going around telling your women we are just fuck buddies? What the fuck, Jaxxon? Why is this woman calling my phone telling me so much about you and me? Did you really take me to her house while you ran in to fight some dude she was entertaining?"

I didn't bother to let Jaxxon answer. My questions kept coming. Angrily I yelled, "You're full of shit! Please get me home. Now, Jaxxon!"

He denied talking to Melissa. He also denied saying we were fuck buddies (even though I heard him with my own ears). He denied pulling up to her apartment—his typical deny, deny, deny behavior.

His phone began ringing off the hook. I guess since he knew I had spoken to Melissa, he wasn't hiding the fact she was calling his phone. He didn't answer it, but it kept ringing.

In between calling Jaxxon's phone, Melissa texted my phone. She texted, telling me about things Jaxxon and I did together, stuff Jaxxon talked to her about. She knew more than she should have even been told.

I texted her, telling her to send me screenshots of their messages. I wanted to believe her, but I didn't know her. I also didn't want to think Jaxxon was this low down. I needed—no, I wanted proof she was having conversations with Jaxxon on the regular, like she said.

Melissa didn't comply with the screenshots, but she sent me something much worse. She sent me pictures of Valentine's night. The romantic night I prepared for Jaxxon. She had pictures of the whole room. Pictures of all the gifts, the cake, the balloons, and all the other decorations I put up that night. She sent them all to me. Melissa sent me the messages that came along with the pictures, where Jaxxon took credit for the room and all the decorations. He told her he did it all for her, hoping she would come visit him. He told her he had the cake specially made for her because red velvet was her favorite.

My soul was crushed.

Jaxxon and I were at least an hour from home, and I wanted to be away from him immediately. I was going to do something stupid if I stayed in his presence. I looked over at Jaxxon, and I started yelling at him. I called him every name in the book except for a child of God. I showed him the pictures she sent me.

I yelled, "How dirty can you get, Jaxxon? You gotta be heartless to do shit like this."

In denial, he said, "Man, I don't know how she got them pictures, and I would never say nothing like that. That woman is ugly as hell. Why would I want her?"

I had to admit he was quick with his lies, but I knew better. Jaxxon kept telling me Melissa was a jealous ex and I was playing into her hands acting the way I was acting.

He said, "She texted me earlier and told me she was going to break us up. I love you, Joss! Please use your eyes and see that for yourself. I'm with you all the time."

As we continued our ride home, Melissa continued to text. She texted and called both of our phones the whole time. I ignored her and Jaxxon the rest of the ride. My feelings were all over the place, and I was mad at myself because deep down I loved him. I knew in my heart I needed to let Jaxxon go once we got home.

The anger I was feeling inside was too much, and it was turning to extreme hurt. I had so many emotions building inside I felt sick. I knew what I had to do, but my heart wouldn't let me do it. Jaxxon's hurt was hitting below the belt, and it was defeating me. I didn't know how to fight back without getting hurt even more. I felt the need to do something revengeful to Jaxxon to make him hurt like he was making me hurt.

I believed Melissa was on some vindictive mess, trying to get me to leave Jaxxon, but pictures were worth a thousand words. I wanted to cry my heart out. The rest of our ride home was silent other than Melissa's calls and texts chiming in the background.

When we pulled into his driveway, he broke the silence. He said, "Can we talk about everything in the morning? When you have calmed down? I want to explain."

It was two in the morning, and all I wanted to do was cry myself to sleep. I hated and loved Jaxxon all at the same time. I agreed, heading straight for his room with our phones still going off.

I removed my clothes and got straight into bed. Jaxxon did the same. I turned my back to him, facing the wall. I silently began to cry to myself. I couldn't help but cry. The pain in my heart. The feeling I couldn't begin to describe. I cooked, cleaned, and took care of this man, playing wifey and giving husband benefits to him, and he was going around telling other people, including his ex, we were just fuck buddies. I cried harder.

Jaxxon rolled over and wrapped his big arms around me. He said, "Please stop crying. I don't ever mean to hurt you intentionally. That woman is always doing stuff like this to ruin whatever relationship I get in. She's mad because I don't want her."

The more Jaxxon talked, the more I cried out loud. Our phones were still chiming in the background. Melissa was still holding on to her agenda to destroy our relationship.

193

Jaxxon held me tight, rubbing me occasionally trying to soothe my cries. He kissed me softly. He said, "I really do love you."

Jaxxon kept kissing my lips until I eventually gave in and began kissing him back. While he kissed me, his hands went between my legs. His kisses went to my breasts, and he started sucking my nipples. As I cried, Jaxxon began to make love to me.

While he slowly stroked my yoni, he told me he loved me. He said it with each stroke. My cries became moans. I moaned loudly with pain and pleasure. My eyes stayed shut while he pleasured me. I felt a pause in his strokes, and I opened my eyes.

Jaxxon had his phone in his hand. He saw me see him, so he increased his stroke, breaking my concentration on what he was doing with his phone, forcing me to focus on what he was doing inside me. He thrust inside me aggressively until I was again moaning loudly, focusing on his lovemaking.

I was still crying on the inside but moaning on the outside. He knew my body. He knew which moves would send me into overdrive and how to keep me there and how to make me cum automatically back-to-back. I moaned and called out his name. I started telling him I was about to cum.

Jaxxon's movements never halted; he was going for number two. I began to moan with excitement. I was already there; I was about to cum again.

I heard him say, "Do you hear that? She will always fuck with me no matter what you say!"

I instantly woke from my sexual slumber to see what the hell Jaxxon was talking about. I quickly rolled over and asked him, "What are you doing, Jaxxon?"

He didn't say a word. He pushed me back onto my side and entered me again. He had his phone in his hand. In the darkness of the room, the screen of his phone lit up the room.

He said, "I'm not finished, and it's Melissa. I want her to know she can't break this up. Hello, I know you're still there, woman."

There was silence. Melissa didn't respond. Jaxxon never stopped stroking in and out of me. His strokes became more and more aggressive. He was close to coming. He was turned on by his actions. My mind was everywhere, but Jaxxon wasn't going to let me focus on anything but his strokes. I was about to cum again for the third time. He started doing all the moaning, calling out my name and telling me he loved me. The phone disconnected, and Melissa was no longer on speakerphone. We came together. Jaxxon was putting on a show for our telephone audience. He said, "She needed to hear that."

I gave Jaxxon a bullshit stare. I said, "Oh really, she needed to hear us fucking? You have been doing some messed-up shit lately, and this—what you just did—is unbelievable."

I got up to get a towel to place over the wet spot in the bed. I climbed back in bed with my back turned to Jaxxon, facing the wall. I was tired. I was emotionally drained. I was going to sleep.

The next morning, Jaxxon and I went at it.

I said, "I have been running into the most disrespectful men as of late, but what you did has taken the cake. You have done enough disrespect in one night compared to all the men combined. What's this relationship between you and Melissa about? How many more secrets do you have? And why the hell am I blocked from seeing your page this time around?" I wanted to know everything. "If you're not going to open up and tell me the truth, then the conversation and our relationship is over."

"Joss, I love you, and whatever I need to do to prove it to you, I will do, even if it means unblocking you from the book."

I made him do it before he finished his sentence. He continued to speak, "I have an agenda with Melissa, so the relationship you think I may have with her is not what you think. But from here on out, I will be an open book to you."

Frustrated, I said, "I can't take too much more of your shit. Something has to change or I'm out."

For the next couple of days, things were a bit shaky for Jaxxon and I. I didn't trust anything he said. He was confirming everything he did two and three times. Melissa wasn't calling and or texting any-more, at least from what I knew.

I started Facebook stalking his page. He had me blocked for a while, so I had posts and comments to look at. I was checking any comments he and Melissa may have been exchanging. None of his posts pertained to me, but a lot of them talked about him wanting someone. Melissa liked every single one of his posts and comments on a majority of them. I didn't have access to Melissa's page, so I didn't know what was being said on her end.

Based on some of the posts he shared or posted, I could tell his relationship with Melissa was far from over. Some of the posts were subliminal to just them. Now that I knew her name, my search went as far back as December, when he and I first met, to see what he was posting around that time. I was trying to be patient especially since I went back almost two years before we met. I was almost close to the present day.

Deep down, I wondered why I was still messing with Jaxxon. I didn't trust him to go to work and not be on some woman's page or inbox. I didn't trust him to go out of town to his hometown because of his ex and his disappearing acts. I didn't trust him when he was home with me, and I didn't trust him not to lie to me. The trust was gone.

I didn't know how to let him go. I definitely deserved better than Jaxxon. He was slick with his words, charming with his touch. And he knew women. He definitely knew how to play with women's emotions. I didn't know if his "I love yous" were true or not.

Things went back to normal for Jaxxon and I. But it only lasted a couple of days. He went to work and came home. I was always there once he got off. I was waiting for the weekend so we could spend time together and talk. The weekend wasn't coming fast enough.

By Thursday, Jaxxon was back on some bullshit. I was at his house waiting for him to come home. Earlier in the day, he kept mentioning he had to go to his older cousin's house, who lived thirty minutes away. I assumed we were going together, but Jaxxon came in the door from work, changed his shirt, and told me he would be back. Thirty minutes later, I received a call from him telling me he was outside his cousin's house.

I fell asleep in the short amount of time it took for him to get to her house. I woke up an hour and a half later. Jaxxon should have already returned home. I called his phone. I received no answer. I called again. The phone went straight to voicemail. I continued to call his phone repeatedly. My gut was telling me Jaxxon was up to something.

I grabbed my keys, hopped in my car, and headed to his cousin's house. The ride took me twenty minutes. I called Jaxxon's phone the whole time I was driving. Still no answer.

I got to his cousin's block, cut my headlights off, and crept by the house. Jaxxon's truck was nowhere in sight. My heart instantly sank. He never came to see his cousin. It was another one of his lies.

I drove back to Jaxxon's house while planning my revenge. I was over wanting to leave him. I wanted to dish the hurt right back at him. I was going to get revenge one way or another. I continued to call him without any luck.

I stopped by Walmart. I didn't really know what I was going to get, but I went straight for the hardware department. I felt like doing something stupid. My mind wasn't letting me think clearly. I grabbed some blades, a hammer, and some other small items that would create big damage.

I purchased my goodies and headed back to Jaxxon's house. To my surprise, Jaxxon's truck was in the driveway. He just got home. I did a quick attitude adjustment right where I stood. I didn't want Jaxxon to know I was on to his bullshit. I was ready to play the fool to catch my fool.

I went into the house and headed straight for his bedroom. Jaxxon was lying across his bed browsing his Facebook page. He was already undressed, and it seemed he already showered. He smiled at me. He said, "I'm drunk! I got drunk with Eric."

I said, "Why didn't you answer my phone calls?"

Jaxxon, being quick on his feet and probably already rehearsed his excuse, had an explanation. He quickly said, "My phone went dead."

I asked another question. "How come you didn't call once you got home, especially after you charged it? You know what? Don't bother answering. It's all going to come back on you! I'm tired, and I'm going to bed."

I shook my head, knowing he was up to something, knowing he was lying. I removed my clothes and got in bed next to him. Nothing else was brought up about that night.

*****

One morning later that week, Jaxxon called to tell me his tire was flat.

I laughed to myself and asked him, "How did that happen? Did you run over a nail or something?"

I left work early to take him to work. Later that day, Jaxxon had Shawn come over to check out the tire. His cousin put air in the tire, and as he was filling the tire, the air seeped right back out. There was definitely a hole in his tire.

Jaxxon and Shawn both agreed it looked like someone flattened his tire. They went back and forth on how the tire became flat over-night, one suggestion being he pissed someone off. I went back inside Jaxxon's bedroom until they were done. He came in the room a little while later.

He asked, "Can you help me find someone to patch my tire?"

Jaxxon's twenty-two-inch rim tires were hard to find, and no one wanted to take a chance patching the tire because the holes were on the side of the tire. It was too dangerous to patch a tire of that size. Jaxxon didn't have the funds to purchase a new tire. Jaxxon apparently had plans I didn't know anything about, and the truck catching a flat put a halt in his plans.

The next day Jaxxon received news his cousin passed away. Jaxxon was very emotional about the death. He couldn't tell me what was going on without crying. I felt sorry for him. I sat on his bed while he called his family to get all the news as to what happened to his cousin.

Jaxxon was in a better place emotionally after he got off the phone. While on the phone, he mentioned to someone he was going to be present at the funeral. He never mentioned to me how he intended to get out of town with his truck indisposed until later that night. He asked me if I could take him home for the funeral. I didn't mind taking him.

The funeral for his cousin was in two days. I couldn't get off work, so we made plans to leave as soon as I got off work the day of the funeral. The trip was going to be a day trip because I had to be back to work that night. I let Jaxxon drive us out of town.

Somehow, we missed the funeral, but we made it to the family gathering that followed. We were at a house party celebrating life. It was a dark road with one streetlight lighting a small corner of the road. His family had fire pits burning, and everyone was celebrating and having a good time. Jaxxon was happy to be around his family. I was glad I was able to share the moment with him.

We stayed at the gathering for a little while. It was almost time for us to go because I had to be at work in four hours. Jaxxon didn't want to go, but he knew we had no other choice. He told his family we were going to come back down that coming up Saturday.

I was shocked he said we were coming back. We didn't discuss or talk it. At that moment, I was willing to keep Jaxxon happy through his rough time. I didn't mind coming back on Saturday. We said our goodbyes, and we left. I let Jaxxon drive since it was his hometown. I wanted to take a nap before going in to work.

We talked about his cousin and family. We discussed the details of us coming back on Saturday, making small talk. I noticed as we were talking, we weren't taking our normal route toward the highway.

I've learned to be observant of my surroundings while with Jaxxon, especially after the last incident when he supposedly took me by Melissa's place. I didn't say anything to Jaxxon as I remembered every left and right turn, remembering landmark after landmark. It was late, almost ten thirty at night, and we were headed to a location unknown to me. Jaxxon came up on some apartment buildings.

"Where are we, Jaxxon?"

Anxiously he said, "I have to leave my baby mama some money for my son."

Looking around, I asked, "When did she move to your hometown? Actually, I know where we are. We are down the street from Zoe's house. When did she move this close, Jaxxon?"

"She doesn't live here. She still stays an hour and a half away. The spot we are going to belongs to her sister."

"Why didn't you tell me we were going to stop somewhere before we went home? It's getting late, and I have to get to work. You waited until the last minute to ride by her sister's house." I was getting pissed. "I feel like you're up to some bullshit."

When we got to the front of the complex Jaxxon pulled in the parking space farthest from the stairway. There were plenty of spaces open in front of the stairway, but he parked away from them. My adrenaline began to run. I didn't trust him. Jaxxon put the car in gear. He said he wasn't going to be long, and then he headed up the stairs.

I watched Jaxxon go up the stairs. My intentions were to watch which apartment he went into. He went upstairs. He had to knock on the door on the left or the right. I could see the door on the right. I couldn't see the door on the left. I told myself to not jump to any conclusions, but my gut was telling me otherwise. I gave Jaxxon five minutes. If he were truly there to drop off some money, it shouldn't take more than that.

I couldn't wait five minutes. I climbed in the driver's seat of my car, backed my car up, and pulled right in front of the steps in a vertical direction. I wanted to see whoever was going to open the door to that apartment. I sat there for a minute. That minute felt like forever. My adrenaline was getting the best of me.

I cut the music up, which was some DMX Rough Rider's hit. I lit the blunt Jaxxon had prerolled before he got out of the car. I got out of the car then leaned against my driver's side door, smoking the blunt while watching the door like a hawk. I was ready for anything. I was ready to run up the stairs and knock on the door myself. I waited for Jaxxon. Five minutes later, he came out the door. No one else appeared at the door with him.

The look on Jaxxon's face was priceless. He watched my every move until he walked up to me. He appeared shaken. He said, "What are you doing?"

I yelled, "I'm not going to play your fool anymore, Jaxxon. You need to tell me who the hell lives in that apartment, or I'm going to walk up the stairs and find out for myself."

Still shaken, he said, "I swear it's her sister's place."

My voice got louder. "Why did it take you almost fifteen minutes to give her some damn money, Jaxxon? None of the shit you're doing tonight is making sense, especially this late at night. You need to tell me the truth."

Jaxxon tried to get angry with me, telling me I was going to mess up his situation with his son. If I went up the stairs, I was going to ruin the peace between him and his baby mama. He knew by my posture and tone his anger was nothing compared to mine at that very moment.

He softly said, "Please get in the car, Joss. Please!"

I got in my car. I was going to get myself to work. The conversation didn't change once we settled in the car to head home. He wanted me to hurry up and pull off. I wanted to go upstairs and knock on the door. I quickly sped off around the entrance of the complex. I went around the corner and got to a stoplight. I was angry, and I wanted to handle the situation right then.

I got out of my car and walked around to the passenger side. Jaxxon got nervous. I needed to let loose. I went back around the car until I got back to the driver's side.

He calmly asked me again. "Please get in the car!"

I got back in the car.

He said, "Can you get us home? Please don't go back to the apartment. If you go back, it's going to cause a lot of drama for me, and I won't be able to see my son."

I sped off. I couldn't recall how we got to the highway. I didn't ask Jaxxon for any directions. He was sitting in the passenger seat sweating like he was in his truck that night he was looking for some smoke. He was guilty about something.

Eventually, Jaxxon went to sleep, like he had no cares in the world. I started speeding down the highway. There was little to no traffic. I had the whole road to myself majority of the ride. I was speeding with my music on blast and my adrenaline rushing. Song after song hit close to my current situation, fueling my anger.

Without slowing down, I pulled over onto the shoulder of the highway. I didn't pull over toward the right like you're lawfully sup-

posed to. I pulled over onto the left shoulder with the passenger side
of the vehicle out toward traffic. Jaxxon jumped up after feeling me
drive on the off-road pavement. He said loudly, "What the hell is
going on?"

I yelled back at him, "Shut up! I don't want you to talk to me!"

I began hitting the steering wheel trying to avoid hitting Jaxxon.
I wanted to hit him. I wanted him to feel pain. I snatched my keys
out of the ignition and got out of the car. I started walking the shoulder of the highway. I began to cry. My anger was winning the emotional battle, and the outcome wasn't going to be good. I cried hard.

I didn't want Jaxxon to see me cry. I didn't want him to know
I was crying. I walked the shoulder of the highway long enough for
me to pray to God to calm me down. I was possibly going to do some
kind of harm to myself or Jaxxon. I quickly and sincerely asked God
to calm me and to give me peace.

I returned to the car, and Jaxxon was looking at me as if I had
lost my mind. I was fuming, but my mind was in a better state of
ease after my prayer. I said, "Dude, you're pushing me, and not in a
good way. I wish I went up those stairs to see who actually lived in
that apartment. I swear I do."

Jaxxon said nothing. We rode the rest of the way home in total
silence.

Upon arriving back in town, I went straight to work. I was a
little late, so I had Jaxxon drop me off at the job. I wasn't comfortable
with him keeping my car, but I needed to get to work, and I didn't
have time to drop him off. I was ready to get away from him, but I
also didn't think I was mentally ready for work. I almost had a mental
breakdown on the side of the highway. I told Jaxxon what time I was
getting off and for him to be at the job in the morning to get me.
I went in to work thinking I needed to decide if Jaxxon was worth
fighting for. His toxic behavior was bringing me down in the worst
kind of way.

The next morning, Jaxxon was outside my job waiting for me.
My car was washed, and my tank was full. It was his way of apologizing. He took me back to his house.

I asked, "Do you have something to tell me?"

He said, "No, crazy. Why, should I?"

"You haven't seen crazy yet, and if you continue with your bull-shit, our relationship is going to end in the worst kind of way."

I was tired from the ride and work. I got in Jaxxon's bed and went straight to sleep. When I awoke, Jaxxon wanted to talk about getting his son for spring break.

He said, "I need you, Joss. I can't do anything without you."

I asked, "Do you think your baby mama is going to let you take your son for the break?"

"She said it was fine, as long as I took one of the other kids with me. Are you cool with that?"

I was okay with it. The timing was all wrong, but he knew I'd help him see his child.

We planned to get his children for spring break. I went to work and requested two weeks off, so I was available for him and the kids. Jaxxon worked days and long nights sometimes. I wanted to make sure someone was with the kids regardless of when Jaxxon had to work.

I came up with different things for the kids to do to make sure they stayed busy. I wanted them to have a good time while they were with us. I wanted Jaxxon to see I had his back. I was excited about the experience, happy to reach another level in our relationship. I was going to meet his son.

After the last incident, Jaxxon was on his best behavior. There were still some things I questioned, but since we weren't arguing as much I might as well leave well enough alone.

By now, I already felt we didn't have a future together. I made up in my mind to slowly disconnect myself from the relationship. He was available to me sexually and was a warm body to sleep next to. That was how I was going to look at our relationship. Jaxxon was never going to change. I wanted more from Jaxxon, but he had to change drastically in order for us to prosper into something that would last. Jaxxon wasn't made for that. He was toxic, and he wanted to play games.

I didn't trust Jaxxon as far as I could throw him. Every chance I got I was sneaking in his phone. He kept his truths in his phone.

He was riding dirty. That was why I couldn't trust him. I had to wait until he went to sleep or take a shower most nights for my chance. I had to hurry and go through his phone each time I invaded it.

Jaxxon knew I was going through his phone. He didn't know when or how often. But he knew. He kept his phone under tight guard 24-7, and he tried hard to keep me out of it. He downloaded so many apps to put passwords on his phone. He even put an app on his phone that took a picture of the person unlocking the phone. Sometimes I'd get in, and other times I didn't care. Sometimes I'd pose for my photo. His password changed a lot because of me.

I learned every password he placed on his phone. I had my ways of learning them all. I used the car window a couple of times. At night, when we would be riding, he would unlock his phone, and I would use the window to watch him put his password in. Other times I'd clean his phone screen and I would wait for him to use it. I would wait until he put his phone back down and then I would take a picture of his screen. I would then figure out his pattern if it was a drawing pattern. If it was numbers, I'd match his prints with my phone keypad and then figure out the sequence order. It was a lot of work, but I figured if he kept changing his password, he had something to hide.

He changed the passwords every time I confronted him about some new shit. I didn't care what he thought or how he felt. I wanted him to know I knew what he was up to.

We would argue about me touching his phone, but I didn't care. I didn't give Jaxxon respect and privacy anymore when it came to his phone. He was disrespecting me, and he didn't act like he cared about my feelings. He constantly called me crazy, and I was showing him how crazy I really was. His phone became my information portal into his misdeeds.

He would delete text messages and phone calls he didn't want me to see before he got home or before he came around me. Anything I found that was suspect or made him appear guilty, he had an excuse. His favorite excuse was "You're the one who is here at my house every day. I come home to you."

He told me I was always worried about other females when I was the one he was giving all his attention to. He claimed his phone was entertainment, and he loved me and only me.

As much as I hated what Jaxxon was doing to me and how much I couldn't trust him, I still loved him. I still did everything for him. I thought if I showed him I wasn't going anywhere, he would eventually stop playing his games. I assumed if I loved him with my whole heart, he would learn how to love me back the same way. I kept trying to nurture the good within him to help him let go of some of the bad. I tried hard to get past his issues with lying, women, his phone, and his disappearing acts. And he didn't make it easy.

Jaxxon was still communicating with Melissa on social media. She was always commenting on his post, and he was always commented back. I was sure there were text messages, but he made sure he deleted those. He was always making subliminal posts that appeared to be directed toward someone, but he never named anyone.

Melissa was always commenting or placing heart emojis on his subliminal posts, like she knew the messages were for her. I wasn't stupid, and Jaxxon knew I saw them all. I sometimes made my own comments, just below Melissa's comments. I refused to be surprised by Jaxxon's games any longer. I watched his posts and his comments. My eyes were now opening wide.

We were arguing on the regular, but we made up with sex every time. It was like sex created a clean slate, and that slate was soiled every day. When we were intimate, I owned his mind, and he owned mine. We called out each other's names each time when either of us reached orgasms, and we came together on the regular, like our bodies were in sync.

*****

Jaxxon had an out-of-town work assignment coming up soon. The assignment was for three days. I didn't feel good about the trip because our relationship's open wounds were still trying to heal. He left that Friday morning with me still asleep in his bed. I slept until noon and then went home. I was always at Jaxxon's house. Sometimes I'd stay there while he was out of town, but I went home this time.

On Jaxxon's work trips, he would text or call me while they were riding. The whole day went by and I hadn't heard from Jaxxon. I called him, and I wouldn't get an answer. I texted him and still got nothing. My carefree ("I hope everything is going good") texts turned into angry ("go screw yourself") texts.

I was letting him know I wasn't up for his shit, and if he was going to ignore me, then it was cool. I knew he saw my text. That greenlight on his Messenger told me he was active, plus he was making posts with his location. I wasn't going to let him piss me off while he was gone. There was nothing I could do, at least for the next three days.

Jaxxon finally hit me up early the next morning. And of course, he had an excuse for why he ignored me the day before. He didn't have a signal where they were working, and I was tripping on him for no reason. He told me he didn't appreciate me going in on him when he wasn't doing anything. He said I should be happy he called me back.

I called him an asshole. I was tired of his shit. He kept denying he was on social media the day before. I previously took a screenshot of one of his posts and the comments. I sent it to him so he couldn't lie anymore. Jaxxon was all about proof. Even though you see it or hear it, he would still deny everything unless you had proof. I told him if he can post on social media, then he had time to text me. I then told him I didn't know how much more of his shit I could take. He said it was going to be my fault he wouldn't be able to see his son. He hung up. I didn't know if we had broken up or not.

I went to work and did everything I normally would do. By midshift, I was curious as to what Jaxxon was up to. He never texted or called me back. I texted him and received no response. I went to his page to see if he made any new posts.

I still loved Jaxxon. I wanted to make sure he was okay. Once I got to his social media page, I noticed he had been busy. He was posting memes like crazy and posting how he was feeling. There were subliminal comments I knew were directed toward me.

One of his posts read, "IT DOESN'T MATTER HOW MUCH YOU TRY TO DO RIGHT BY SOMEONE… IT WILL NEVER BE ENOUGH FOR SOMEONE WHO ALWAYS WANTS SOMETHING TO BE WRONG."

He also made a post talking about him giving up on love and he was tired of trying to make certain people happy.

I was getting angry. I commented under his post asking him why he was bringing our relationship to social media. Why didn't he just text me so we could talk? Why was he being petty and childish, putting our business on the 'book? He didn't reply to any of my comments.

Every one of his posts Melissa was busy commenting on. She had something to say about everything he posted and our relationship. And he replied to all her comments. One comment he told her he tried to do right by me. I couldn't believe he was talking about me to her. They were going back and forth on his page conversing. Jaxxon knew I was reading the comments. Melissa did too.

She tagged him in a post, asking him, "Can I be the one to take you away from all the things that you are going through to relieve you of your pain?"

I didn't know why his answer surprised me. He told her she could. Jaxxon was coldhearted, and he didn't care who he hurt. I didn't know if he said she could to get a rise from me or not, but it worked. I replied under his comment, "OH! So, she can?"

Jaxxon finally responded to one of my comments. He said, "Since you asked, yes, she can!"

Melissa was loving our back-and-forth banter because she was placing heart emojis under each comment.

My heart was crushed as I read his comment. He asked her, "Did she mind?" She asked him, "Did he mind?"

I left the post alone, and I got offline. I told myself they could have each other.

I began to think to myself, *I'm free*. I didn't have to deal with Jaxxon's lies anymore. I felt the hurt of his deceit, but I was strong enough to get over it. I didn't need his mess in my life anymore. I was too good of a woman with lots of things going for me. I was worth more, and I deserved more.

Melissa was what Jaxxon wanted, and I had no intentions of standing in the way of it happening. I had a vacation coming up, and I didn't have to worry about watching his kids. I was going to make my own plans—plans to move ahead, to be happy without Jaxxon.

Later that night, I went back on the 'book. I forgot I had Jaxxon's posts on "See First" (an option you can select on the 'book). When I logged on, his post was the first thing I saw. It was a picture of his hotel room and all the alcohol and beer he was drinking. The first comment was his saying he was drunk. I was curious what was being said in the comments. And of course, he and Melissa were chatting back and forth.

Melissa was telling him how drunk he was. He reminded her how he got down in bed when he was drunk. Melissa commented she didn't want to sleep with him while he was drunk. She said she remembered and asked him did he mind again.

I don't know why I felt like being petty, but I went to every comment they made to each other and hit the Like button. Then I commented, "This shit is funny to me!" I left them to their conversations. I continued scrolling on my page, and I noticed a post where Jaxxon said, "He was single, and he didn't do titles." I made sure to like that post as well.

I was done for the night. I was going to bed, and I was going to figure out what I was going to do with my newfound freedom. I planned to go to Jaxxon's house to get my stuff later while he was gone.

I wasn't planning on jumping into anything new anytime soon. I needed the peace. I wanted to be single. Over the years and the heartbreak, it seemed as if the drama of love was all that existed in the world. I didn't want to get involved with anyone like Jaxxon ever again. I was going to find my focus again, enjoy my vacation, and bounce back.

As I was about to jump into bed, Jaxxon called. Something deep down told me to ignore his call and continue what I was doing, but I wanted to know how he was going to try to fix this fuckup this time. He had to know he messed up with me big time. Against my better judgment, I answered the phone.

Once I said hello, Jaxxon started in with his bullshit. He sounded annoyed. He asked, "Why did you have to say something on my posts. You just gave her the ammo to fire at our relationship. What I say and do on the 'book is entertainment."

Jaxxon continued to point the finger back at me as to why things went down the way they did on the 'book with his posts.

I said, "I don't care! Our whole relationship has been a joke to you, and now you want me to act like what you do on the 'book is something new. I don't think so. I'm not going to let you disrespect me and sit back and take it.

Jaxxon was drunk, high, and angry. I could tell it in his voice. He kept trying to make me feel guilty about what was said on the post.

"It doesn't matter, Jaxxon. You're single now, and I am no longer your problem. Good luck with your future."

I hung up.

He called right back and continued to call, but I ignored his calls and went to bed.

For the next two days, while he was still on the road, Jaxxon continued to call and text. At first, he was sending me hateful texts, blaming me for our relationship going bad. He told me I was blind and stupid because I couldn't see his actions. He implied I couldn't see how he was messing with me and me only. He said he was always with me and I never saw that part. And now I wanted to listen to other women and question his every move.

As it grew closer for him to come home from his assignment, his attitude changed, so did his comments. He started telling me he needed me. He wasn't going to be able to get his kids if I didn't help him. He professed his love for me repeatedly. Jaxxon wasn't going to let me go. When he got home, I was going to be his focus and attention.

Two days later, it went down just as I assumed. Jaxxon called my phone nonstop. He called and he called and he called. He texted my phone day in and day out. He left messages begging and pleading for another chance. He promised me things would be different. I just had to give him a chance to show me. He told me he needed to see his son, and I was his ticket to doing that.

After a while, Jaxxon's calls started getting to me. I started feeling sorry for him and his son. I thought maybe he would see how dedicated I was to him if I helped him get a chance to see his son. I didn't know if I wanted Jaxxon back or not, but I wanted him to be able to see his son.

I thought I could show him I was the right woman for him by helping him with the kids over the break. I didn't have to have a relationship with Jaxxon to do that much. But my mind knew differently. This was Jaxxon's golden ticket back into my life.

I finally answered one of his calls. "Hey, I don't know why you have the urge to keep calling my phone. Please stop!"

He said, "No, you stop. You need to stop ignoring me when I call you. We need to talk. Can you please meet with me after work so we can talk? Please don't say no!"

Against my better judgment, I agreed.

I found myself at Jaxxon's house, in his room, waiting for him to get off. I had to work later that night, so I was growing impatient while I waited. I was no stranger to being at his house, and eventually I fell asleep. I awoke to Jaxxon walking through his front door. I could tell by the look on his face he was happy to see me, but I wasn't too sure I was happy to see him. Jaxxon got settled, and we talked about what he did while he was on the road.

He said, "You were the one fueling Melissa by making comments. If you would have left well enough alone, things wouldn't have gotten as bad as they did."

He proceeded to tell me he loved me and he wanted to be with me. He told me his future was with me.

I told him he had a lot to prove, and I didn't know where we stood as far as a relationship was concerned, but I was going to help him with his son and the other child while they were in town for spring break.

Even though I knew the decision to watch Jaxxon's children was easy for me, I knew Jaxxon was somehow going to make it difficult. We talked until I had to go to work.

I went to work thinking, maybe Jaxxon could change, thinking the good that I knew existed inside of him could actually come out. He could love me the way I should be loved. I wondered if I loved Jaxxon harder, he would see I was truly down for him, and I was worth having and fighting for.

I was so confused by the love I felt for Jaxxon and the resentment that was building in my heart from all the pain he was throwing my way. I admitted I was fooling myself thinking I wanted to let Jaxxon go. I wanted to be with him, and being around him and his child for two weeks was going to draw me closer to loving him. I was fighting a battle with myself, trying to figure out where I wanted to be in Jaxxon's life.

After work, I went straight to Jaxxon's house. I wanted to talk about my feelings as well as clear the air about his behavior. I wanted to get some of the things in my mind and heart out to the surface. I wanted him to know exactly how I felt even though I didn't know exactly what I was feeling. I wanted him to know what battles I was fighting, dealing with him and his lies. I was ready to tell Jaxxon I was willing to give us another chance at a relationship.

After Jaxxon and I talked, we made love—the medicine for almost all heartache and pain. Jaxxon was gentle with his touches. His hands were warm and soft as he caressed my body like the first time we made love.

Jaxxon whispered to me as he stroked inside of me. In between his moans, he whispered, "I love you!" "I'm sorry," and "I can't live without you."

As he made love to me and I heard his words, I silently cried to myself. Deep down I was hurt, and I was losing the battle to love once again.

Jaxxon and I took the two weeks before the kids arrived to try and mend what was broken in our relationship. We talked day and night. Every day he became a bit more open with me. He didn't hide his phone. He answered all his phone calls in front of me. I could see he was working hard to help rebuild the trust.

Spring break came quickly. I couldn't take off work to take Jaxxon to get the kids. Jaxxon decided he was going to take his truck, which was still indisposed and hadn't been moved since the tire situation.

The next day Jaxxon came home with an air compressor he borrowed from Shawn. I questioned his motives with the compressor.

He said, "I borrowed it so I can inflate the tire on the truck. I noticed the tire never went completely flat. So, I'm going to use the compressor to fill the tire every time I stop. I'm going to have to make a lot of stops, but it's my only possible solution, Joss."

We both got up early the day he had to leave to get the kids. We talked about our plans and concerns as far as the children were concerned. We talked about the trip itself, making sure he contacted me no matter what, especially with his air compressor idea. He was excited; he was going to spend time with his son.

I was happy for him as well. In the back of my mind, I was concerned about the trip. I didn't like when he went out of town, and every time he left something happened. And the air compressor idea was a dangerous idea because he was going to have the kids in the truck with him with a messed-up tire.

I felt like I was being selfish. I wanted spring break to be fun and exciting for all of us. But I also didn't want Jaxxon to leave. I pushed my fears and negative thoughts to the side and prayed for a safe trip and a blessed couple of weeks.

Jaxxon and I continued to get things together for his trip. After everything was loaded and ready to go, Jaxxon and I took a few moments for ourselves. We made love. Afterward, I lay in his bed, watching him as he got dressed to leave. He kissed me on the forehead, then he left.

To ease some of the stress of worrying about Jaxxon on his trip, he told me he was going to call me as much as I needed him to. He called me the first time he had to stop to refill the tire with the air compressor. He informed me the tire was holding up better than he thought.

Around the time I estimated Jaxxon to arrive to get the kids, I began to call him. My calls went unanswered. I didn't want to assume the worse, but I also knew the feeling that was gathering in my stomach was telling me he was up to something.

Jaxxon was unreachable for hours. But he called me after a while to tell me he was at Trina's (his baby mama) house. I wanted to get on him when he called because he should have arrived at her house much sooner than he did. He also had three hours unaccounted for.

"It's ten fifteen, Jaxxon. Where have you been, and why are you just getting to her house?"

He said, "I went to see Zoe before I came here, and you forgot I have to drive an extra hour and a half to get the kids. I'm late, and she still doesn't have the kids ready. I'm going to have to wait until they get ready. I'll call you back when I'm getting on the highway."

I said okay, then we hung up.

Two hours later, Jaxxon hit me back. All the time that passed, I presumed they were already on the road heading back. Of course, I was wrong in thinking that.

When I picked up the phone, Jaxxon told me Trina needed to go to the store to get the kids some traveling snacks and some other daily essential items she forgot to get earlier in the day.

It was getting late, and Jaxxon should have been on the road heading home by now. I couldn't help but feel like it was all some bullshit. My demeanor for the situation was changing quickly. I was ready to renege on him and the kids. I felt the anger building inside of me. "Jaxxon, just let me know when you get on the road to come home."

He called me back two hours later. He said, "I'm letting you know we are getting on the road and we are heading home now."

I wanted to ask him where the time had gone, but I digressed because I didn't feel like arguing. I didn't want the vacation to start off on a negative vibe, and I was happy he was on his way back.

We talked for a little while longer. I could hear the kids in the background talking. I was happy Jaxxon was getting what he wanted. I told him to keep me informed on the rest of the trip, and then we hung up. By my calculations, they should be arriving home around six in the morning.

Around five in the morning, Jaxxon was calling my phone. I got a little scared because I thought something happened.

He said, "Baby, I'm tired. I don't think I can drive any longer. I'm going to pull over on the side of the highway to take a nap. The kids are already asleep. I just need you to wake me up in an hour, okay?"

I tried to convince him to keep driving at least until he got to a truck stop because I wasn't okay with him resting just anywhere with the kids in the truck.

He said, "I'm too tired, Joss. I won't make it."

I was concerned, but I said, "Please be careful, and make sure you pull over somewhere safe. I'll call you in an hour."

I had my alarm set to call Jaxxon within the hour. I was glad this part of the journey was almost over. After an hour passed, I called Jaxxon to wake him up.

He said, "I'm about an hour and a half away. I'm going to pump the tire up, and we will be back on the road."

I again told him to be careful and for him to call if he needed me.

Around eight in the morning, as I was leaving work, Jaxxon called to tell me he was home. The kids were watching TV, and he was going to get some sleep.

My anxiety kicked in as soon as I pulled into Jaxxon's driveway. I didn't know what I was walking into. I didn't know how his kids were going to respond to me. I didn't even know if I was going to bring up Jaxxon's lapse in time while he was gone. I shook it all off and headed in the house.

Jaxxon was still asleep in his bed, and the kids were sitting at the foot of the bed watching. They looked up at me as I walked in the room. Excitedly, I said, "Hey, you guys! My name is Joss, and I'm a friend of your dad!"

I sat down in the chair beside the bed. They immediately scrambled to the chair. The oldest child Jaxxon helped raise asked, "Who are you?"

Jaxxon's son had the most questions for me. He was small and petite. He looked like a mini version of Jaxxon. His son was a tad bit darker than Jaxxon. His four-year-old squeaky voice was to die for. He asked question after question. I didn't know which one to answer first. He wanted to know why I was there. How did I get in the house? How did I know his daddy? He even asked me if I knew his mother. I laughed because he wouldn't let me get a word in otherwise.

The other child watched on, not saying much at all. She was a couple of years older than Jaxxon's son. She was slim, tall, and light-skinned. I was looking for some kind of resemblance to Jaxxon to make sure she wasn't his. I didn't want to be subjected to another one of Jaxxon's surprises.

I previously asked Jaxxon why Trina insisted the other child come along. The little girl and his son were extremely close, and when he was with Trina, he always took care of the little girl because her father wasn't in the picture. He told me he and the little girl were close as well.

I took the kids out of the bedroom to talk while Jaxxon slept. Jaxxon knew I was there because during my mini interrogation by his son, he woke up briefly to tell his son to stop asking so many questions.

While in the living room, I tried to answer every question his son asked. I told them my name again. I told them I was their father's girlfriend, and I told them I had a key to get in the house because I was always there.

I said, "While you guys are in town for spring break, you guys will be spending a lot of time with me while your dad is at work. I have a lot of cool stuff planned for us to do, and we're going to have a lot of fun."

They both gave me a big smile, then they went back to their TV show. I sat with the children for a little longer. I answered more of their questions. I was relieved the children took to me, and I was happy. Between one of the questions they had for me, I was able to fit in a question of my own.

I asked, "Are you guys hungry?"

They both chimed in with "Yes."

They both agreed to have cereal. I helped them make their own bowl of cereal, and they went back to the room to finish watching TV while they ate. I followed behind them with a smile.

I watched Jaxxon sleep while the kids were occupied with their food and the TV. I saw the peace on his face while he slept. Jaxxon told me so many stories about him and his son. They used to be inseparable before he left town. His son had to go live with his mother after he lost his job. Jaxxon has been trying to get him back ever since. He said his only wish was to get his son back.

I wanted this break to be a happy event for all of them. I wanted to show Jaxxon I was there for him and willing to help. I thought maybe the bullshit would stop. I hoped what I was doing for him was going to be the eye-opener he needed to see that.

As soon as Jaxxon woke up, he started playing with his son. I saw the bond automatically. They played, laughed, and had their own special chemistry. I smiled watching them play around. Every so often Jaxxon would look up at me and smile, and that made my heart melt.

Jaxxon enjoyed his day with his kids. We took them to the store and brought toys and stuff for them while they were at the house. They played outside until dark. We took them riding to show them around the town. By the end of the night, the kids were worn out, but they didn't want to sleep. Eventually they fell asleep.

After they fell asleep, Jaxxon and I had time alone. He said, "Thank you for making everything possible for my son to be here with me. I wouldn't have been able to pull this off if it weren't for you. I need you in my life, and I'm so glad my son likes you."

I could see the happiness on Jaxxon's face. He hugged me briefly and then disappeared into the bedroom to check on the kids. He crawled in bed behind his son and held him, eventually falling asleep. I watched them sleep for a little while before I crawled in bed behind Jaxxon and held him.

The next morning Jaxxon went to work, I was alone with the kids. His son looked over in the bed and saw me. He asked, "Did you stay the night?"

I laughed and said, "I always stay the night."

He said, "Even when my daddy isn't here?"

I smiled and said, "Yup!"

The other child asked, "Do you live there?"

I happily said, "Nope, you will see my house later if you're good."

I fed the kids. I had them straighten up the room, and then they got dressed to leave. I was taking them to my house for a bit while I freshened up and changed my clothes. I thought it would be fun for them to meet my daughter and my new Yorkie puppy Cole. I had a basketball goal in my yard and other things to keep them busy while I got myself ready. I wanted them to get to know me, and it didn't take long.

By the third day, everything started going wrong. It just so happened to be my birthday.

I planned to spend the day with his kids and my daughter as a gift to myself. We were going to the movies, out for lunch, and then grab some snow cones before heading back to Jaxxon's house. Everything I did with the kids I captured with pictures to share with him later.

After our fun-filled day and doing everything as planned, the kids were tired. I took my daughter home and then went back to Jaxxon's house with the kids. The kids bathed and got themselves ready for bed.

I texted Jaxxon to update him on the big day and how they were probably going to be asleep before he got home. He never texted back. I realized he didn't text the whole time I had his kids. He never texted to see how they were doing or how they were acting. It was getting late, and I realized I never received a "Happy Birthday" text from him either.

I waited patiently for Jaxxon to come home. I thought he was going to have some flowers in his hands or at least a birthday card or something. I thought maybe he was going to surprise me. The kids were worn out, but they were waiting patiently for Jaxxon to arrive home too.

When Jaxxon walked through the door, the kids ran to him screaming, "Daddy, daddy, daddy!" They quickly started telling him about everything we did. When they couldn't remember specific details, they looked over at me so I could fill in the blanks. Their happiness made me smile. Once they were done talking, they returned to the bed and finished watching TV until they fell asleep. Jaxxon sat down in his chair and watched the kids watch TV.

I thought he was going to wait until the kids were asleep to shower me with love and attention, maybe even some birthday sex, but Jaxxon sat back in his chair pretty much ignoring me. I went in the bathroom to change my clothes for bed. I realized by his demeanor Jaxxon wasn't going to entertain any of my thoughts. I climbed up toward the top half of the bed to get comfortable for bed.

As I dozed off to sleep, I wondered what the hell I was fighting for. Why did I stay and continue to take Jaxxon's lying and blunt disregard for me and my feelings? Sawyer or Drew didn't care about my feelings either. Neither did Micah. Why should Jaxxon be any different? What a way to end my birthday, I thought. My feelings were a little hurt.

The next day, things with the kids continued. Jaxxon left for work already. He slept in his chair the whole night. The kids ate then got dressed, and we headed to my house. We spent most of the day at my house, and toward the end of the day, we went to the park so the children could play on the playground.

Jaxxon texted while we were at the park and mentioned they were coming home from work early. I told the kids to get ready so we could head over to his house.

While we were riding to the house, the kids talked about not wanting to go back home to South Carolina. They talked about their mom and where they lived. They told me about the apartment they lived in and who stayed in the apartment with them. I started to ask them questions of my own to get some clarification on what they were telling me.

I asked, "Who all live in the apartment with you guys?" They told me their mom and two other brothers lived in the apartment. I asked them if their auntie or grandmother stayed with them. The kids said no. The oldest one offered up the address to where their aunt and grandmother lived. I asked them if they stayed in Georgetown. The kids again told me no. When they said no to my last question, my mind went straight into overload. Jaxxon had been lying to me again.

The kids continued talking about where they lived. They told me about the other kids that lived in the apartment complex. I asked them if their apartment was on the second floor. They told me yes. They told me they stayed on Day Spring Road. All I could do was shake my head after I heard the address. I didn't want the kids to pick up on my anger, so I continued to listen to them talk.

By the time we got to Jaxxon's house, my mind was in thinking mode. I wasn't sure how I was going to approach Jaxxon with the information I just found out. I didn't know how I was going to keep my anger from growing out of control.

Jaxxon arrived at the house a few minutes after we did. He went straight for the kids. He said "hey" to me and proceeded into the house.

I got even more upset because all I got from him was a simple "hey." The whole time the kids had been in town Jaxxon not once hugged or kissed me. He treated me like a damn nanny, and that was exactly how I felt. I took off work to watch his kids for him. I spent my money spoiling them and trying to make sure they had a good time. I was the one they spent every day with, just to find out he lied to me yet again. It was no one's fault but my own, and I got madder.

I went in the house and told Jaxxon I was going home for a few and I might come back later. He didn't like the fact that I was leaving. He asked, "Why are you leaving?"

I said, "I have something to do at home [I really didn't have anything to do]."

I didn't wait for his next reply. I looked at the kids and told them I would see them soon. I walked out of Jaxxon's house confused as to what my next step would be.

When I got home Jaxxon called me. "What's your problem?"

I said, "I don't have a problem, Jaxxon. Worry about spending time with your kids."

Jaxxon told me I had issues. I reiterated to him I was fine. He kept on talking, telling me I was jealous of his kids and the relationship he had with them. He told me I was acting funny and I've been acting funny since the kids arrived in town.

Shocked by his assumption, I asked him, "How did you come up with that bit of information? You're the one acting funny. You haven't touched me since the kids arrived, and that's not like you. You even dismissed me on my birthday!"

He said, "I don't want you around my kids if you're going to act funny toward me."

I was tired of arguing with him. I said, "I told you I wasn't acting funny, and I'm about to argue with your lying ass. Where does your baby mama live?"

He yelled, "Georgetown. What's that have to do with our conversation?"

I was getting angry and frustrated all at the same time. "Tell me the truth, Jaxxon. Does your baby mama stay on Day Spring Road?"

"Wherever you're getting your information from is wrong."

I got loud and said, "And you're a liar, Jaxxon."

He hung up on me.

I called Jaxxon right back. As soon as he answered, I told him I was coming to get my stuff. He told me not to come to his house and I wasn't allowed around his kids anymore.

"You won't have to worry about me anymore after I get my stuff! I'm coming to get my stuff, and you wouldn't ever have to worry about me again."

"You're not getting your stuff, Joss! Your stuff is in my house, so it belongs to me."

I laughed. "I'm on my way!"

He yelled, "I'll burn it before I give it to you!"

I was getting pissed. I didn't care about the stuff in my Nike overnight bag I kept at his place. Other than some clothes and some other odds and ends, I just wanted my velvet waterproof vibrator. That was the most expensive thing in the whole bag, and I wasn't about to let him keep my favorite vibrator hostage. Again, I said, "I'm on my way!"

He threatened me, "I'll call the police if you show up at my house."

By this time, I was super pissed and didn't care what he decided to do. I was getting my stuff one way or another. The fifteen-minute drive to his house had me emotionally messed up. I told myself I was done with him. I couldn't believe he said I was jealous of his kids when I was the one taking care of them every day.

I always knew something wasn't right in Jaxxon's head, but after he threatened to set my stuff on fire, I confirmed he lost his damn mind. I didn't understand where his anger was coming from. I should have been the one pissed off, not him.

When I arrived at Jaxxon's house, I went to the door and tried to go in. The door was locked. I knocked on the door. No answer. I called Jaxxon. Surprisingly, he answered.

I said, "I'm outside, and I would like my stuff."

Jaxxon showed up at the door in a matter of seconds. He didn't let me go inside; he stepped outside and looked at me. It was dark outside, but I could see the whites of his eyes staring at me. His tone and demeanor appeared different from what it was on the phone.

He softly said, "I want to talk to you in a calm manner. With no yelling. The kids are lying down."

I said, "I don't have anything to talk to you about. I want my stuff and I'll be on my merry way."

Jaxxon reached his hands out for me, like he was trying to hug me. "Can you listen to me, please?"

Annoyed, I said, "Talk, Jaxxon!"

"You need to drop the attitude, Joss!"

"I want my stuff, Jaxxon."

Jaxxon walked to the door to let me in the house. My bag was sitting in between the threshold of the living room and his bedroom. I walked past Jaxxon to his bedroom. The kids looked up from the bed and smiled at me. They asked what I was doing. I smiled at them and told them I was grabbing some of my things. They were satisfied with the answer and lay back down.

Jaxxon stood at the doorway watching everything. I grabbed my things and walked out of the room. Jaxxon turned angry again. "You never listen to me, Joss!"

I said, "I always listen to you, and the only thing that comes out of your mouth is lies. I'm sick of you and your lies."

I grabbed my belongings and walked out. Jaxxon stepped outside with me. As I walked to my car, Jaxxon stood on his porch, watching me.

When I got in my car, I felt a sense of relief. I didn't have to deal with any more of his drama, but my ride home was filled with tears—tears for the kids and tears because I let Jaxxon get the best of me yet again.

Everything happened so quickly. I didn't know what really went wrong other than Jaxxon losing his ever-loving mind. I went home, got in bed, and went to sleep.

The next morning, I woke up thinking about Jaxxon's kids. I wondered if Jaxxon stayed home with them. I was hoping he did, but knowing him, he'd let the seven-year-old watch the four-year-old. Curiosity got the best of me. I got dressed and drove over to Jaxxon's house.

When I got there, I knocked on the door, and his son opened the door. I looked for the other child, and she was in the room watching TV. Jaxxon was nowhere in sight. I asked the kids if they'd eaten, and they told me no. I asked them if their dad went to work; they told me yes. I pushed all my feelings aside, and I told them to get dressed. They were coming with me to my house.

I called Jaxxon, and he picked up on the third ring.

I said, "I'm at your house with the kids. Your son opened the door for me when I got here, and that's not cool. He didn't ask who was at the door or anything before he opened it. I don't think they should be at the house by themselves. If you're cool, I'm going to take them to my house. You can call me when you get home and I'll drop them off."

Jaxxon said, "I'm cool with that. I'll call you when I'm on my way home."

While the kids were at my house, I told them I enjoyed hanging with them and getting to know them. They were going home soon, and I wanted to get my goodbyes out the way. It was Friday, and Jaxxon was off for the weekend. He didn't need me to watch the kids after today.

Later that day, I took the kids back to Jaxxon's house. We got to the house before Jaxxon called. The kids bathed while I made their dinner. After they ate, we sat and watched TV, laughed, and played until Jaxxon arrived home.

When Jaxxon got home, his mood was different from the night before. He wanted to let the kids play outside before it got too dark. The kids started playing basketball.

Jaxxon asked, "Can we talk? What happened last night shouldn't have happened. I felt like you were threatened by my kids. I need you, Joss."

I said, "I don't know where you got the idea of me being threatened by your kids. I have been treating your kids like they were my own from day one. The kids have been giving you daily praise reports telling you just that."

"I want us, and I need you! I want you to get along with the kids so we can have a future together."

Jaxxon wasn't lying. I knew he needed me. His truck wasn't running, and he needed me to help him get the kids back home. He wasn't fooling me. I told him the shit he did wasn't called for. I told him we would have to see how things went from here on out as far as we were concerned. We took the kids inside and got them ready for bed.

Jaxxon and I stayed up talking while the kids slept. His birthday was the next day. It was also the last full day we had with the kids. I asked him what he wanted to do to celebrate his day. I also mentioned the carnival that was in town. I told him it would be fun for the kids, plus I wanted a funnel cake.

He laughed. He saw the kids were out cold, and he motioned me out of his room and into the living room.

When we were clear of the bedroom, Jaxxon grabbed me and moved me closer to him. He looked me in the eyes as he kissed my lips. He grabbed my ass and bit into my neck, softly pushing me up against the wall. He lifted my legs to wrap around his waist as he kissed me aggressively from lips to neck.

He carried me slowly to the couch, laid me down, and started to take my sundress off. As he lifted my dress over my head, he began to suck on my breasts. He grabbed them, pushing them together, as he went back and forth sucking and nibbling on them.

I felt myself grow wet between my legs. I felt his bulge in his pants. I wanted him. I wanted him to make me feel good—good enough to forget the past couple of days.

Jaxxon kissed me all over my body. Finally, he lowered himself below my waist. He grabbed my hips and pulled me closer to him. He slowly started licking my wetness, tasting my juices. I lay there, back arched, and head tilted back, enjoying his tongue slowly playing with my yoni.

His tongue traced my clit, and then he gently sucked. He alternated between sucking and licking, bringing heat to my yoni. I felt my yoni swelling in his mouth.

My body gyrated to his movements. I reached for his head to aid in his licking. My movements paused. I was about to cum. I whispered to Jaxxon, "I'm cumming!"

He sucked my clit until I was done. He stood up to remove his pants. I could see his hard-on in the dark. He pushed my legs open and lowered himself between my legs. We kissed. He slowly slid inside of me. My mouth opened slightly, and my eyes rolled as he entered me. He slowly stroked my yoni.

I came; he knew I came. He went deeper inside of me. A moan tried to exit my mouth but couldn't. I was taken over by his strokes. I could feel wetness leaving my body. He moaned and whispered he loved me.

Jaxxon placed my legs on his shoulder. He knew my body, and he made me cum again. He stroked my G-spot over and over, causing multiple orgasms to roll from my body. I was losing control, and he knew it. He slowly removed himself from inside of me. He fell back onto his knees, sucking up my juices. I was overwhelmed with emotions. I wanted him back inside of me.

He stood up and motioned me to stand up as well. He bent me over the edge of the couch, lifting my leg onto the arm of the couch. He licked me from behind, putting his two fingers inside of me as he tasted me. He fingered and licked me until I came again. While my body was in the middle of its orgasm, Jaxxon entered me, going straight for my G-spot. I came again instantly.

Jaxxon went from making love to me to fucking me—slow then fast. His hands around my waist guided my hips toward his body as he went deeper with each stroke. His moans matched mine. He wanted to cum. He slowed his strokes to gather control; I began to push back into him, welcoming his orgasm. Jaxxon grew harder inside of me. He gripped my hips to slow my movements, but he was losing control. He lightly moaned my name, and I felt his release inside of me. I stroked him until he was done.

I quickly turned around and fell to my knees and took Jaxxon in my mouth. He twitched as I sucked on him. He grabbed my head, trying to get me to stop. I sucked him off until he repeated my name and begged for me to stop. I stopped, we kissed, and I told him, "Happy birthday." We lay on the couch until we fell asleep.

The next day, Jaxxon, the kids, and I went to the park, the movies, out to eat, and then to the carnival. The kids were having fun, and they were excited to spend a whole day with Jaxxon. I was happy they were happy. Jaxxon, on the other hand, was having mood swings. After the night we had and the wonderful day, he should have been happy, but he wasn't.

One minute he would join me and the kids in excitement, and the next minute he was angry and snappy toward me. I didn't know why he was acting the way he was acting. I let it slide and continued to have fun with the kids.

We rode the rides and played the vendor games. We all won prizes of all kinds. To end the fun, we went to grab some funnel cakes. The kids were happy, and they didn't want to leave; they were tired, and it was getting late. We got the kids home and into bed. Jaxxon sat in his chair, looking sad.

I asked, "What's wrong with you? Why have you been distant with an attitude?"

He said, "I'm not acting no kind of way. Stop assuming things."

I didn't want to argue with him, so I changed the subject. "Happy birthday again, baby!"

I handed him his birthday gifts. I made him a banana pudding cake, which was his favorite, a jacket, a hat, and a special photo album.

I knew how much Jaxxon loved his kids. I took pictures of everything we did and everywhere we went. I developed the pictures and made a small scrapbook photo album for Jaxxon. I also included his favorite pictures of me. He was excited about the book. He looked at the pictures repeatedly. I was happy to see him smile.

The next morning, Jaxxon's attitude was worse. I didn't play too much into it; I assumed his attitude had a lot to do with his kids having to go home later. His mood swings were off and on throughout the day. He was happy, talking and playing with the kids, but toward me, he was snappy and angry.

I didn't let his bipolar mood faze me, but it was making me a little angry. I knew something was going on with him, but he didn't want to tell me. I wasn't going to bring up some of the things I noticed he was doing (like sneaking to talk on his phone and disappearing for moments at a time) while the kids were in town. I figured I'd wait until we had time to sit and actually talk about it all. I knew eventually we had to talk about our relationship and what was next for us.

Later that night, we loaded the car and started on our way out of town to drop the kids off. The kids talked and asked questions the first hour, and they fell asleep shortly afterward.

I was doing the driving. I asked, "Where are we going exactly?"

He said, "Once we got close to my hometown, I'll take over the driving. It will be easier that way."

His demeanor toward me was still the same. He fell asleep minutes later.

Jaxxon didn't know I already knew exactly where we were going. I was hoping he'd confess and tell me himself. I turned the music up louder and continued driving.

All I could do was think the whole ride. Every time we went to his hometown, something happened. I couldn't stop thinking about Jaxxon, his lies, his phone, and how he treated me.

I sacrificed my vacation to make sure he was happy by taking care of his kids. I did everything for him, and I always ended up with the regret. I continued driving, still thinking about Jaxxon's deception.

We got closer to our destination, and I became nervous. I wanted to remember the route to Day Spring Road on my own. On our previous visits, just in case I had to do a pop-up on Jaxxon, if he tried to disappear on me again, I would remember different landmarks and street names.

Jaxxon would wake up from time to time, checking to see how far we had gotten. I didn't say anything to him; I wanted him to stay asleep until I got us where we were going.

I drove right to Day Spring Road. I drove past the first turn-in by accident, causing me to turn around. Jaxxon shifted, sat up, and looked around. It was too soon for him to wake up. I wanted to be right in front of the apartment he took me to the night of his cousin's funeral—the apartment complex he told me was his baby mama's sister. He didn't wake up completely; he adjusted himself, then he dozed back off.

I completed my U-turn and turned into the correct entrance for the apartment complex. I drove by the dumpster I remembered seeing. I pulled into the middle parking spot in front of the upstairs apartment. I wanted to be 100 percent visible from the apartment door. I turned the music down, opened my door, and said, "We're here."

Jaxxon jumped up. He was nervous. He said, "We are where?"

Amused by his reaction, I said, "At your baby mama's house. Isn't this where she lives?"

Jaxxon looked at me and then looked back at the kids. I opened the back door for his son to get out of the car. Jaxxon was already standing by my side before I could fully reach in the car to help his son out. He picked his son up and then told the other child to grab their stuff.

Sarcastically I said, "I can help bring some of the stuff in the apartment!"

Jaxxon looked at me and said, "No."

He told his son to give me a hug. Then he rushed up the stairs with the kids and all their belongings.

I gave Jaxxon five good minutes in the apartment before I went up the stairs to introduce myself. Jaxxon was mad. I saw it on his face when he got out of the car to bring the kids in. I was laughing my ass off on the inside. This time, I caught Jaxxon in a cold, hard lie, and there was no talking his way around it.

Before I could shut the back door of my car after making sure there was nothing left behind by the children, Jaxxon was back in my car sweating bullets and looking nervous. He said, "Let's go! I need to go by the store to get something and bring it back."

I looked over at him with a smirk and said, "We're coming back?"

He just looked at me. I asked, "What store are we going to, Jaxxon?"

He said, "The one around the corner."

By his tone and statement, I knew he knew I knew where I was. We were around the corner from his best friend Zoe's house.

I pulled up to a gas pump when we got to the store. My adrenaline was running high. I was ready for whatever could or might pop off. I was ready if baby mama wanted to get down or if Jaxxon wanted to have an all-out brawl-out argument. At his point, I didn't care; I was ready for any and everything.

Jaxxon got out of the car, and I got out behind him.

I said, "I need gas, and you're paying for it!"

He said yes and kept walking in the store. I walked into the store behind him. I found what I wanted, paid for it, and went to pump the gas.

I sat in the car for a while after I was done pumping the gas. Jaxxon hadn't come out of the bathroom yet. I picked up my phone and started calling him. I was ready to get home, and he needed to hurry up.

My calls went straight to voicemail. I called a few more times; again they went straight to voicemail. I got out of the car and headed back into the store. I stood by the bathroom door. I called his phone again. It went straight to voice mail again. I didn't hear his phone ring while I was standing at the bathroom door. I called his phone again. Still no answer. I called a few more times, and then I got angry. I opened the men's bathroom door, and I went inside. Jaxxon was inside one of the stalls, taking a shit. He was on his phone.

I yelled, "What's taking you so long, and why aren't you answering my calls?"

Jaxxon jumped as if he was scared. "I can't stop shitting. I didn't get any of your calls, Joss!"

Sarcastically, I said, "Whatever, Jaxxon!"

I walked out of the bathroom. I was beyond pissed. I wasn't going back to the car until Jaxxon came out of the bathroom. I walked around the store, brought some more stuff, and made small talk with the cashier.

After an hour, Jaxxon emerged from the bathroom. We walked to the car in silence. As we got in the car, I asked, "Are we going to another store to get whatever it was you needed before we head back to your baby mama's house?"

He said, "We aren't going back."

I asked, "Why?"

Jaxxon didn't answer any of my questions. I started to drive toward the highway. The ride home was silent. An hour into the drive, I looked over at Jaxxon. "Why did you lie to me?"

Surprised, he said, "What are you talking about? I haven't lied about anything."

"Something has got to be mentally wrong with you! Do you really believe your own lies? You have been lying to me since the very first time we came out of town together. Actually, you have been lying our whole damn relationship! You lied when you had me sitting at Zoe's house by myself for over five hours when you were literally five minutes away, less than five miles away. You told me you were over an hour and a half away! You are a downright dirty, lying-ass bitch, and your secrets are coming back to bite you!"

By the look on Jaxxon's face, I could tell he was fuming. I didn't care.

The ride home was silent other than his phone going off. It was his baby mama, Trina. I saw her name flash across the screen as he let the phone continue to ring.

She called repeatedly. As I listened to the phone ring, I thought the kids must have told her about me or she was wondering why he didn't return with whatever it was he was supposed to bring back from the store.

Amused, I said, "Why don't you answer your phone, Jaxxon?"

He said, "I don't want to hear her mouth, and she's nothing to be concerned about."

We got home safely. Spring break was over, and it was back to our regularly scheduled program. It was time to go back to work.

*****

Jaxxon and I didn't talk much more about that night, but our relationship was on shaky ground. I suggested many things to Jaxxon on how we could improve our relationship. I told him the biggest thing he needed to do was earn my trust. He needed to remove all the passwords on his phone and be home when he says he was going to be home. I told him he needed to stop blocking me on Facebook, and most importantly, he needed to delete Melissa from his page.

Jaxxon agreed to some of my requests. I didn't expect him to change everything right away. I didn't force his hand. I wanted him to become an open book as far as our relationship was concerned.

We started eating breakfast together on Sunday mornings. On his weekends off, we went on long country rides to nowhere. We would sit at the house drinking and have a good time. We were making love all the time, and it kept getting better with every session. His phone wasn't an issue as much, and it wasn't ringing all the time. Jaxxon's actions had me believing he wanted us.

On occasion, I took my hour lunch break from work to run to Jaxxon's house for a quickie. One random night before I went to work, Jaxxon and I talked about me coming through on my lunch break for our usual quickie. Knowing what the plan was, I left his front door unlocked so I could get back in the house later. I didn't want to use my key (the spare I made a while ago after Jaxxon threatened to burn my stuff). Plus, Jaxxon didn't know about the key, and he didn't know I made it when he first started giving me his keys.

On this night on break, I walked in the house and headed straight for the bedroom. Jaxxon was still asleep. I placed my phone on the stand by his bed. I then leaned in to kiss his face. As I was bending over, his phone (which was right by his ear) made a rustling sound. I grabbed his phone and saw her name light up across the phone screen. It was Melissa.

Jaxxon had fallen asleep while he was on the phone with Melissa. I said hello a couple of times and then hung the phone up. She called right back. I threw his phone at him, and it hit him in the head. He looked at me, and I yelled, "You're a piece of shit!"

Jaxxon looked at me, acting confused.

"Are you seriously talking to her while I am at work? How long have you been talking to her, Jaxxon?" In anger I screamed, "WHAT AM I DOING WRONG? WHY DO YOU KEEP DOING THIS? WHAT THE HELL IS YOUR PROBLEM?"

While I was steadily yelling at him, I started packing up my stuff. I was through with all his games and the emotional rollercoaster he kept taking me on. I grabbed all the things that mattered and headed for the door.

Jaxxon didn't try to stop me. I looked back and told him, "I'M DONE!"

I went back to work an emotional wreck. I didn't know if I was relieved we were finally over or if I just gave another woman my man. I walked off the production floor to cry a couple of times throughout the rest of my shift. I knew the hurt was real, but I knew I couldn't take his shit anymore.

After work, I went home and started bringing my stuff in from Jaxxon's house into my house. In the heat of the moment, I left a lot of stuff at his house I didn't want him to have. It was early in the morning, so I knew he was at work, and that meant he was not at home. I rode back to Jaxxon's house to get the rest of my belongings. I had my key.

Jaxxon wasn't there as expected. I went inside and took my time grabbing all my things. As I was grabbing stuff, I realized all the things I did for him, all the stuff I brought him. I was careful not to miss anything. When I was done grabbing everything, I scanned the room once more. Along with all the feminine touches I made to his room, I kept his room clean and smelling good. I kept things organized. I gave him stability.

I said, "Fuck it!"

I was tired. From Drew to Jaxxon, I was sick of men taking advantage of my love. Love is a battle, never playing fair. But this time, I was going to get my licks in.

I went to his kitchen to grab another bag. I put everything I ever brought him or had given him in the bag. I took the jacket, the hat, pictures, teddy bears, cologne, and the scrapbook I made him of his kids. I took it all. I put it all in my car and drove home. I had no sense of regret, just relief.

I was expecting Jaxxon to call or text when he got home, especially after he noticed the stuff missing from his house. It wasn't any surprise when he called. When I picked up, he asked, "What's up, and did you eat?"

He was calling acting like everything was good between us. I knew he hadn't been home.

I said, "I'm busy unpacking my stuff, and I've been too busy to eat."

He asked, "Can I take you to your favorite wing spot so we could talk."

I quickly said, "I don't think that's a good idea, and I'm not interested in anything you have to say."

"I need to talk to you about last night. I'm not happy how things went. Can you at least come by the house when I get off to talk?"

"I'd rather get something to eat."

I didn't want to go to his house. I wanted him to get what he needed to say out. All the other men didn't get this chance, and they began to call and pop up. I needed Jaxxon to get everything he needed to say off his chest because I didn't want him calling me anymore. Going to his house would only get me caught up in his charm, allowing him to seduce me again.

I said, "At least I'll get a good meal, listening to your bullshit."

He said, "I'll be at your house within the hour."

Jaxxon and I went to my wing spot. On the ride, he told me I was looking for an excuse to leave him every week.

With an attitude, I said, "What part do you play in my weekly decisions?"

He wanted to get the food to go, and I was cool with that. I wanted to get away from Jaxxon as soon as I could. We sat in the parking lot of the wing spot after we got our food.

I said, "Start talking!"

He said, "Are we going to talk here? I thought we were going back to my house to talk while we ate."

Jaxxon was a sweet talker, and he had plenty of charm. He was good with his words, having you believe everything coming out of his mouth. You could catch him in a lie, and he would lie his way out of that lie while lying about the original lie. He was manipulative with his gestures, and he had a way of throwing things back at you to benefit himself. As I got to know Jaxxon and his ways, I started seeing these things for myself. I didn't want to be alone with him. My love for him kept getting the best of me, and that was what corrupted my decision to go back to his house.

When we got to his place, we sat in the driveway for a few minutes. I was being hesitant. I knew what was going to happen once I went inside his house. I knew he was going to convince me to give him another chance. He was going to take advantage of my love for him. And I knew I wasn't strong enough to stand my ground. I didn't want to be vulnerable, and I didn't want to fall under his trance. But I was lying to myself if I said I wouldn't give in to him.

Sure enough, once we got in Jaxxon's bedroom, things went in a different direction. We didn't talk or eat. Jaxxon grabbed me by my waist and pushed me against the wall. His grip was soft and warm. He looked at me and told me he loved me. He pushed his body closer to mine and began to kiss me. He knew how to manipulate my body as well as my mind.

Jaxxon's hands reached up inside my shirt. He grabbed my boobs with both his hands as he kissed and licked on my neck. I wanted to tell him to stop, but my body was giving in to the pleasure. He was off to a good start; he was on his way to seducing me. In between his kisses, he kept telling me he loved me. While kissing, he walked us in the direction of his bed. We went past the dresser, around the chair, and onto the bed.

He removed his clothes, and I didn't say a word. He was completely naked; he walked over to me and undressed me until I was naked too.

As I lay back on the bed, Jaxxon stood in front of me between my legs. Through the darkness, I could see his member standing at attention. We were just getting started.

He lifted my legs onto his shoulders and grabbed my hips, bringing me closer to him. His member was standing hard and swollen, aiming right for my yoni. His member slid inside of me as I gasped for air. An empty moan escaped my lips as I felt him fill me. He stroked left then right. He teased in and out.

Our lips matched, and we kissed as he stroked my love. His hands reached for my waist, and he held them as he ground inside of me. He kissed my lips then my breasts as I moaned with satisfaction.

Jaxxon lifted his face to mine to look me in my eyes as I moaned. He watched the outcome of his art. I let him see the pain and love in my eyes as he stroked inside of me. He watched the faces I made as his body pleasured mine.

He said, "Look at me!" I did.

"You belong to me! Never try to leave me again! No one else matters but you and me. Nothing else matters right now other than what we are doing right here and now."

I said nothing. I moaned as he stroked and spoke.

He said, "Whose is it?"

I sternly said, "Mine."

He thrust harder inside of me, causing me to lose my breath. He asked me again, "Whose yoni is this?"

This time I said nothing. He asked again. I continued to say nothing. His thrusting became rapid and harder after each unanswered question. My moans grew louder with each thrust. I refused to tell him my yoni was his. As he thrust inside of me, he told me again I was his and that my yoni belonged to him. His thrusting became intense—so intense I was ready to cum again.

Jaxxon removed himself from inside of me while turning me over. He pushed my head down into the pillow, raising my hips in the air. He grabbed the back of my neck and pushed it down into the bed, and he entered me from behind. I gasped again. My yoni invited his movements. He stroked inside me until I was moaning uncontrollably. Both hands found their way to my hips as he stroked forward. I threw my ass back into him. We went on and on for what seemed like a lifetime. We got lost in pleasure, and love took over until we came.

We laid on the bed out of breath and high off pleasure. Jaxxon rolled over to look me in the face. He said, "Don't ever leave. You are all that matters, and you should see it in my actions when we are together."

No longer drunk in love, I said, "I'm not concerned with your actions while we are together. It's your actions when we aren't together I'm concerned with. This shit with you and Melissa is on a whole other level. I don't understand why you keep reaching out to her. What is she doing that I'm not doing, Jaxxon?"

"It's not what you think, Joss! I'm keeping in touch with her for a reason. I can't explain or tell you about it yet."

"Bullshit, Jaxxon!"

He insisted, "If you can be patient with the situation, I promise it will all be revealed in time."

I wanted to believe him for my heart's sake. I wanted to believe he genuinely loved me and he wasn't hurting me repeatedly on purpose.

Deep down I didn't believe a damn thing he said. I told Jaxxon I would give him some time to handle the situation. I told him I wouldn't leave him just yet. He and I made love again until we fell asleep.

The next morning, Jaxxon went to work, and I stayed at his place. I lay in his bed thinking about everything. Why do I keep falling for the same shit? Why was it so easy to be dick-matized by him? I couldn't help but wonder if I was afraid of leaving him or more afraid of being alone. Was I afraid of someone else taking my spot? Why couldn't I just walk away? I was afraid of being wrong about Jaxxon, and he was actually a good dude. Honestly, I didn't know. I prayed to God and asked him to fix it.

When Jaxxon got off work, I was at his house where he'd left me. I went home earlier to get some of my stuff, and I bought back some of his stuff I took. I made up my mind. I was going to stick it out with him—with my eyes wide open.

When I got up for work, Jaxxon was asleep. I went on a mission. I went on a search for evidence. Jaxxon liked to keep things in his wallet, so I checked in there first. From the first day that I met Jaxxon, I knew he kept two condoms in his wallet and a giant bag of condoms in his nightstand. I checked the nightstand on a regular to make sure the bag wasn't lacking. His wallet, on the other hand, I didn't check it all the time, but I memorized the brand and expiration date of the two condoms, just in case.

I checked his wallet, and the condoms were still there. I looked in all the folds and pockets of the wallet, and nothing was out of the ordinary. I returned the wallet to his dresser where I got it.

Next, I located his phone and started looking through his messages. Of course, I saw baby mama's messages and calls. Random messages, calls, and texts, but nothing that left me thinking, until I reached Melissa's name. I saw the messages they shared. I saw they video chatted on the regular, and I noticed the times in which they chatted. They chatted when I was at work or while he was at work. I closed his phone and decided I was going to keep praying for God to show me the truth.

When I got to work, I started compiling my evidence against Jaxxon. I was going to have evidence of all his dirt and confront him the right way. I was giving him one more chance to change, or I was going to play him at his own game. I was going to take my lunch around the same time I found out he was video chatting with Melissa, starting tonight.

Jaxxon didn't know I was planning to come through at lunch. We didn't make plans for a quickie. He didn't know I had already left the front door unlocked so I could sneak in unheard. I arrived at Jaxxon's house right at five in the morning, around the time they chatted, based off the message log.

I walked inside to find Jaxxon already up and moving around. I looked for his phone, and it was still sitting on the nightstand attached to the charger. He was surprised to see me. He said, "I just got up to use the bathroom. Are you here for another round?"

I searched the room. I didn't see anything that could put me in my feelings, so I quickly said, "Sure."

Jaxxon and I made love again. I had twenty minutes left from my hour lunch break, so I closed my eyes for a few minutes. I always had time for a quickie and a nap.

My alarm went off, and I had to get back to work. I wasn't worried about Jaxxon getting up. I rightfully put his ass back to sleep. I finished dressing, then I took my butt back to work. In the back of my mind, I wondered if I didn't show up, would he had been on video chat with Melissa? All I knew was the score was Joss, one, and Jaxxon, zero.

We had a good run for two weeks without any drama. He wasn't working as late as much, and he came straight home afterward. I was looking for dead giveaways he was possibly doing something shady or dirty between his phone, his wallet, the truck, and the bag of condoms in the nightstand. There was no evidence he was playing games.

Jaxxon was charming me, kissing me, taking care of me, loving me, sexing me, and spoiling me. He was making sure I was straight in every way. It felt like the calm before the storm. He was distracting me from something, but I played along anyways.

*****

One night when he came home, he had some food from one of my favorite spots. We ate, and he urged me to take a nap before work. I was busy the whole day, and I was tired. I didn't think anything of his gesture.

As I slept, I tossed and turned. Every time I turned in Jaxxon's direction, he would be sitting in the chair, watching TV. Eventually, I stopped trying to watch him, and I was finally able to doze off. I slept so hard I didn't realize Jaxxon had gotten in bed with me. My alarm went off, and I got up and got ready for work.

I got to work a little early, so I checked out what was going on, on the 'book. I knew if Jaxxon posted anything, his post would show up on my timeline first. I befriended Melissa on the 'book a while back when she first hit my inbox, telling me about Jaxxon running up in her house. I could see her posts as well. Jaxxon had a couple of posts, but nothing out of the norm. Melissa had some posts, but I didn't really care to read them.

After scrolling for a few, my gut told me to check her comments on some of her posts. To my surprise, Jaxxon and Melissa were going back and forth having a good ole conversation about their past and their relationship under a random post. He was telling her what he would do for her if she lived close to him. They talked about missing each other. I went on to the next post she made, and again, another conversation was going on in the comment section between the two of them.

All I could do was shake my head. I hit Like on both posts and comments so both of them would know I saw the comments. I then reread the comments between the two of them. I did a double take when I noticed the time stamp on the comments. They were going back and forth while I was asleep in his bed just hours before. I couldn't believe it. I didn't want to think he could be so heartless, he couldn't be that bold, but he was. From that moment, the disrespect got really real.

The rest of the night at work, I continued to think about the post. I kept thinking about Jaxxon. I kept thinking about how much more I could take from him. I wanted to get even. The situation between him and her wasn't going to stop, and it was time to start playing their games.

My first thought was to go sleep with someone else and not give a damn. That was too easy. I wanted to do something that hurt. I thought about doing damage to his truck, but that wasn't going to satisfy me enough. My thoughts grew. I wanted revenge. I wanted to get Jaxxon back for all the pain he caused me. I wanted him to pay and to know I wasn't playing with him.

I was going to confront Jaxxon. I went back on Facebook and took screenshots of their conversation and printed them out. I couldn't wait until it was time to get off work. I was going to let him know what I knew, and I had more than enough proof.

When I got off work, I went straight to Jaxxon's house. Papers in hand, I went into his bedroom, calling his name. He was still asleep. I sat on his bed beside him. He slowly woke up. He said "hey" as if nothing happened the night before. He acted as if he hadn't disrespected me.

Jaxxon got out of the bed and went into the bathroom. When he came out of the bathroom, he sat opposite me in the chair across from his bed. He looked at me and asked, "What's wrong?"

I didn't respond. He asked me again. Instead of saying anything, I handed him the printouts of the screenshots I took of his and Melissa's conversation.

Jaxxon looked at the printouts for two seconds and placed them on his table in front of him. "What's the deal?"

I went from zero to one hundred real quick. I looked at him. Fuming, I said, "Your disrespect for me was and is out of control! You don't love me! And why the hell do you keep dealing with me when apparently I'm not who you want! Karma is a bitch, Jaxxon, and she is coming for that ass. I don't understand what I could have possibly done to deserve you putting me through all of this. I have been nothing but disrespected and hurt by you over the past five months. I'm over sitting around taking your shit, grinning and bearing it! All you ever try to do to win me back is seduce me. That's all you're about, your sex. That's it!"

I got up and left his house. I went home and went to sleep. I was emotionally drained. I didn't take any of my things when I left. I went home to sleep and plot.

Jaxxon texted and called my phone nonstop while he was at work. He was making inappropriate subliminal posts on the 'book, trying to get my attention. I ignored him most of the day. I finally answered one of his texts. I asked him, "What do you want, Jaxxon?"

He replied, "You!"

I said, "You're full of it, and you don't know what you want."

Truth was, I wanted Jaxxon to sweat me. I wasn't going to chase him or any other man anymore. If he wasn't sweating me or harassing me through texts or calls, he was texting or calling someone else. Possibly Melissa.

It was part of my plan to be less available to his every call or text. I didn't know if I wanted to be with him or if I was truly in search of revenge. I wanted Jaxxon to hurt like I was hurting. He was selfish, only caring about himself. Expecting him to feel my pain was probably a waste of time.

I continued to ignore the rest of his texts and calls. As it got late, Jaxxon's persistence wore me down. I wondered how long he was going to continue to pursue me. How far would he go?

Jaxxon continued with the calls and texts until late in the night. By eleven thirty that night, he was calling my phone back-to-back. In between calls, he was texting. I was lying in my bed entertained by my phone, but at the same time, I was annoyed.

Finally, after midnight, I picked up one of his calls. As soon as I picked up, Jaxxon said, "Stop playing around!"

Amused I said, "What makes you think I'm playing, Jaxxon?"

"I didn't call you to argue, Joss. I'm calling because I want to see you. I don't want anything. I just want to make sure everything is okay between us. I need a haircut, and you are the only person who knows how to cut my hair the way I like it cut."

I laughed. "Dude, it's too late to cut your hair! We can talk about your head in the morning."

Jaxxon wasn't taking no for an answer. He started talking about all the things he was going to do to me if I came over. His details were sweet and seductive. He told me I was crazy and I always took everything out of proportion. He said I was in the same state as he was, and Melissa didn't matter because she was in another state. He said I shouldn't be mad about her. He continued to say everything and anything to convince me to come see him and to woo me into believing his side of the story.

And again, my dumb ass gave in to his pleas and begging.

I didn't trust him, but my heart wanted to be with him. I was struggling with my own self as to why he had such a hold on me. Deep down I knew better. In my heart, I knew we were never going to work. I knew things were only going to get worse.

Within the hour I was headed to Jaxxon's house. It was one thirty in the morning. His front door was already unlocked, waiting for me. His room was dark, music was playing, and he was lying in his bed with his back toward me.

I mentally prepared myself. I wasn't there to be seduced. If anything, I was there to talk, to find out why I wasn't good enough for him to go on the straight and narrow, and possibly to cut his hair.

I sat in the chair across from his bed, waiting for him to turn around and face me. He didn't move. I made a lot of noise closing his bedroom door, so I knew he heard me come in. We sat in utter silence.

I broke the silence by asking, "Are you getting up so I can cut your hair or what?"

He finally rolled over. It appeared he had been crying.

I said, "What's wrong with you now, Jaxxon?"

He sat up in the bed. He said, "Nothing, I'm good. I just want my hair cut."

"Well, let's get started then!"

"Are you in a rush?

"No, but it's almost two in the morning, and I want to get some sleep, eventually."

He looked at me and told me I could sleep at his house. He said I could take a nap and do his hair when I got up. I sat on the end of his chair waiting for him to make a move, waiting for him to get all the items I used to cut his hair. Jaxxon never moved off the bed. He lay back down.

I knew what he was trying to do. I knew he was trying to get me to stay at his house for as long as he could. Or he was waiting me out, trying to seduce me yet again.

A couple of minutes went by. He said, "Are you tired?"

"Jaxxon, I'm more than tired. More like annoyed!"

"I'm tired, and I need to get up for work in a couple of hours. Six o'clock comes quickly."

"Well, when do you expect to get your hair cut if you're not going to get up now to get it done?"

He looked at me. "Don't worry about it." He pulled the blankets back. He said, "Come to bed, Joss!"

"I'm not staying the night, Jaxxon."

He sat up in the bed and said, "Please!"

We sat in silence for what seemed like forever. He looked at me again. "Please come to bed."

After a minute or two, I stood up and began to remove my clothes. I went to the side of the bed I was going to occupy and sat for a moment. I hesitated and shook my head, knowing what lying in his bed was going to lead to.

Jaxxon sat up and began rubbing my back. He said, "Lie down and get some sleep."

I sighed as I laid down. I got comfortable in the bed. I moved away from Jaxxon to create space between us. He said nothing. I assumed he was already asleep, so I began to fall asleep.

I lay in the bed with my back toward Jaxxon. As I dozed off, Jaxxon's hand touched my thigh. He moved closer to me. His hands were touching different parts of my body while he moved. I didn't say anything. He moved closer to my ear and whispered, "You will always be mine!" He grabbed my face gently, turning it to face him. "Do you understand?"

I pulled my face from his hand and said, "I belong to myself. If you want me to belong to you, you got a whole lot of work to do!"

Jaxxon wasn't in the mood for talking. He grabbed me by my waist and pulled me to the center of the bed. There was no need for me to put up a fight. I knew what he was after, and he was going to get it one way or another. He opened my legs and climbed on top of me.

I felt like my body had a Jaxxon mode, and when he wanted me to be submissive to him, he just hit the button. He knew how to make me hot and wet in all the right places. While he kissed me, he started grinding between my legs. I could feel his member getting hard. It brushed my yoni. I tried not to give in, but he wasn't letting up. He lifted my legs to his shoulder and slowly entered me. I gasped as he filled me. He watched my facial expressions as he entered me.

He said, "I told you before to never think about leaving me! How many times do I have to tell you, you belong to me?"

I said nothing. I lay there with him on top of me, listening to his empty words.

My silence wasn't what Jaxxon expected because his thrust going inside of me became harder as he continued to ask me if I understood. The only thing that could escape my mouth were moans. No words, just moans.

My moans grew louder than the music. His aggressive strokes continued, sending my body to a level of ecstasy. I put all the other emotions I had aside and began to thrust right back at him. I thrust my yoni into every one of his thrust.

We didn't make love this time. We fucked hard and long. He came. I came. At times we came together. Nothing else mattered in that moment. I realized as we finished out our session, Jaxxon was never going to let me walk away from him. He was going to do everything in his power to keep me in his life, one way or another. Leaving Jaxxon wasn't going to be easy.

We both passed out until his alarm went off for work. When he got up to get in the shower, I got up too. While he was in the bathroom, I got dressed. I was standing in front of his dresser when I placed my hand on his wallet. It felt funny and off-balance.

I rubbed my hand across it once again and noticed there was only one imprint of a condom. There were always two condoms. I opened his wallet and looked to make sure I wasn't tripping. When I looked inside, there was only one condom in his wallet.

My heart sank. Adrenaline ran through my body. So many thoughts ran through my mind. I wanted to go postal, but I did nothing. From that moment, I was done with Jaxxon. No ifs, ands, or buts about it. I was done.

Jaxxon walked back into the room. I walked out.

"What's wrong now, Joss?"

I didn't say a word. He came behind me as I reached the front door and said, "I love you! Are we going to see each other later after I get off work?"

"I honestly don't know, Jaxxon."

With the missing condom playing on my mind, I called Jaxxon as I drove home. "I know you have a condom missing out of your wallet. Why is the condom missing, Jaxxon?"

Jaxxon's tone turned angry. He said, "Whatever I do is none of your business. You're stupid for not seeing what is right before your eyes! You're always looking for stuff to destroy our relationship. You never fucking listen to me, ever!"

"You're full of shit, Jaxxon. Just because you do what you're supposed to do while in front of me isn't all that matters! The shit you do every time you go to work and out of town is the shit that is destroying our relationship. You expect me to play dumb and naive. You want me to be okay with you fooling around, lying, and playing with my emotions. Go fuck yourself and leave me the hell alone!"

I hung the phone up. Jaxxon immediately called back. I didn't answer the first couple of times. After a few calls went unanswered, I answered. With an attitude, I said, "Stop calling my phone."

He said, "Seriously, Joss, you need to either get in line or fall back. It is what it is, and I'm not changing for anyone. You deserve everything you get from me."

I hung up on him again. I was furious. I knew he was on his way to work. I hopped in my car and headed for Jaxxon's house. I used the spare key I made to let myself in. I started gathering my stuff for what I wanted to be the last time.

My phone continued to ring. I thought it was Jaxxon, but surprisingly when I answered it, it was Melissa. I was curious as to why she was calling my phone. I answered.

She instantly said, "Hey (like we were friends or something!)."
I said, "Hello."

I listened to hear what was going to be said next. She went straight to the point. She asked, "What is your relationship status with Jaxxon?"

I didn't feel like I had to answer her by any means, but I humored her anyways. I said, "He was my man up until today, and what business is it of yours?"

She calmly told me she was calling out of concern. I was trying to figure out what concern did she have for me. This girl didn't know me, nor did she know about anything I was going through.

She said, "Jaxxon told me you guys were still just fuck buddies. He said you guys were never in a relationship."

Anger built up in me. I said, "Jaxxon is a liar. I know what the truth is. And why are you calling my phone again?"

"Well, Jaxxon and I have been working on our relationship since the beginning of the year. I knew about you, and it didn't bother me he had a fuck buddy. But if there is something more going on between you two, I need to know."

I sat down on Jaxxon's bed as she continued to talk. When she was finally done with her rant, I said, "Jaxxon and I been in a relationship up until this morning. I have the keys to his place, and I practically live here!"

"Jaxxon said you were crazy because you assumed ya were in a relationship because ya were having sex. Jaxxon and I are together as a couple, so you guys can't be a couple!"

I wasn't surprised or angry by Melissa's words. "You calling me right now, Melissa, is the last nail in the coffin. You can have his no-good ass! I'm at his house now at this very moment getting the rest of my things."

She said, "Are you mad? You don't have to get your stuff. Continue fucking him! Keep playing wifey, since you're washing his clothes, cooking his dinner, and taking care of his house."

I sensed in her smart-ass comments she was trying to be funny, so I said, "Bye, thanks for calling." Then I hung up.

I went through Jaxxon's room like a fine-tooth comb, gathering all my things. I went in the bathroom and packed up all my hygiene items. In his bedroom, I grabbed everything I had ever brought him, gifts and all, including the photo album I made of his kids. By the time I started moving all the stuff to the car, my phone rang. It was Melissa again. I answered my phone. "Yes! What can I do for you, Melissa?"

Calmly she said, "Are you mad, Joss?"

I angrily said, "I'm upset, not mad. And I'm not on *Fear Factor* either, so stop asking me if I am mad. I'm not in the mood for any more shit! You don't have to worry about me, Melissa. Jaxxon is all yours!"

Melissa wanted to prove to me Jaxxon said he and I were only fuck buddies. I told her at that point I didn't care. She asked me would I do a three-way call with her if she could get him on the line. She said she and I needed to know the truth. He was lying to her as well. I told her I didn't care about Jaxxon's lies anymore. She asked again to do the call. I told her I'd listen, but I didn't care either way anymore.

She clicked over to dial Jaxxon. I put my phone on mute while I waited. Jaxxon's cousin Shawn answered his phone. Melissa said, "Hi."

Shawn said, "Hi. What's up?"

"Let me speak to Jaxxon."

Shawn told her to hold on for a second; Jaxxon had his hands full at the moment. While waiting for Jaxxon to come to the phone, Melissa and Shawn continued to talk about random shit. I was on the other end, getting furious.

Shawn knew about Jaxxon and I. Why was he holding conversations with Jaxxon's so-called ex? I knew this call was going to be an eye-opener. I was about to find out some shit I wasn't supposed to know.

Jaxxon finally got on the phone. He didn't hesitate when she said who she was. They proceeded to talk and laugh. They talked as if nothing were out of the ordinary. Their chemistry was normal, without anger, animosity, or betrayal. She asked, "Are your plans still in effect to come see me?"

He said, "As soon as my shift is over on Saturday, I'll be there."

As I listened, I realized he already preplanned a trip out of town to see her, and not once did he say a word to me. I kept listening to them talk as the adrenaline rose inside of me.

Melissa shifted the conversation to me. She asked, "What about Joss? Is she coming with you?"

He quickly said, "No! Why would I bring her out of town with me if I'm trying to bring you back home with me? You better be ready to leave with me for North Carolina when I get there."

My mind went for a spin. I couldn't figure out who the hell Jaxxon thought he was. He was steady trying to be with me, making plans with me, but he was busy making plans with Melissa as well. I snapped out of my thoughts when I heard them say "I love you" to each other.

Melissa hung up the phone and clicked back over to my line. Excited she proved her point, she said, "Honey, I told you, Jaxxon and I are always going to exist! Whether we are together or in a different state. Even if he found someone, we will always be."

I wanted to hang the phone up on her, but I had questions. I wanted to know who Melissa was to Jaxxon. I wanted to know where she came from and why she had such a hold on him.

I came right out and told her Jaxxon and I started talking six months ago. "He told me you were no one to him from the beginning. I'm practically living at his house maintaining things there. I met his kids and most of his family members." I told her things I wanted her to know. I wanted to get her to start telling me things—things I didn't know.

Melissa began by telling me that even after Jaxxon moved out of state, he never really left her alone. Every time he came to town, he was staying with her. She said he had been trying to get her to move to North Carolina with him since he left. She told me she and Jaxxon talked every day, especially when he was at work. She informed me they video chatted every morning, and some days they had phone sex. She said she was his alarm clock, waking him up every morning he had to work.

How could all this be going on? How was he able to do all this right under my nose? My third-shift hours made it easy for some of it, but I was with him every day, almost every second. Other than when he went to the bathroom or to work, I was always with him.

She told me he told her about me and I was just someone to sleep with until she came to live with him.

She said, "I was never out of the picture! I know how Jaxxon is. He craves women. He loves yoni! I allowed him a pass to sleep with other women until I decide to move. I love Jaxxon, and I always will! You love him, and I can hear it in your voice. We are not the only ones."

I couldn't hear any more of the bullshit. I reminded Melissa I was out of the picture from that point further. I said, "I'm over Jaxxon's mess, and you can have all of it. Everything you're telling me is a giant Jaxxon pandora box, and it's going to explode. I'm too good for all of it. No offense, Melissa, but something is wrong with you for letting him treat you the way he does! Have a nice life!" Then I hung up the phone.

The rest of the morning and most of the afternoon went by peacefully. I was feeling a bit of a rush since I was newly single. A load called Jaxxon was lifted off my shoulders. I made up my mind. Someone else can deal with him and his bullshit. He had a lot of it and a whole lot of nerve.

As the evening crept in, my phone started to ring again. This time it was Jaxxon. He had been texting throughout the day, but I ignored them too. I didn't answer his call.

He asked, "Do you want to pick up some food from one of your food spots? I'm coming to your house when I get off work!"

I knew he was getting angry because I wasn't answering his calls or text. I texted him back and told him he better not ever show up at my house.

Later that evening, Jaxxon showed his face at my house anyways. I was scared and surprised at the same time. I didn't know what he was thinking, but I knew things could easily get out of hand.

I went outside to meet him.

He said, "What's your deal, Joss? Stop playing with my emotions! What reason have you found to leave me this time around? You're the one always walking away every time something goes wrong."

I couldn't believe him. He had the nerve to act like he was mad at me and it was my fault we were going through this drama.

Jaxxon couldn't have gone home before he came to see me. I knew because he didn't say anything about his stuff being gone. He would have noticed, considering his room looked mighty different without the things I brought laying around. By the way he was acting, Jaxxon wasn't aware of the conversation Melissa and I had earlier.

I stared at Jaxxon, pretending to listen to him. I really and truly just wanted him to leave. I said, "Karma is a bitch. Now leave! She's catching up to your ass, Jaxxon."

He looked at me as if I were crazy. "What do you mean by that?"

With an attitude, I said, "I spoke to Melissa, Jaxxon! I've heard more than I wanted to hear about your relationship with her."

By the look on Jaxxon's face, he wasn't expecting me to tell him what I just told him.

He said, "You're stupid if you believe anything she said! She's going to say and do anything to break us up! I've told you that already."

I shook my head and laughed. "Your accusations may be true, but it was the three-way call she made to you earlier that kept me from telling her to kick rocks!"

Jaxxon became even more surprised.

"I was on the other line when you told her you loved her. Oh, and you're going to see her this weekend?"

"You're bullshitting, Joss! Are you coming to the house or not?"

I looked him in his face. I walked closer to him, and I said, "I will not be seeing you ever again."

Jaxxon told me I was stupid as he got in his truck. I stood in my driveway and watched him leave. He called my phone shortly after he pulled off.

I said, "What could you possibly want?"

I think I was wanting a reason not to hate him. I wanted him to give me a reason to believe he really wasn't a coldhearted, conniving asshole.

He said, "You shouldn't always believe everything you hear, Joss. I have a reason for playing with Melissa's emotions. I set a plan in motion to get back at her right before you and I hooked up. I'm not going to renege on my plans because of you. If I really wanted that woman, she would be at my house instead of you!"

"Jaxxon, please leave me alone! Have fun playing your games. If you didn't already know, you're too damn old to be playing games with anyone's emotions. Grow up!"

I hung my phone up.

Fifteen or so minutes passed, and my phone started ringing. It was Jaxxon calling again. My heart instantly sank into my stomach. A slight case of fear took over my body.

Jaxxon arrived home, and he noticed all my stuff was gone. I continued to let the phone ring. While I ignored his calls, Melissa called.

I was curious as to what she had to say now, so I answered. "Hello."

She said, "Are you all right?"

"I'm fine! And you're calling for what again?"

I wondered if Jaxxon already updated her on our conversation. She said, "Jaxxon just called me. He's mad about something. He said you took some stuff from his house that didn't belong to you."

"I took what's mine and anything I paid for. I'm amused at how quickly he reached out to you! I don't have time for this shit!"

"I'm not trying to cause any drama or pain. Believe it or not, I'm hurting too! I didn't know Jaxxon was in a full-blown relationship with you. I was led to believe you guys were just having sex."

I quickly said, "There was way more to our relationship than sex! That man told me he loved me on a regular basis. We made love almost every day. I took care of his kids when they came to town for spring break. We were definitely more than just fuck buddies!"

I didn't want to be on the phone with Melissa anymore, but I needed to talk to someone. She knew my situation all too well. She, too, was in love with Jaxxon. The pain, the betrayal, and the hurt were falling on me hard. I couldn't think, and saying everything out loud to her was making me feel better. I couldn't tell anyone the guy I was in a relationship with was playing me the whole damn relationship. I didn't want to be judged for being naive or for being an idiot to a man's bullshit. I didn't want anyone to know. I felt stupid for being in the position I was in.

Melissa sounded concerned. She asked, "Has he really been telling you he loves you every day?"

I could sense a change in her emotions when she asked me the question. I said, "Yes, he has! Multiple times a day. I have text messages from him as early as this morning with him saying it to me. He told me after we made love this morning before he left for work."

"He called me this morning as soon as he got in the car with Shawn. He told me he missed me and he couldn't wait until I came to live with him."

I shook my head as she spoke. "So, you mean to tell me he called you as soon as he got in the car to go to work? This morning?"

"Yup, this morning, because I said hey to Shawn too!"

"This crap is unbelievable! How is Jaxxon able to pull any of this mess off? How was he keeping his stories together?"

Melissa sent me screenshots of phone records and text messages between her and Jaxxon. I read them all in disbelief. She told me he was calling her while she was on the phone with me.

I laughed. "You got to be to shitting me! He's texting me at the same damn time he is calling you! Hang up with me and speak to your man, Melissa. Life goes on, and I'll be fine! You love him and have already made plans with him. Go talk to him. If you want to talk afterward, you can call me back."

She said, "Okay." Then she hung up.

Jaxxon was still texting me. He was texting me, asking me if we could talk. He texted me telling me he had some explaining to do and that he didn't want to lose me.

He asked me if I ate and if I would at least get something to eat with him. I agreed to meet with him as long as it was a public place.

I wanted to see his lying face as he told me even more lies to cover his ass.

As I hung up the phone with Jaxxon, my phone rang. It was Melissa again. When I picked up the phone, she said Jaxxon was still planning to come get her on Saturday.

She laughed. "He still thinks I'm coming back with him to live with him. He said everything was ready on his end for us to be together. He said I was the only thing missing."

I remained silent as Melissa spoke. When she was done telling me about the rest of the call, I said, "He just texted me asking me to get something to eat with him all while on the phone with you, telling you he was ready for you!"

The short time I knew Melissa, I could tell she was smart. She knew Jaxxon longer than I had. I was sure she knew a lot about how he moved and did things. I didn't know how deep her love was for him, but I knew she cared enough to not see him hurt.

After I told her I was going to meet up with Jaxxon, she made a comment under her breath. I asked her to repeat herself. She said, "Jaxxon just asked me for some money to help with the gas to come get me."

I knew Jaxxon didn't have any extra cash to go out of town, so I knew she was telling the truth.

"Joss, he asked me for seventy dollars!"

"I hope this doesn't hurt your feelings, but you're stupid if you send him a dime."

To my surprise, Melissa said, "I'm gonna just send him the money. I want him to come get me. I want us to confront him together."

Since Jaxxon was unaware of what Melissa and I discovered about his betrayal, she wanted to set him up. I agreed it was a good idea, but it wasn't worth the extra drama it might steer up. And I honestly didn't want her around the man I loved, who had more feelings for her than he did for me.

Jaxxon always had excuses for every lie. Someone was always trying to set him up, or they were lying to him. And in Melissa's case, he swore she was trying to set him up or she was trying to break his relationships up.

I hung up with Melissa then called my cousin Roxanne. I tried to explain the situation to her the best way I knew how. I told her our plan to get Jaxxon back. I said, "Roxanne, we can be in his hometown by nightfall, pick Melissa up, and be back in North Carolina by eleven o'clock. There's enough time to get all this done before Jaxxon's scheduled trip out of town tomorrow. Enough time for Melissa and I to set him up and mess up his world."

Roxanne has always been my outlet and voice of clarity. She said, "You don't know Melissa like that! That boy—and I mean boy, because a man doesn't do shit like this—that boy isn't worth the trouble you're going to get yourself into. The situation isn't going to end well, and someone is going to get hurt, cousin."

I had to listen to her. Out of the whole conversation of reasoning with Roxanne, the only thing I took away from it was that I didn't know Melissa. I knew Jaxxon, or at least so I thought.

After hanging up with my cousin, I called Melissa back. "I'm going to come up with my own revenge plan for Jaxxon. You can stick to your original plan of coming here to North Carolina. You can call me when you get here, and I will show up at his house. We could set him up that way."

Melissa accepted the idea. Together we were going to seal the deal to make sure Jaxxon left to get her. She was going to call Jaxxon back to get an exact time of his departure. She wanted to three-way the call. She wanted to prove to me she was a woman of her word and she had nothing to hide.

Melissa called Jaxxon. He picked up on the second ring. Melissa didn't hesitate; she went straight to the point. She asked, "When are you leaving, and where will I be staying?"

He said, "I'm just getting off work, Melissa. I'm leaving as soon as I get off work tomorrow."

I listened on as he continued to answer Melissa's questions. He told her she was going to be living with him, at his cousin's house.

Melissa came right out and asked Jaxxon if I was going to be staying there with them too. She became sarcastic with her questions.

She said, "Are we all going to be one big happy family sleeping in the same bed together?"

Jaxxon didn't say anything for what seemed like forever. "Why are you tripping? And she doesn't stay here because we are not together."

Melissa told Jaxxon she had spoken to me. She told him I updated her on the type of relationship he and I had. She continued to tell him all the things she found out about me.

He said, "Melissa, she is not an issue for us! All you need to be worried about is being ready for me when I come for you."

It was hurting me to listen to them talk back and forth about me and their plans. I really couldn't believe my ears. It was like listening to or watching a movie. Melissa and Jaxxon finished talking about their plans. Then they said goodbye to each other and hung up. Melissa clicked back over to my line.

She said, "Did you hear the whole conversation?" She sounded agitated.

I said, "Yes."

"Joss, I don't know you, and I'm not out to get you. I have no reason to lie to you."

I agreed and told her the same. "I would be lying to you, Melissa, if I said my feelings weren't hurt. I just want answers. And after all this time, I want Jaxxon to pay for playing so many games with my heart."

"I know you're hurt. I can tell by talking to you that you love Jaxxon."

I quickly said, "That doesn't matter anymore. When he comes to get you, you can have him. Everything I knew to be true about Jaxxon was all a lie. You have the upper hand with Jaxxon between the two of us. You know him better. You know who he is and the things he does, how he moves and all his actions. That man is a liar, and all he knows how to do is lie! He lied about you. He talked shit about you and how you looked. And apparently, he has been telling you lies about me. I wish we were just fucking. Then I wouldn't be hurting so much right now."

I added, "He failed to tell you I was at his house every day, scratching his back, rubbing his pains, feeding him, fucking him, and washing his clothes. We were just fucking! Apparently, there was no relationship, just a big misunderstanding on my part! Oh, and let's not forget about him telling me he loved me every day. All that accounts to just us fucking!"

She said, "I agree with everything you said, Joss." She said I wasn't the only woman she had to come to terms with in Jaxxon's life. She caught him cheating multiple times, confronting other females on a regular. "Sadly, no matter how many times Jaxxon and I break up or wherever we are in life, we will always deal with each other. We will always exist."

I asked, "What do you mean by always exist? How was Jaxxon able to have a whole relationship with me for over five months and you never come to North Carolina to check on anything he was doing? Why didn't his people mention you when I came home with him? The only time he could have been communicating with you had to be when he was at work. After work, he was with me or sleeping. How was he doing all this, Melissa?"

She told me he called her on his way to work every morning. They talked while he was working and on his breaks. She mentioned they video chatted on a regular, mostly when it was late or in the early morning. She said they had phone sex on the regular as well.

I was surprised by the things she was telling me. I didn't realize how far Jaxxon had gone to keep up a relationship with his so-called ex. I became curious about how much Melissa knew about me, let alone our relationship.

Melissa was eager in wanting to set Jaxxon up. She threw idea after idea at me. I wanted revenge as well, but Melissa sounded like she had a score to settle with him. Like they had their own agreement and he didn't comply. Now she can enact her vengeance. She wanted to three-way him again. I suggested she call him. After all I'd learned, I didn't care about what they had planned.

Jaxxon picked up the phone, and Melissa didn't hold back her intentions for the call. She said, "Are you coming to get me or not, Jaxxon? And don't lie!"

Jaxxon seemed frustrated by her question. This was the second time she asked him the same question. Jaxxon told her he was coming.

He quickly changed the subject, telling Melissa he needed at least seventy bucks in order to get to her. While sitting on the other end listening to their conversation, I just shook my head. He was trying to get Melissa to send him some money so he could pick her up and bring her back home with him.

I thought, *Wow!* I sat wondering if Melissa was going to send him the money. Jaxxon was really lame and sneaky. He was smooth with his tactics. I continued to listen to the rest of their conversation.

Melissa informed Jaxxon she was going to have to find a ride to the store in order to send him the money. He told her to find somebody fast. The sooner she sent the money, the quicker he could be on the road. Melissa told him to give her an hour to come up with something. Seconds later they hung up.

Melissa clicked back over to my line. She let me know she was going to call me back after she found a ride to the store. When I hung up the phone with Melissa, I sat in disbelief at how everything was playing out, wondering at how quickly my life was being turned upside down in such a short amount of time. I sat wondering, why me? The life I thought I had with Jaxxon was nothing but a lie. I sat in my room in pure silence, with just my thoughts.

As I sat thinking, my phone beeped. It was Jaxxon messaging me. In his text, he was asking me how I was doing and if he was going to see me tonight, making sure I was still going to get something to eat with him later. I shook my head in disgust. I couldn't believe this dude had the nerve to think he was going to keep entertaining me, knowing he had plans with Melissa. It briefly dawned on me. Jaxxon didn't know Melissa and I were still communicating. He didn't know I knew he had plans with her.

I didn't know Melissa or her agenda. She had no reason to trust my words, and I had no reason to trust hers. She had no reason to keep my secrets. And her not telling Jaxxon about us communicating made me believe she was truly down for setting up his ass. It was my turn to play the part. It was my opportunity to convince Jaxxon everything was all right between he and I.

I texted Jaxxon back and told him I was ready to link up whenever he was ready. I told him I needed to take a shower, get dressed, and I'd be at his place afterward. While I was getting ready for my so-called date with Jaxxon, Mellissa called back. "I found a ride. I can send Jaxxon the money. After I send him this money, everything will be in place for us to confront him."

I said, "I'm ready for it!"

"And I can't wait."

"I'm meeting up with him soon. It's going to take everything in me to not spazz on his ass, but I'll keep my cool until you get in town."

With a humorous laugh, she said, "Don't have too much fun without me!"

My tone turned serious. "This whole thing isn't fun, and it sure as hell isn't funny. Jaxxon has been playing with people's emotions, treating women like they are trash and disrespecting their feelings and all."

He was telling me he loved me, and he wanted to be with me. He was playing house with me while he was apparently loving someone else. I knew all this drama was going to end, but I was curious on how it was going to end.

Within the hour, I was driving to Jaxxon's place to pick him up. We were going to get something to eat, and so I could hear him lie some more. When I pulled into his driveway, he was already standing outside. Jaxxon got in the car and kissed me. I didn't say anything. Jaxxon stared at me while I drove. He finally broke the silence.

He said, "What's wrong, Joss?"

I turned my head to face him. I was biting my tongue. I said, "Nothing."

"You're lying. You're too quiet over there."

"I'm fine, I'm just tired."

"We can grab something to eat and head back to my place to watch movies or something, if you want. I don't care what we do as long as you don't shut me out."

I continued to drive in silence. I was trying so hard to contain what I knew. I wanted to call him out on everything I had learned earlier. I needed to see his reaction when I told him about what I knew about his relationship with Melissa. I wanted to let it all out so bad. But something inside of me wouldn't let me.

We finally made it to our eating spot. I wondered if Jaxxon was going to tell me he had plans to go out of town, but he didn't. I asked, "Do you have any other plans for this weekend? Can we go see a movie tomorrow?"

He said, "Maybe. Let's play it by ear and see how the day goes."

I was getting irritated. "Why can't you just tell me yes or no, Jaxxon? It's just a movie."

He didn't say anything.

The waitress took our order. She disappeared, returning with our food and total. The total amount was $27.87. Jaxxon pulled out his money and began to count the total out. He put twenty dollars on the counter.

He looked over at me. "Can you cover the rest? I need the rest of the money for a bill."

When he was counting his funds earlier, I was counting as well. I totaled his dollar bills to be exactly seventy dollars.

I laughed out loud to myself.

Jaxxon asked, "What's so funny, baby?"

I told him nothing and continued to laugh to myself. I couldn't believe this dude had the nerve to pay for our food (or should I say some of our food, since I had to pay for the remaining balance) with the same money he received from Melissa. He told her he needed the money for gas to pick her up, yet he was spending it on me. And he didn't know I knew the rest of the money he had wasn't going to bills. He was using it to go get Melissa.

The only thing I could do was laugh. I was laughing to keep from crying. Inside I was pissed.

We got our food and started to the car. I had a sudden urge to snap. I knew I couldn't. I turned to Jaxxon. "Can I ask you a question?"

Without waiting for his response, I calmly said, "How old will you be before you stop bullshitting and playing games, Jaxxon? When are you going to start acting like a man and start taking responsibility for the things you do to others?"

Jaxxon looked at me. "Where are your questions coming from? Everything is going smooth and you're trying to mess it up by asking stupid questions."

I quickly said, "My questions aren't stupid! You're just mad I'm asking you the right ones."

I was tired of holding back what I needed to say to him. But I was afraid of his reaction.

He said, "I don't want to argue with you while we were out."

"I'm not arguing with you, Jaxxon. Just stating facts."

He started getting loud. "Everything bad that has happened to us, in our relationship, is your fault. You're the one not listening to me, acting stupid and shit, all the damn time."

By the time Jaxxon finished his sentence, I was pissed. "No one deserves to be disrespected or hurt by anyone who claims they love them. You're a piece of shit who only thinks about himself! One day, Jaxxon, your bad karma is going to catch up to you! And I pray it does."

I could see the anger flaring on Jaxxon's face—an anger I saw him have toward other people but never toward me. Jaxxon walked off from me. He started walking toward the middle of the parking lot. I could tell he was mad as hell. We were thirty minutes away from his house. And I wondered what Jaxxon planned on doing.

I yelled, "Are you going to get in the car?"

He didn't acknowledge me. I got in my car and placed the food in the backseat. I backed out of the parking spot and started driving in Jaxxon's direction. I pulled next to him.

I yelled again, "Are you getting in the car or not? I'm ready to go! We don't have to speak to each other anymore. Just get in the car and I'll take you home."

We drove home in silence. I got off the exit ramp closest to my house. I wanted to drive the street route to Jaxxon's house.

He said, "Go by your house first!"

I said, "WHY?"

"Because you need to give me my photo album of my kids! The album was a gift from you to me. It's mine! Those are my kids in them photos, and you can't have them."

"I'm not giving you a damn thing, Jaxxon! How do you know I even have the album? I could have very well left it at your house [but I know damn well I took it]."

I ignored Jaxxon's request to go by my house, taking him straight to his house. When we arrived in his driveway, I said, "Have a good night! Oh, and I hope you have a safe trip!"

Jaxxon gave me a look of surprise and confusion. He said, "What trip are you talking about, Joss?"

"Never mind, Jaxxon."

With the look on his face, I could sense he had more to say, or he was hoping I was coming in behind him, but instead I pulled off. After a few minutes of driving, my phone started ringing. It was Jaxxon messaging me. He asked why was I acting funny toward him? He said he wanted me to stay the night and he was going to look for the photo album. But he was sure it wasn't in his house. He told me he loved me and I needed to come back to his house.

As the messages rolled in from Jaxxon, I chose not to respond. I had so many mixed emotions running through me. I really couldn't wait until Melissa arrived. Jaxxon needed a taste of his own medicine.

I thought about Melissa, and I decided to call her. I wanted to make sure she wasn't going to back out of the plan. "What's up?

She said, "I just got off the phone with Jaxxon."

I was astonished at how Jaxxon played his game. As soon as I was out of sight, Melissa was on his brain. He was on my line trying to get me to come over but was calling Melissa, trying to pick her up from another state. This dude was unbelievable.

I said, "I just dropped him off at his house."

"He told her he was about to lie down for a quick nap. I want to three-way him again, Joss."

I didn't stop her. She clicked over to call Jaxxon. They started talking, and their conversation was normal until my name came up. Melissa asked Jaxxon if he was going to show her around town and take her to all the good eating spots. She said, "Will I meet your fuck buddy friend too?"

Jaxxon's voice changed. His tone turning angry. He said, "Why do you keep asking about her? She isn't a part of my life like you think she is! It's your fault she is around anyways! You were supposed to have been here in North Carolina, with me. Joss knew she was only temporary until you got here."

I was on the other end of the phone getting livid. I had my phone on mute, so Jaxxon couldn't hear all the names I was calling him on my end. It was taking everything in me to not unmute my phone and cuss his ass out. He was now blaming Melissa for his bullshit. I couldn't believe I fell in love with someone like Jaxxon. I was caught up in a real-life double-life drama.

I questioned so much. I thought about Drew. I thought he took me for a ride, but he was nothing like Jaxxon. Jaxxon was the worst. I was listening to his deception, listening to it all unfold.

I listened as they talked about everything, from the past to the future. Melissa would steer the topic back to me every so often. And Jaxxon quickly dismissed the topic. He told her she needed to get herself under control and she better be ready when he got there. Melissa agreed and said goodbye before she clicked back over to me.

She sadly said, "He doesn't know how much you care about him, Joss. I don't think he knows how deep your feelings are. I can't believe he said you guys were nothing, though! Joss, this is what he does. It's a cycle. I've gone through this with him so many times."

I said, "Is this some kind of sick game you guys like to play? Why do you keep taking him back, Melissa? Why do you keep putting herself through the pain and frustration?"

Her voice changed. "Because I love him! And the only reason I'm sharing so much with you about him is because he and I are working things out. Whether I come to North Carolina or stay where I am, we are going to stay working on us. If you want him, just tell me, and I'll step aside. I can tell you love him just as much as I do. If you really wanted him, I'll let him go. After all is said and done, you are going to be another one of his women that he charmed."

Jaxxon was giving Melissa hope for a future and steadily making promises to her all the while making promises to me and leading me to believe he and I would have a future.

Even with all the things I've learned, nothing Melissa and I shared or talked about would matter. Jaxxon was just going to try to seduce me to smooth things over, and in his mind, everything would be fine.

Melissa knew Jaxxon well. She was right. He charmed and manipulated me through sex. That was how he kept me involved with him, with his charm and seduction. He had practice according to Melissa. He had practice manipulating women, and this was his game of life.

We sat on the phone talking about some of the things Jaxxon did to me, to the both of us. I told her about the first time I met Jaxxon, right before Christmas, telling her how he disappeared on me New Year's Eve night, telling me his cousin got shot. It was too much for him, and he needed time to think.

She laughed. "His cousin never got shot!"

Melissa told me around that time I wasn't the only chick Jaxxon was talking to. She reached out to that chick, just like she hit me up. She told the other chick not to get too attached. The woman wasn't as understanding as I was. When Melissa told the woman who she was to Jaxxon, the woman started kissing and telling. She told Melissa New Year's Eve was the first time she and Jaxxon hooked up.

I said, "Was the woman's name, Sandy?

Melissa laughed. She asked, "How did you know?"

I told Melissa about Liz calling Jaxxon's phone. I told her that was the first time he lied to me. She said he wasn't at his aunt's house; he was really with Liz. I suspected he was messing around with someone. I never had the evidence to back my suspicions, so I never said anything. I just watched him and his precious phone.

Melissa told me of her encounters with Liz, telling me they went back and forth on Jaxxon's page, exchanging comments under his post. She said they eventually swapped telephone numbers, and they did the exact same thing she and I were doing right now.

Melissa said she didn't know about me at that time, and apparently neither did Liz, because my name never came up while they talked.

I said, "Yeah, that must have been when Jaxxon had me blocked from his page. He disappeared on me for a week too."

Melissa cut me off and began to snicker.

I asked her, "Why are you snickering?"

She laughed. "What do you mean by missing, Joss?"

"Girl, I couldn't find him anywhere for a whole week."

Laughing, she said, "That boy has never been missing."

"What do you mean?"

"He was with me. He came home that week to do something for his cousin Shawn. He didn't do shit. He was with me the whole entire week!"

I knew she was telling the truth because she knew he was doing a favor for Shawn. I continued to listen to Melissa. We were connecting pieces, filling holes in with his lies. I was in complete shock. Jaxxon was a damn pro.

I said, "That man is a piece of work. He knows how to play women, and he used them for whatever it was he needed in that moment. Honestly, I was happy when he moved away. He is toxic."

"Don't feel stupid for falling for Jaxxon's shit, Joss! Remember, I've been where you are, so I know how you're feeling."

"I met the family. I met his best friend, Zoe. I even met the kids."

Melissa laughed again. "I saw Jaxxon every time he came to town. He always came to visit me."

It was all making sense as to why he was always leaving me at someone's house while he made a quick play.

She said, "Girl, if he let you meet them kids, he really do love you though. He doesn't introduce his kids to just anyone."

Her voice changed while she talked.

I sensed she felt some kind of way because I met Jaxxon's children. Her finding out about the kids showed Jaxxon's true feelings for me. She knew I had a piece of his heart.

We talked and exchanged screenshots and pictures of our conversations with Jaxxon. We came to the realization when he wasn't around one or the other, he was talking to the other.

She had so much information on Jaxxon. She knew the dates when he was out of town on work assignments. She told me about some of the other women he was involved with. Some of them had told Melissa they had been in a relationship with Jaxxon for months. My mind was blown. I was getting a headache from the overload of information.

Melissa told me one girl drove to his house to confront Jaxxon, but she didn't do anything because she saw a black Nissan in his yard. She didn't want to cause a scene, and she ended up leaving him a note telling him it was over between them.

Surprised, I said, "Wow!"

She said, "What's wrong, Joss?"

Amused I said, "The black Nissan is mine."

My phone started ringing. I was relieved. I needed a break. Jaxxon's deceit was too much for me. I wondered how he was doing it all. He was always complaining he was tired, but damn, it was his fault. He was in his forties, playing games like he had the rest of his life to live.

My phone screen lit the way to further disappointment when I saw it was Jaxxon calling. It was getting late, and I was wondering why he was calling. I told Melissa I would hit her back, and then I answered Jaxxon's call. "What do you want?"

I was really in my feelings after hearing everything. I couldn't disguise it any longer. I wasn't expecting to see Jaxxon anymore, so I saw no reason for our current conversation.

He yelled, "I can't find my photo album, and I know you have it. I want it!"

I yelled back at him, "I took what I paid for! I gave you the album. I paid for the album and the photos. They were mine to take."

I could sense Jaxxon's anger through the phone when he said, "WHAT?"

I was getting angry too. "I don't care if you get upset. After all the bullshit you have put me through, especially lying about Melissa, you don't deserve shit. Nor do I give a damn about your feelings."

"Joss, you better give me back my damn album. And whatever that girl is talking to you about isn't true! You're quick to believe everything she tells you, but you don't want to believe anything I have to say. You're ready to end everything we have, listening to someone you don't know."

"Man, you're hilarious. You're right, I don't know Melissa, so tell me why she knows so much about me? She recited the text message I sent to you earlier, verbatim. How would she know what I sent you, Jaxxon? It's because you're telling her."

"You're tripping, and I want my photo album!"

"Whatever!" Then I hung the phone up on Jaxxon.

Jaxxon called back. I ignored him. He kept calling. I was getting frustrated and angry. It wasn't fair he got what he wanted from me, and now he was calling harassing me even more over a photo album, not giving a damn about the people he actually hurt. I wanted his stupid ass to look me in my face and lie to me. I wanted to confront him. I wanted him to see my hurt.

I grabbed my car keys and headed to his house. I didn't know if going to his house was a good idea. My mind was full of stories that pierced my heart, and it hurt. It hurt like hell, and I wanted the man I loved to see my pain. I wanted Jaxxon to apologize and mean it.

I called Melissa back on my way to Jaxxon's house. I told her I was tired of Jaxxon's games. I let her know I was on my way to his house to confront him. Screw a plan. I was tired of him right now—him and every other man that lied to me.

She genuinely sounded concerned. She said, "Please be careful. Don't get yourself bent out of shape over him. If you go over there, you know he is going to try to have his way with you, and you're going to forget about everything. It's going to happen. Jaxxon is good like that, and you're going to forgive him once he starts seducing you. Your anger will be null and void."

Her taunting was adding fuel to my flame.

I said, "He will not be getting any more of my yoni. You can stay on the phone while I talk to him, but I'm going to say my piece, Melissa!"

I tried to calm down before I got to Jaxxon's house, but once I pulled into the driveway, I started getting angry all over again. The house was dark, and it looked as if everyone was asleep. I wanted to use the key I made to let myself in, but I hesitated. I didn't want him to know about the key. I didn't want him to know just in case I needed to get back in his house for some reason.

I called Jaxxon's phone. He didn't answer. I walked to the front door and knocked softly. He didn't answer. I sat at the door waiting and thinking. I was waiting to see if he was going to come to the door. I thought about whether I should just get back in my car and go home or not.

I went down the stairs of his porch and walked to the side of the house where Jaxxon's bedroom window was located. I began knocking on his window. I noticed some movement in the curtains, and I started knocking a little harder. Jaxxon peeped his head through the curtains.

When he made eye contact with me, I yelled loud enough for him to hear me through the window, "We need to talk! Can you open the door and let me in?"

He said, "Yeah, okay!"

I walked back to the front of the house. I quickly called Melissa and told her I was at his house. "I just want you to listen to our conversation. Put your phone on mute until I leave."

She said, "Okay, Joss. Please be careful!"

Jaxxon pulled the door open for me with force. I could tell he had an attitude. Sadly, I knew why he was dismissing me. It was mainly because he was going to get Melissa, all without telling me a mumbling word. He walked to his bedroom, and I followed. He went to the bed and lay down. I sat down in his chair.

I started the conversation off. I asked, "Jaxxon, what's going on with you?"

He said, "Nothing is wrong with me."

I didn't expect him to tell me the truth. Jaxxon sat up in his bed, looking directly at me. "Did you come to bring me my photo album? You have pictures of my kids, and those pictures don't belong to you. You don't need to have pictures of my kids."

"I didn't come over to give you anything! You forfeited everything I gave you when you lied and used me."

He sighed. "Man, you're trippin'. You don't know what you're talking about, as always."

"Tell me the truth then, Jaxxon."

The room was dark, and only a dim light from the moon outside lit the room. Jaxxon lay back down on the bed. He ignored the fact I was in the room. I sat back in the chair with my phone on the nightstand. It was lying face down with the speaker side up so Melissa could hear everything Jaxxon and I were talking about. I didn't want Jaxxon to see the indicator light showing my phone was in use.

I noticed while sitting in the chair he cleaned his room—something he hadn't done since we had been together. He had a small incense burning, making the room smell fresh. I noticed while he was moving around on the bed he had changed the sheets on the bed from the sheets we had previously made love on.

I grew angry. I couldn't help myself anymore. I was going to tell him everything I knew.

I asked him, "Are you planning a trip out of town?"

Surprised by the question, he said, "No, why?"

I started yelling, "You're a liar! Why do you gotta lie all the damn time? Why did you clean your room, Jaxxon?"

He didn't say anything; he just looked at me.

I continued my rant. "You're wrong for bringing Melissa back here to sleep in the same bed we made love in just hours before. Changing the sheet isn't going to change the fact the bed is still wet, Jaxxon. Did you check it? Is the bed still wet, or did you just lay a towel over the wet spot? You're a nasty, conniving piece of shit!"

He said, "You don't know what you're talking about, Joss!"

I said, "I know more than you think. Mostly from your lips to my ears, I heard more than I should have. I have been enlightened by your actions and misdeeds. I've been on three-way with you and

Melissa a couple of times today. I know more than you think I do, Jaxxon. I know you're going to get her today. I know you told her I was just your fuck buddy. I also know the twenty dollars you spent earlier came from her. At this point, Jaxxon, just stop lying!"

Jaxxon became furious, and I didn't care. I was just as mad. "Melissa can have you because I don't want you! She is on the phone right now, listening to our whole conversation."

I reached toward the nightstand to grab my phone. At the same time, I heard ruffling on the other end of the phone. Melissa had taken her phone off mute, but she still didn't say anything.

Jaxxon watched as I grabbed my phone. He shook his head. I put my phone on speaker. I said, "Melissa, are you still there."

She said, "Yes."

I looked over at Jaxxon to see his facial expression. As I turned toward him, he jumped up out of his bed. He was on his feet in seconds. Before I had time to react, Jaxxon was standing over me as I sat in the chair. He said, "All I want from you is the pictures of my kids! You don't have any rights to my pictures."

I stood up. "I'm not giving you a damn thing. I spent the money on the kids and developed the pictures I took with my phone. Those pictures are mine."

Jaxxon lunged at me. He said, "You deserved everything I've ever done to you! You're not leaving this house until I get my shit."

I said, "We will see!"

I walked toward the bedroom door. As I opened the door, Jaxxon came from behind me and pushed the door shut. He pushed himself in front of me, putting himself between me and the door. Jaxxon was leaning down into my face. We were face-to-face with each other.

As I backed up away from him, he pushed me back into the chair. I quickly stood back up. I was surprised he had the nerve to put his hands on me. I wasn't afraid, but I was unsure of how things were about to play out.

I looked at Jaxxon in disbelief. I couldn't believe his actions toward me over a woman and some pictures. I thought I meant more to him than all this mess he was putting me through. But I didn't.

I quickly hung up my phone and placed it in my pocket. I grabbed for my keys, putting them in my other pocket. I was getting out of his house before things got worse. I was sure of that much.

I quickly began plotting my way out. He wasn't going to let me just walk out of his house. He didn't have any clothes on, so if he was going to chase me out of the house, he was going to have to put some clothes on. I prepared myself to make a mad dash to the front door.

Jaxxon blocked me from opening the door. We tussled at his bedroom door. His almost three hundred pounds to my hundred and eighty pounds was a difficult fight. The whole time, he was telling me to give him the pictures of his kids.

I maneuvered around him to get closest to the door. I began pulling the door toward me to try to get it open. At the same time, he was pushing the door shut. I was trying to pull the door open wide enough for me to get through it. I placed all my weight against Jaxxon, pushing him away from the door. I opened the room bedroom door. I ran for the front door, and Jaxxon ran to put some clothes on.

I sprinted to my car as soon as I stepped outside. I knew all I had to do was start my car and take off. I quickly cranked the car and started for the gear shift to go in reverse. Suddenly, Jaxxon was standing at my driver's side window pulling the door open. He placed his body in between me and the steering wheel. He placed his body weight on me, reaching around the steering wheel. He was going for my keys in the ignition. I placed my hand over the keys to keep him from pulling the key out of the ignition.

We nudged back and forth. I was putting all the strength I had on the keys in the ignition, trying to keep him from taking them. My hands stayed on my keys. Jaxxon's hands covered mine while he tried to pry my hands off the keys. He used his strength, squeezing my fingers. His body weight pressed against me, and his grip on my hand became unbearable.

He said, "You're not going anywhere without giving me what I want! If you try to move this car, I'm going to snatch the fucking door off!"

Jaxxon was putting all his strength on my hands. I was trying my best to keep my keys in the ignition. My grip was strong, but it was loosening as Jaxxon's grip got stronger. He was stronger than me, and I kept trying to fight him off the keys so I could find a way to take off. The pain from him pressing and squeezing my hands was beginning to hurt. I had to let go.

When Jaxxon felt my hands loosening around the keys, he quickly snatched the keys out of the ignition across my face and arms. Pain shot through my arm as he scratched me with the keys. I was in total shock. I couldn't believe what just happened, let alone his actions toward me. Jaxxon disappeared into his house.

My first instinct was to call Melissa back. She was calling my phone the whole time we were fighting, assumingly because I disconnected our call so abruptly when Jaxxon found out she was on the line. I dialed her number. As soon as she answered, I told her what happened. I told her he had my keys and he was refusing to let me leave.

I said, "He had put his hands on me, Melissa, fighting me over my keys."

She sounded surprised. "Are you okay? Stay where you are. Don't go back in his house. I'm going to call him and tell him to give you your keys back. He will listen to me. I know he will."

I shouted, "This is some bullshit! He's only doing this crap to me because he got caught. And if you have that much influence over him, then he is all yours. I'm done with his shit from here on out."

I hung the phone up and went to the house for my keys. I knew I was half to blame for our fight because I went to his house. I didn't plan to give Jaxxon the album, but if I had to give it to him to get my keys, so be it. But he was going to have to give me the keys first because the album was sitting on my kitchen counter.

As I was heading toward the house, Jaxxon reappeared on the porch. He had a cigarette in his mouth. I went up the porch stairs toward him, asking him for my keys. My phone steadily kept ringing. I knew it was Melissa calling. I wasn't going to answer anyone's call. I wanted my car keys.

I said, "You need to give me my keys, Jaxxon."

Jaxxon, said, "Nope, I will not."

I reached for my keys, which were in Jaxxon's left hand. Pain shot through my arm. I was bruised worse than I thought from my struggle with Jaxxon. I stepped back a couple of steps. "I need you to give me my keys before I call the police."

Jaxxon laughed and said, "You can call the police all you want, but I'm not giving you shit."

I knew he was bluffing about calling the police because he didn't like the police. He recently found out he had a bench warrant as well, so he didn't really want me to call them. He was calling my bluff.

He said, "You need to fix this, Joss."

I looked at him like he was crazy. I said, "You're a joke, Jaxxon!"

I turned and walked off the porch and headed to my car. As I walked to my car, I dialed 911. The dispatcher picked up and asked me what was going on. I told her the guy I was dating took my car keys and he was refusing to give them back.

She asked me where Jaxxon was located. I told her he was sitting on his porch watching me while I was on the phone with her. I let her know I was at my vehicle. She asked me if I was afraid for my life, and I told her no. She said, "The cops are on their way."

I sat in my car waiting for the police. I answered one of Melissa's calls as I waited. As soon as I answered, she asked me if I was okay. I told her I'd be fine as soon as I got my keys from Jaxxon. I told her I didn't have any worries because I called the police.

She said, "Why did you do that?"

"After he just tried to fight me to keep me from leaving, do you really think he is going to just give me my keys, Melissa?"

"You shouldn't have called the police, though. He has a history with the police. You know he doesn't need them around."

I knew what she meant about Jaxxon and the police. He was the one who forced me into calling them. I was praying they got my keys so I could leave. I didn't want Jaxxon to go to jail or for him to be handle unjustly by the cops. But I did want my keys.

I said, "Police or no police, I'm done with Jaxxon and all of his bullshit! I don't care about his wants or his history with the police.

We are over because he put his hands on me. I'm done. And I'm getting off this phone!"

The police arrived a few seconds later. Two officers approached me. They quickly pulled me to the side and asked me what was going on. They asked me if I lived at the residence. I told them I stayed there every night, but I had my own place. They then asked me who Jaxxon was to me. I told them he was an ex-boyfriend. I told them we had just broken up.

One of the other cops went over to Jaxxon, who was just coming down from his porch. The cop asked him for his side of the story as he approached Jaxxon. I could hear Jaxxon tell the cop more lies. He said I had broken into his house earlier that day while he was at work and I had stolen some things that didn't belong to me. The cop asked him what I took. He told the cop I took pictures of his kids and he wanted them back. He told the cops he was at home, minding his own business, when I came knocking on his window trying to pick a fight. The cop asked him if he put his hands on me, and Jaxxon quickly said, "No."

The other cop that was with me asked me if I was hurt. I told him I had a scratch on my arm, but I would be fine. I told the cop I didn't want to press charges; I just wanted my keys so I could leave. I told him Jaxxon would never have to worry about me ever again. I just wanted my keys.

The cop that spoke to Jaxxon asked me about the photos. I told the cop they were photos I took on my phone of his kids when they were in town for spring break. I told the cop I took the pictures and I had copies of them on my phone. I told the cop things went bad between Jaxxon and I, and we broke up because he was a liar and a cheater.

The cops asked Jaxxon for my keys. He told the cops he didn't have them. I told the cops he was lying. The cops asked him again for my keys. Jaxxon quickly told the cops he didn't have them again. Jaxxon told the cops he had thrown them in the yard after he snatched them from me.

I looked at Jaxxon in disbelief. I couldn't believe he did that. It was the dead of night, with almost an acre of yard, and this dude threw my keys in the yard. I wanted to do something awful to him.

The officer asked him where he threw the keys. Jaxxon walked to the area and pointed around in a circle. The cops pulled out their flashlights, and we all began to search for my keys. After ten minutes of searching, Jaxxon (of all people) found my keys. The cops grabbed the keys from him and passed them to me. I asked the cops if I could leave. The cop who took my statement asked me for my number. I gave him my number, hopped in my car, and left.

I was glad I was able to leave Jaxxon's house safely and without getting seriously hurt. I was in complete disbelief at everything that had taken place—Jaxxon chasing me down and struggling with me all because he was caught in his own lies and betrayal. I cried on my way back to my place.

When I got back to my house, I called Melissa. I apologized for hanging the phone up on her. After she accepted my apology, I recapped everything that had happened. I told her Jaxxon was now all hers. I told her his actions tonight proved where his loyalty was, and that loyalty was with her.

Melissa truly acted as if she felt my pain. She told me she was in shock as well, and she didn't think Jaxxon was that kind of a guy to put his hands on any woman. She asked was I hurt and if I needed to go to the hospital. I told her I was fine, telling her my arm and shoulder was still hurting a bit from struggling with Jaxxon through the car window and door. I had some scratches on my arm, but I was more emotionally hurt than anything.

I let Melissa know I was going to bed. I needed to sleep the night away. We said bye to each other and hung up. I crawled in my bed and cried myself to sleep. I tossed and turned all night.

The next morning, I woke up with a different agenda on my mind. I considered myself free, and I no longer had Jaxxon's escapades to distract me.

It was a Saturday, and I needed to do something with the extra adrenaline that was running through me. I wanted to go out. I wanted someone to make me smile, if only for one night. I called Roxanne to see if she had any plans for later. She had plans.

Either way I wasn't going to get into my feelings about Jaxxon anymore. I quickly tried to find some trouble to get into. Just as soon as I made up my mind about Jaxxon, Melissa called.

She said, "How are you feeling?"

I said, "I'm better than I was the night before."

She was calling to tell me she had just gotten off the phone with Jaxxon. He was on his way to get her. "He didn't speak on anything that happened last night."

"I don't care! He's all yours to deal with. I'm no longer concerned about him and what he does."

Melissa quickly reminded me that I loved Jaxxon. As of that moment, love didn't matter anymore. I asked Melissa if we could change the subject. And she started talking about a car show event she was planning on attending later that night. I wanted to make plans myself. I was trying to get into some good trouble for once.

We both laughed. We chatted a little while longer, then we hung up.

Melissa appeared to be a good person, but her actions were a little bias when it came to Jaxxon because she loved him too. It was a shame we had to meet each other through Jaxxon's betrayal.

By noon, I was done with everything I needed to get done. I ran all my errands for the day, and my plans for the evening was to stay in, watch some movies, and order some Chinese food. I was ready to lie back and chill.

My peace of mind was interrupted by my phone. It started to ring. I went to the nightstand, where I had placed it earlier. It was Melissa.

When I picked up, she said, "Girl, Jaxxon just called me and said he was stuck on the side of the road."

Melissa informed me Jaxxon was over an hour away from her when his gas light came on, and he pulled over somewhere. He called her because he needed her to send him some more money.

I laughed, and Melissa laughed as well. She quickly made a joke, or I took it as a joke, because I knew it wasn't going to happen. She said, "You need to go pick Jaxxon up from off the side of the road or send him some money."

I said, "He's on his way to come get you. You send him some more money or let him sit and rot."

We both laughed.

While we went back and forth making jokes about Jaxxon's dilemma, he started calling her phone. Melissa would click over for a few minutes and then click back over to me to tell me what he was saying. I had no sympathy for him.

After the third or fourth call, Melissa said she was going to call him on three-way so I could hear him for myself. I was highly amused by Jaxxon's situation. Karma arrived quicker than I thought. She went ahead and called him.

Melissa clicked over to dial Jaxxon. She clicked back over to me while it was still ringing him. As soon as he answered the phone, he started asking her if she was sending him the money or not. He told her to stop playing games and to hurry up with sending the money.

Melissa asked, "Where are you again?"

Jaxxon said, "I don't know. Hold up, let me ask this man."

I heard Jaxxon stop someone. He asked the man if he knew their location. The man said they were in Lawndale. Melissa told Jaxxon she wasn't going to send him any more money. She told him he needed to call me or another one of his hoes. She was no longer interested in seeing him, and she wasn't going back home with him. She told him to figure his situation out for himself.

Jaxxon wasn't taking Melissa seriously. He said, "What are you talking about, Melissa? Just be ready when I get there. I'm in this situation because of you."

She quickly said, "No, Jaxxon, you're in the situation you're in because of your own actions."

He hung up on her.

Melissa clicked back over to me. I could tell she was tired of his crap. She said she didn't know how she dealt with his shit for so long. She had plenty of dudes that wanted her, and she didn't want to deal with Jaxxon's mess anymore. She told me I could have him if I wanted him.

I hurriedly said, "I don't want him."

Melissa and I ended our call.

Five minutes had passed, and my phone was ringing again. I thought it was Melissa telling me something else Jaxxon had done, but it wasn't her. It was Jaxxon. I laughed on the inside. "Hello, Jaxxon, what do you want?"

He said, "Oh, so it's like that?"

"How am I supposed to be toward you, Jaxxon?"

"I thought we were better than that, Joss!"

I laughed and said, "You are very much mistaken."

"What are you doing? Do you have plans for later tonight?"

I was getting annoyed. "I'm chillin', Jaxxon. What can I do for you?"

Jaxxon told me he was at work, and they (he and Shawn) stopped at Walmart and he needed me to send him some money. He'd return the money to me as soon as he got home later. I humored him a bit and asked him where he was. He told me he was in Durham.

I asked, "You're in Durham, North Carolina?"

He said, "Why are you asking me so many questions?"

"Because I know you're not in Durham and you're stuck on the side of the road in Lawndale on your so-called trip to get Melissa."

Jaxxon was silent. "You still don't know what you're talking about."

I laughed. "Jaxxon, I know plenty! I was on the phone when you were talking to Melissa, and the guy told you where you were."

He said, "Fuck ya!"

Then he hung up.

Unbothered by Jaxxon's call, I continued doing what I was doing before the daily Jaxxon update from Melissa. I didn't care what Jaxxon was up to, but I knew deep down he wasn't through with me yet.

Melissa and I spoke off and on throughout the day. Talking to her eased my mind from thinking about Jaxxon. It was weird talking to her at times because of who she was and how we met, but we did have a lot in common, especially when it came to being involved with Jaxxon.

Melissa filled in a lot of missing time, or should I say the times Jaxxon was away and I wasn't around. She hadn't heard from Jaxxon, but she heard from mutual friends of theirs that he had been seen around town.

Melissa and I talked about our weekend plans. She was going to another car show with one of her male friends later, so she felt well protected just in case Jaxxon showed up. I told her I didn't have any plans. I told her I was going to chill at the house with my daughter and probably watch some movies. She insisted I get out of the house. I was cool with doing nothing. I had to work the next day, and I just wanted to relax before then.

We chatted for a little longer, talking about what she was going to wear for the car show later that night. After a while, our conversations became less and less about Jaxxon. Melissa agreed to call me once she got in for the night. We hung up, and I began to plan my day.

I ran to the store, got some hair, went home, and started to microbraid my hair. As I was doing my hair, I realized how at ease I was not having Jaxxon in my life. In the back of my mind, I was concerned for his well-being, but I was damn sure happy he wasn't my problem anymore.

The next morning, while I was getting ready for work, Melissa texted me. She always started our conversations asking me if I was okay. She hadn't heard from Jaxxon, and neither had I, and that was a good thing. Maybe he moved on from the both of us.

I was halfway through my shift when my phone rang. It was Melissa. As quickly as I could say hello, she was already saying my name. "Joss, Jaxxon just ran up in my house! He broke my phone, stole my money, and took some alcohol!"

I stopped walking to my desk and stood in disbelief. I said, "What? When did all this happen, Melissa?"

She was out of breath. She said while she was getting ready to go out, she kept seeing what she thought was Jaxxon's truck riding by her house. After the third time, she realized it was him. She said she assumed he was trying to see if she was at home. She didn't think he had the balls to come to the door, so she went back to getting ready to hang out.

A few minutes later, she heard a knock on her front door. When she opened the door, Jaxxon busted in. He demanded Melissa get her stuff because she was going back to North Carolina with him. She said that was all he kept repeating as he grabbed some of her clothes. He told her he came in town to get her, and he wasn't leaving without her. She said she told him she wasn't going anywhere with him.

She smelled alcohol in his breath. She threatened to call the police on him if he didn't leave her house. When she reached in her pocket to get her phone, Jaxxon grabbed it and threw it across the room. She demanded he leave at that point, but when he realized she wasn't going anywhere with him, he went into her bedroom, in her dresser where she normally kept her money, and took all her money. He also took the bottle of 1800 that was on top of the dresser and left.

She said, "Joss, he is going to jail! I already called the police!"

While talking to the police officer, she found out he had an existing warrant for his arrest. She gave the cops all the information they needed as well as a description of his truck. Melissa said it again, "Joss, he is going to jail."

I asked, "Are you okay? I'm sorry, Melissa. Now you have to deal with him."

I didn't know why I was sorry. I just felt the hurt she was feeling, seeing this other side of Jaxxon—the side where he was aggressive toward the people whom he swore he loved. Just like me. I could tell Melissa was in shock over Jaxxon's actions. I could tell by her tone he had done the ultimate no-no in her eyes.

Melissa repeated the events that just took place to me, this time a bit slower. She said Jaxxon didn't seem like himself. She was sure Jaxxon wouldn't have run up in her house if her guy friend were there. She assumed he was watching her house because her guy friend just left her house a few minutes before Jaxxon showed up.

Her phone was messed up after Jaxxon threw it. It wouldn't let her dial out or look up any numbers. My number was the last number she dialed. She asked if I could reach out to her guy friend for her. She had given it to me in a previous conversation some days back. Instead of calling him, I texted him and told him Melissa had an emergency and she needed him to call her ASAP. I didn't hear anything else from Melissa until the next day. She called me first thing in the morning.

I asked, "Have you heard from Jaxxon? Has he called or texted you?"

She said, "I don't think he will show his face around here anytime soon. I can't believe he had the nerve to run up on me like he did."

She told me her male friend was going to stay with her for a while. She didn't think Jaxxon was crazy enough to show up while her guy friend was there. Jaxxon was becoming unpredictable. I was glad she had someone there with her just in case something happened.

Melissa told me she asked around for any news on Jaxxon. One of their mutual friends told her he was around town getting high and drunk. She heard he hid his truck and was riding around in someone else's car because the police were looking for him and his truck.

Jaxxon really messed up. If he kept on the path he was on, he was going to get himself hurt. He was in his hometown hiding out from the police with no money. He was probably going to jail. I was glad in some ways; I wanted him to hurt. I wanted him to get the karma that was due to him.

Once Melissa was done recapping the night before, I told her I didn't want to speak about Jaxxon anymore. He deserved whatever it was he got, and he was no longer my concern. She accepted my request. We changed the subject to her male friend until I hung up to get some rest.

*****

Melissa and I talked every day for over a week. We talked about everything. We laughed and joked about things we had in common. We found out we had the same astrology sign. She was looking for a new job, and I was about to take a mini vacation. She started dating her male friend exclusively, and I was supposed to go on a friendly date with a newly divorced Drew. A week without Jaxxon in both of our lives was looking promising.

I believed if Melissa and I would have met on different terms, we might have been good friends. We were cool with chatting with each other, but with each conversation, we knew a giant elephant named Jaxxon lingered in the shadows. Sadly, he was what brought us together.

Another week had gone by. I was in the middle of my vacation when Melissa called. As soon as I picked up, she started talking about Jaxxon. My heart went into my stomach at the mention of his name.

She said, "Joss, I found out Jaxxon is stuck here. I found out from a mutual friend of ours he was trying to find a way home because his truck was messed up. He is asking everyone he knew for money to get home." Jokingly, she added, "Joss, why don't you come get your man or send him some money to get home?"

I laughed. "I wish I would!"

We both laughed.

A couple of more weeks passed with no Jaxxon in my life. No word on where he was or what he was doing. I was enjoying the peace.

It was a Friday night, and I was planning on chilling around the house. I already had my daily talk with Melissa, and she had plans too. She was going out with her boyfriend. I really didn't know what I had in mind to do, but I had a lot of TV shows to catch up on.

I began to start my night when my phone beeped. My heart skipped a beat. It was Jaxxon's unique beep. I became nervous and anxious all at the same time. I didn't know why he was texting me, but he was.

I reached for my phone to see if I was correct in my assumption. It was Jaxxon, as I assumed. I laughed as I looked at the name glaring at me from my phone. I laughed because he had the nerve to text me, and I forgot I had changed his name to LIAR in my phone.

It'd been almost a month since Jaxxon and I communicated. I knew what he was up to, thanks to Melissa. I knew he was only texting because he needed something. I didn't bother to read the message. I continued with my night as if he never reached out to me, and he never texted back.

With all the time that had passed, I was surprised Jaxxon tried to reach out. That was Jaxxon for you, though. His thought process was totally different from the average person, and he thought he was a great manipulator to get you to forget the things you know you knew. It was impressive, especially how he kept his lies together and how he had a story for everything.

The next morning, on my daily talk with Melissa, I told her about Jaxxon texting. We both laughed at Jaxxon's stupidity and talked about our plans for the day. I was going to a comedy show. I brought tickets for us a while I was with Jaxxon. Melissa was going out with some friends. Before we hung up, Melissa told me she heard Jaxxon was back home, in North Carolina. She told me to watch myself, then we said goodbye.

I received another text from Jaxxon later that afternoon. This time I read it. He had the nerve to think he was still going with me to see Katt Williams at the comedy show I was attending later that night.

I brought the tickets two months ago for Jaxxon and I, and the plan then was for us to go together. After all this time, he still thought he was going to go to the show with me. The thought of it made me laugh.

I laughed a little harder when I wondered how Jaxxon would feel if he found out I was going to the show with Drew. I reached out to Drew, as a friend, to see if he would accompany me to the show. I had an extra ticket, and I didn't want to go alone. Drew was a comedian, so I gave him the extra ticket. I laughed even harder thinking about Jaxxon's reaction.

I couldn't help myself; I had to respond. I texted him back saying, "Really! Are you seriously asking me about going to a show I paid for after dealing with all your bullshit?"

He said, "What are you talking about?"

I said, "Leave me alone, Jaxxon!"

I felt myself getting heated. I hung up the phone and went back to getting ready for the show.

As dumb as Jaxxon tried to play, he had to know better than that. I honestly couldn't believe he thought he was going to weasel his way into going to the show, trying to walk back into my life. He believed himself and his lies.

I went on to the show. I went on to trying to live my life happily. I went to work, I took care of my kids, and I took care of me. I was speaking to Melissa every day. And Jaxxon was now texting every day. And every day I ignored him.

On Facebook, we were all friends, Melissa, Jaxxon, and I. A while back, I changed my following instructions for Jaxxon's profile. I didn't want to see his posts first anymore. I didn't care about anything he said and did.

When I posted something; he was sure to put a thumbs-up. I didn't want to call it stalking, but I knew he knew my every move on the book. I didn't know if he was riding by my house and sitting in the parking lot of my job. His daily texts and calls showed his persistence.

At work one day, I had a couple of coworkers (Ninja and Oneida) come up to me and asked me who was the guy professing his love for me on Facebook. I wasn't aware of any posts because I was working two jobs and I hadn't been on Facebook.

I said, "I don't know what man you guys are talking about."

They said almost in unison, "Girl, you're being tagged in a whole lot of posts. Some guy is on Facebook professing his love for you."

I knew I was a good woman, but I was wondering who was in love with me that much to tell the world.

In shock, I pulled my phone out and logged on to the 'book. The guy professing his undying love, pleading for forgiveness and a second chance, was Jaxxon. Every day for well over a week, he tagged me in posts, telling me he loved me, he was sorry, he needed me, and he will always love me. He posted old pictures of us together, asking for a second chance.

I read the posts I was tagged in. I was moved by his show of affection. I knew Melissa was seeing the posts as well. She threatened to come whoop my ass if I ever got back with Jaxxon. I was too good for him, she said. Even though I never responded to any of the posts, he continued to tag me in posts, and he continued to call every day.

As time went on, nothing had changed on Jaxxon's part. He texted, "Good morning, beautiful," every single day. He was sending pages worth of text messages, poems professing his love, making promise after promise to never hurt me again. Jaxxon wanted another chance to prove himself. His actions were lightening my heart, and I remembered the love I had for him.

I loved Jaxxon, and I wasn't too sure I wanted to be with him. As much as I didn't want the feelings for him to not exist, they did. With the pictures he posted, memories of us together popped into my mind. My heart was swelling from memories of love. He was reminding me of all the times he made me laugh, easing some of the tears he caused me to cry. I hated how he made me feel inside.

It was a Friday night, and I was working my second job when Jaxxon called. I was having a good day, so I answered. As soon as I answered, there was an awkward pause.

I said, "Hello."

Jaxxon said, "Hey, I wasn't expecting you to pick up. I'm used to talking to your voicemail. When I heard your actual voice, I froze. I'm sorry!"

I asked, "What can I help you with?"

"How are you?"

"As good as to be expected. It's Friday, and I have my whole weekend to myself. I'm in a good mood. Hence me answering the phone for you!"

"Why are you in such a good mood, though?

I happily said, "It's payday! Everyone is happy on payday!"

He laughed.

"You never told me why you are calling."

He quickly said, "I want to see you."

I told Jaxxon I didn't think that was a good idea. He said I'd never know unless I let it happen. I had to get back to work, so I told him to call me back later.

He asked, "Are you going to answer the phone when I call back?"

"Well, Jaxxon, I guess you're going to have to wait and see."

Then I hung up. My phone beeped two seconds later. It was Jaxxon's personal message beep. He sent a heart emoji with the comment, "Thanks for answering the phone."

I got done with work, went home, and started looking for something to get into for the night. I called Roxanne to see if she wanted to play out on the town. She didn't have a babysitter, so nothing happened there. My daughter was going out with her friends, and Melissa was going out with her man. Everyone I reached out to had plans.

I gave in to myself and decided to Netflix and chill by myself. I didn't have any problems hanging by myself. I was content chilling at the house. Plus, I was in a good-ass mood. I finally had a whole weekend off, and it was payday.

I took a shower, lit some candles, and conjured up some food. I set the TV up to watch my movie, then I prepared to relax. I was happy sitting and watching TV by myself. To myself, I gave the Lord thanks while I counted my blessings. I had no worries. My family was good. My kids were doing their own thing. I had a job, a car, and a house. I had no immediate worries, and I was happy and content. And I didn't need a man to be happy with myself.

The night was still young, and I was halfway through my movie when my phone rang. I wasn't expecting a call from anyone. But apparently someone wanted to speak to me. I glanced at my phone which was lying on my nightstand. When I saw the name on the screen, I just sighed to myself. I forgot I told Jaxxon he could call me later. With no hesitation, I answered.

I don't know why I answered the phone. I should have just kept ignoring his calls.

I was feeling good about myself, and I was proud of my growth in self-love. I felt strong enough to face my demons, strong enough to resist Jaxxon with his charms and advances.

I don't know what made me think that love played fair, what made me think I was emotionally stronger than love.

I said, "Hello."

He said, "Hey, beautiful. What are you doing tonight?"

"I'm just chilling around the house, I don't have any plans for tonight."

I asked him how his day at work was. I was making small talk, hoping he would give up and say goodbye. Wishful thinking on my part. With his persistence, Jaxxon wasn't going to give up that easily, especially since he had me on the phone after all this time.

Jaxxon answered my question about his workday and proceeded to ask me questions about the rest of my night. He asked could he come over and watch movies with me. I quickly said, "No!"

"Dang, Joss, you didn't even think about it."

"I don't have to! I don't think it's wise for us to be around each other."

Jaxxon asked me if I still loved him. For a moment I paused and thought about it. Deep down, I did love him. I loved him for how he made me feel when I thought it was just the two of us. I loved him for the things he did for me and to me. I loved the person he had the potential to become. I'd truly be lying if I said I didn't love him. But I knew I hated him for all he put me through. I came back from my thoughts and told Jaxxon I still loved him.

In telling him I still loved him, I wasn't expecting anything to come from it. I was being truthful with myself. I had feelings, and those feeling were going to heal in time, but not overnight. Saying I didn't love him was me lying to myself. I had to be truthful with myself, admitting my truths.

Jaxon told me he loved me too. He asked me to consider giving him another chance. And I asked him about his drama, basically, wanting to know if he had been speaking with Melissa. He told me I didn't have anything to worry about anymore. I just needed to give him a chance to prove to me he could be the man I needed him to be.

Almost begging, he asked, "Can I see you tonight?"

"Again, I don't think that is a good idea."

"I don't want anything from you, Joss. I just wanted to lay eyes on you. Even if it's for a moment, a second, or for the last time. Can you do that for me?"

Annoyed, I said, "I'm sorry, but I don't want to see you! I'm not ready to see you, because of the feelings I still have for you."

"I understand where you're coming from, but you have nothing to worry about. I'm not going to try to seduce you or anything. I promise I just want to talk face-to-face."

After a few minutes of thinking about it, I gave in. I told him he could come over for a little while but only to talk. Jaxxon's voice got high in excitement, and he said, "Cool, I'll be there in less than an hour."

I said, "Call me when you're outside."

As soon as I hung up the phone, I questioned what I had just agreed to. I wanted to call someone to tell them so they could talk some sense into me. I thought about my cousin Roxanne. I quickly changed my mind, because I had realized I hadn't told her the whole story about Jaxxon yet. I then thought about Melissa. I knew with everything we shared that wasn't a good idea, because she was still the other woman. Or was I the other woman? Either way, I saw it. I didn't have anyone to knock some sense into me. I had only myself to count on. My own willpower.

I got up and started to straighten myself up. My hair was in a hair wrap, so I took it off. I found one of my dresses I normally wear around the house and slid it on. I looked around the house and started putting stuff up and out of the way.

From the time Jaxxon and I hung up the phone to when he called my phone to tell me he was at the door seemed liked seconds. Everything was going too fast. And I wasn't ready. I didn't have time to get ready. Time to get my feelings in check. For some reason, as soon as I touched the door handle to open the door for Jaxxon, I knew I was doomed.

Jaxxon was good with his words, his actions, and even better with his hands. He had a plan set in motion from the moment I opened the door. He knew what he wanted and how he was going to get it. I couldn't get mad because even I knew better.

How he moved was how he got me the first time. I knew better than to believe him when he said he wasn't going to try to seduce me. I should have just stood firm and never agreed to see him.

I opened the door. We stood in front of each other, face-to-face. He looked at me, and I looked at him. He said, "You look good." He motioned his hands for me to come closer to him. I hesitated, but as if I were in a trace, I moved closer to him.

His hands and arms reached out for me. Once he made contact with my body, he held me close into his chest, engulfing me within his arms—the same way he did when we met for the first time. His hug covered me. The warmth of his hug took over. The feelings I had for him began to rise back to the surface.

As he held me, he whispered in my ear he missed me. His arms moved up and down my back slowly and softly. He told me he loved me. He said he never thought he would ever hold me in his arms again. His embrace never eased up, and I could tell he wasn't going to let go. I just stood there and let it all happen.

A few long minutes went by before he let me go. When he loosened up, he pulled back from me slightly, looking me in my face. I looked up at him as well. Without hesitation, he kissed me.

Jaxxon knew me. He knew exactly how to make me weak. He kissed my lips slowly and sensually. His hands moved up and down my arms, bringing me closer to him. He kissed me deeper. He went for my neck and began to kiss me there. My body wouldn't let me lie. My body reacted to every tingle he caused. I forced myself to pull away. I forced myself out of his spell.

He was surprised I jerked away. He said, "Are you okay? Am I doing something wrong?"

I reminded him about our phone conversation. "Remember, you said face-to-face, not touching."

He laughed. "You can't fight what the heart wants."

I laughed. "Right, but I only agreed to talk."

"Well, let's talk then."

Relieved at his response, we headed toward the living room. I sat down on the couch.

He asked, "What are you doing?"

"I'm sitting down so we can talk."

"Joss, you never sit in your living room. Why don't we just go in your room like any other time? You're not going to be comfortable in the living room, and you know it."

Sadly, he was right. I shook my head and headed to my bedroom. In the room, I motioned for him to sit on the chaise across from my bed, as I sat on my bed. I wasn't nervous or scared. But I was anxious to get him taken care of so I could continue with my night. Alone.

Prior to tonight, I hadn't been in Jaxxon's presence for over two months—two months of stress-free living. I gained a sense of clarity on relationships and what I wanted out of them. I was able to focus on my future and heal from the pain of men. It was just the beginning of my process, and I knew it was going to take time. But I wasn't planning on letting another man take advantage of my heart anymore, and that included Jaxxon.

Jaxxon sat in silence. He looked tired, so to break the silence, I asked him if he was tired. He told me he had a tough route at work and he was really tired, but he wasn't going to pass up a chance to see me.

I said, "Your gesture was sweet, but we can talk at another time if you're that tired."

"Now, Joss, you know good damn well you would have stopped taking my calls again. I had an opportunity, and I took it."

I laughed. "You're right!"

After another awkward pause, I said, "Why are you here, Jaxxon? Don't you have a bunch of other females to entertain? My life has been peaceful without you and all your drama. And I'm not about to deal with your shit all over again."

"I'm not trying to be about no drama, Joss. Honestly, I want you and only you, and I am here to show you that."

Jaxxon pulled out his phone. "Look at it. I took all the passwords off my phone. I don't want to hide anything from you anymore, Joss. I'm coming to you as an open book. I know I hurt you, and I will try to make it up to you for the rest of my life if you would just let me show you."

While he was talking, he got up from the chaise and slowly started walking toward the bed, toward me. He stood in front of me and dropped to his knees. He laid his head on my lap, and he said, "Please, Joss, please!"

My posture didn't change. I couldn't give him an answer right then. I tried to adjust myself while his head laid on my lap. I said, "Jaxxon, I need time. Time to figure out if I can look past all the hurt you have caused me."

"Okay, please don't shut me out while you consider our future together. Promise me you will answer my calls and you will really truly think about us."

I looked down at him and told him I promise.

Jaxxon came off his knees, moving closer to my face. Before I knew it, we were kissing. He used his body weight while kissing me to slowly guide my body flat onto the bed. I didn't hesitate, and I didn't stop him. He was on top of me completely, kissing my lips and neck. Low moans escaped my mouth.

I said, "We can't do this! The timing is all wrong!"

Jaxxon didn't stop, and truthfully, I didn't want him to stop.

Jaxxon kissed my neck while his hands went under my dress. He placed himself perfectly between my legs. He slowly ground between my legs as he kissed me. He was teasing me, making me wet, mind fucking me, before he took me.

Jaxxon backed off me to loosen his pants. He told me to take my dress off.

I slowly complied. He pulled me to the end of the bed, then he dropped to his knees. I braced myself because I knew he was about to make my body call out his name.

Jaxxon kissed my inner thigh, whispering to me everything he was going to do to me. He told me I was going to like it.

He whispered, "I'm going to kiss your yoni lips until it's nice and wet. I'm not going to stop until you're satisfied. Then I'm going to fuck the shit out of you!"

My yoni instantly got wet. I opened my legs and welcomed him to my body. He kissed, licked, and sucked. I clenched the sheets and grabbed for walls that weren't there. I felt nothing but heat streaming through my body as he pleased me from within.

When he stood up, I knew what was coming next. I knew I was about to be screaming his name. I knew he was about to work my body. I knew, I knew, I knew!

Jaxxon climbed on top of me, lowered himself to my ear, and whispered, "I love you, Joss Love!"

He eased slightly back between my legs, lowering himself as he got ready to enter me. He whispered, "I love you," again. He entered my body, and I gasped. My body gave into him without putting up a fight. Every stroke he made, he said, "I love you!" And just like that, I was back under his spell.

I felt him thrusting inside of me. My yoni was getting wetter with every stroke. I heard his words as he whispered and moaned in between his "I love yous." I heard my moans and whimpers as I called his name softly. I felt my body giving in to the love and pain of Jaxxon. I felt the tears roll down the side of my face as I gave in to him once more. I felt all these emotions at one time, flowing through my body. Love overpowered them all. Jaxxon stroked my love for him right back to the surface of my heart.

My mouth opened slightly as if I had something to say. My head tilted back as if I was looking for something above me. My hands spread out beside me as if I were about to fly. My feet planted on the bed, as if I were preparing to run. I couldn't help myself. I couldn't help what was about to happen to me. My mouth moaned a moan, and I was about to cum. I threw myself into Jaxxon's thrust, cumming as if I never came before.

I moaned with pleasure as my yoni pulsed repeatedly until I was done. Jaxxon followed my every movement. And just like that, in less than an hour, I was his all over again.

Jaxxon and I talked after we were done. He promised me no more secrets. If I didn't want him doing something, all I had to do was say the word. He didn't care if I went through his phone. His words sounded good. And if he wanted me back, I expected nothing less.

We talked about what we had going on during our hiatus. We made love again, and then went to sleep. It was late, and Jaxxon had to work in the morning.

The next morning, I woke up to Jaxxon standing over me. He was praying, thanking God for me giving him a second chance. It was a cute gesture, and it warmed my heart. I didn't know how I felt being back with Jaxxon. But I did feel some kind of way.

Later in the day, I received my daily call from Melissa. I wanted to tell her about Jaxxon and I hooking up, but I didn't. I felt in some ways I was betraying her. She and I talked like normal, about plans and things for the day. Jaxxon's name didn't come up during our chat, and I was relieved.

Melissa had become someone I respected. She was kind of like the friend I never had. She was a cool person to know, and I was glad I met her. I made up my mind to tell her about Jaxxon. Just not at that moment. I didn't think it was important to tell Jaxxon I befriended her either. I didn't know if I was 100 percent invested in Jaxxon.

Jaxxon texted me all day long, telling me his every move. If he wasn't texting, he was calling. He was trying too hard, but I wasn't ready for him to stop. Everything he was giving me I was going to take, and then some.

As soon as Jaxxon's shift was over, he was back at my house, ready to get dinner and to do anything I asked of him. He gave me his phone as soon as he walked through the door. I thought he was going a bit too far with the phone, but I didn't trust him, and until I did, I was going to check up on him.

*****

Two months passed, and Jaxxon was on his best behavior. He was living up to everything he said he was going to be about. We were on our way to being happy. We were hanging out and spending time together every chance we could. He came home when he said he was, and he was at my house when he was off. Sex was never an issue, but it somehow got even better. I was surprised at how we were getting along, but I wasn't complaining either. We still had some things to work out, though nothing that I felt was major. Jaxxon was getting high and drinking more, but it wasn't something I felt was out of control. I was happy, and I knew for sure Jaxxon was too.

I gradually stopped speaking to Melissa. I never told her directly Jaxxon and I were back together, but I was sure she saw the posts he and I made and the things he tagged me in. Before I knew it, she and I stopped texting and calling each other. I knew in order for my relationship with Jaxxon to work, Melissa couldn't be a part of my life. I knew it was all for the best.

One morning, Jaxxon's phone started ringing. It was on the nightstand by the bed, and I was closest to it. It was barely after five in the morning. The face of the phone illuminated the room. While squinting at the phone, trying to see who was calling, I saw his baby mama's name come across the screen. I assumed something was wrong with his son for her to call so early in the morning. Jaxxon was asleep behind me, not at all fazed by the phone and its ringing. I shook him awake and handed him his phone. He quickly hit the Ignore button.

I was half asleep, but I noticed he wasn't speaking. I looked over at him while his phone began to ring again. He looked at the phone screen and ignored it once again. A few seconds later, I heard a beep from his phone, indicating a text message. Without saying a word, Jaxxon got out of my bed and left out of the room.

Some time had gone by, and I noticed the morning sun was starting to appear through the curtains. I had fallen back to sleep. I reached next to me and noticed Jaxxon wasn't in the bed. I looked around the room, thinking he was probably on the chaise, but he wasn't.

I got out of bed, put my robe on, and then headed out of my bedroom. I quietly peeped around the corner to see if he was in the living room. He wasn't. I stepped into the living room and peeped around the other corner to see if he was in the kitchen. He wasn't. My house wasn't that big, so I assumed he was in the bathroom or he was gone.

Something was going on with him. I felt it in my gut. I walked back through the living room from the kitchen and headed toward the bathroom, which was right across from my bedroom. For a moment, I hesitated. I wasn't sure if I was going to catch him doing something he had no business doing. I damn sure wasn't sure how I was going to react if he was.

I stood outside the door and tried to listen for some noises or him talking. I didn't hear a thing. I said, "Screw it." I walked into the bathroom.

Jaxxon jumped as the door opened. I looked at him as he sat on the toilet, texting someone. At that moment I didn't know who it was, but I knew he didn't offer up any details or information. He gave me a surprised look—a look I knew all too well from past issues. He didn't say a word. I asked him if he was going to get ready for work sometime soon. He looked up at me and said, "Yeah."

I left Jaxxon in the bathroom and returned to my bedroom. I wasn't about to start this drama over with him, and I definitely wasn't about to argue with him this early in the morning.

Jaxxon came in the room to get ready for work. His movements were uneasy. I could tell something was on his mind. I didn't say anything to him while he got ready. When he was done, he kissed me and said, "I love you," and goodbye.

I went about my day as normal. It was the first time in a long time I wanted to reach out to Melissa. I just wanted someone to talk to. Plus, I missed our conversations. But I also knew I couldn't have a relationship with her and Jaxxon both. It wouldn't have been fair to either of them. Apparently, I chose Jaxxon over Melissa because I never called her again.

That night, when Jaxxon got to my house, he was tired. He went straight for the bed. I knew as soon as he set his phone down, it was mine for the taking. He placed it on the nightstand by the bed. I watched him as he changed his clothes, kissed my cheek, and then hopped in the bed behind me. He said goodnight, and he was snoring shortly after.

For a while, I told myself his darkness would come to light. I thought I shouldn't get too attached because he showed me who he was before. Deep down I didn't want to go through his phone because this time around I was scared—scared of what I might find and scared of how I was going to react. Having him in my presence while finding out he was doing me dirty wasn't going to end well.

For thirty minutes, I fought off the urge to go through his phone. I reminded myself he told me I could. He said he was an open book and he had nothing to hide. I was allowed to operate his phone as if it were mine. Ever since we had gotten back together, I told myself I was going to leave the past in the past. I never looked through his phone prior to this moment.

I checked his call log first. Nothing suspicious at first glance. His baby mama called a handful of times throughout the day, and there were some unlisted numbers in his phone. Some numbers I recognized and others I just shrugged off. I remembered the call from early that morning. I knew it was his baby mama, but I was wondering if there was another call while he was in the bathroom. When I checked for the call, all records of his baby mama calling were gone. I wondered why he deleted her call when he knew I knew she called.

I checked his text messages. Again, nothing out of the ordinary. I did notice he deleted parts of a conversation with his baby mama because the conversation pieces that remained didn't make sense. There were answers, but no questions. There were LOL and yeses randomly placed. I saw where she was asking for some money so she and the kids could move. She was then asking for money for daycare fees. Jaxxon mentioned to me a couple of times he needed to send her some money. I assumed he had already done so. I was wrong. I told myself I'd ask him about the texts later.

I went on to look at his photos. Jaxxon had a lot of apps on his phone that served a secretive purpose. In the beginning, these apps had passwords, so I wasn't able to look in them, but since he removed all the passwords, I had all access. In his regular photo gallery, there were pictures of his son and some work stuff. Jaxxon was a picture taker, so I knew there had to be more photos. I saw another app that resembled a camera roll. When I clicked on it, I instantly hit the jackpot.

There were pictures of me, his child, cars, some other women, and a whole lot of memes. My heart kind of skipped a beat. I knew I was in for a surprise as I went through the pictures. The ones of me, his kids, and the cars I quickly skimmed by. The ones of the other women I stared and looked at them in disbelief. I was checking time stamps and dates. Some of the photos were taken while we were together. Some of the women looked familiar. Melissa had shared some of the same photos with me when we were exchanging information about Jaxxon.

Here we were, months later, and Jaxxon's lies were still unfolding before my eyes. He had the audacity to get involved with women that were strong in the face. I couldn't stop looking at the photos. I scrolled until I saw a video. I hit Play. It was a video of Jaxxon and Melissa at a fair. They were laughing and having fun. They were smiling and enjoying themselves. She looked happy, and so did he. A knot formed in my stomach.

After watching the video, I checked the timestamp on it. I almost dropped the phone. It was the same date as the week Jaxxon went missing. I couldn't believe it. I already knew he was with Melissa because she told me so, but he fabricated a completely different story. I watched the video again. I listened to Jaxxon's words. I even heard him tell her he loved her. I deleted the video out of spite.

I saw more pictures that increased my anger. I deleted them after I finished viewing them as well. I didn't care if Jaxxon knew what I was doing. If he were really trying to be with me, he wouldn't care either. I went to his search engine to see what he was looking at online. I checked his search history.

As I read his online history, I saw something that caught my eye. I saw it again a couple more times. It said, "Man looking for female." I clicked on one of the tabs. It directed me to a sex ad on Craigslist. He was searching these ads while he was at work. I was disgusted with Jaxxon.

I realized having me was never going to be enough for Jaxxon. He was shopping for females—on Craigslist of all places. I wondered if all the other women he messed with came from Backpage or Craigslist as well.

Out of disgust, I put Jaxxon's phone back on the nightstand. I shifted on the bed so I was facing him. I just stared at him while he slept. I sat there wondering how his mind worked—how a forty-year-old man played games like a five-year-old daycare child. How and why were all I could think. I debated with myself to say anything to Jaxxon.

When Jaxxon's work alarm went off, I got up with him. I hesitated about telling him what I saw in his phone. I didn't want any more secrets between us, so I had to tell him.

I said, "Jaxxon!"

He quickly said, "Yes, baby!"

I went straight to the question. "Are you looking for females to screw on Craigslist?"

Before speaking, he gave me a surprised look. He said, "Why would I need to do that when I have you?"

"That's why I was asking, Jaxxon. Why do you have searches for a male looking for a female on Craigslist?"

He started getting mad and his tone changed. "I don't know what you're talking about."

I said, "Whatever, Jaxxon!" I walked out of the room. I felt myself getting mad, and I didn't feel like arguing with a liar. Jaxxon and I didn't say anything else to each other that morning or that night.

The next day, while Jaxxon was at work, he texted me, asking about plans for later. I told him I'd leave the plans up to him. You could feel the tension through the phone. Before we hung up the phone, Jaxxon told me he loved me. He said I didn't have any reason to be mad at him because he found out his coworker was behind the Craigslist searches. I listened to him speak, but in my head, I told myself it was all just another lie. I wanted to give him the benefit of a doubt.

Later that night, when Jaxxon got home, we made up. He took me out to get something to eat. When we got back to my house, we made love and put the day and all the previous drama behind us.

Things were going well for us. We took turns staying at each other's houses, but we mostly stayed at mine. Some days after work, he would get dropped off at his house and I'd pick him up afterward to bring him to my house. Everything worked. But with Jaxxon, the good doesn't always last long.

Early one morning, Jaxxon's phone started to ring. It was five in the morning again. I reached for the phone. It was his baby mama, Trina. I passed the phone to Jaxxon, who was lying beside me in my bed. I saw him hit Ignore. Instantly the phone started ringing again. This time I rolled over and shook Jaxxon awake.

I said, "Your baby mama is calling. Something might be wrong."

He lifted his head, looked at the phone, and said, "Nothing is wrong."

Trina called a couple more times. By around six o'clock, Jaxxon was getting up out of the bed. He headed to the bathroom, phone in hand. My anxiety was starting to get the best of me. My gut was telling me something was up. I knew Jaxxon, though. If Trina's calling was nothing, he would have answered the phone. It was something.

Jaxxon was in the bathroom for a good amount of time. I walked past the bathroom. I heard the clicks from pressing on his phone keys. I heard incoming beeps as well. Jaxxon was texting. I quickly reminded myself that I wasn't going to take any more of his shit. I tried to keep my composure. I tried not to explode. I said, "Fuck it."

I took two steps back toward the bathroom, grabbed the door handle, and stormed in. Jaxxon's eye grew wide as he saw my face. I looked at him sitting on the toilet with his phone in his hand. We maintained direct eye contact, and he said nothing. I grabbed the bathroom door handle and walked back out of the bathroom.

Jaxxon quickly finished whatever it was he was doing. I heard the toilet flush, and the door opened.

He was walking in the room and speaking at the same time. "It's not what you think, Joss. It's Trina, asking for more money because she has to move."

I turned to look him in his eyes. I said, "Why does everything have to be so secretive with you? I don't care if your baby mother was asking you for money to move. You guys have a child together. You are obligated to help her to a certain extent. You didn't have to be sneaky about any of it. You could have just told me what was going on, Jaxxon."

I could see the relief exit his face. I assumed he was relieved to know I wouldn't leave him over this situation. He stood in front of me, dropping down to his knees. He placed his head on my lap, and he just held me. I felt the love I had for him flow through my body. It was warm and inviting. I felt the need to be a part of his life. I wanted everything about us.

Jaxxon eventually got up to get ready to go to work. He was off the next couple days, and I knew that meant we were going to be spending every sleeping and waking breath together. I loved being under Jaxxon, and I knew he loved being under me.

The next day happened quickly. Jaxxon woke up earlier than me. He wasn't in the bedroom with me when I woke up, so I knew he was either in the living room watching TV or playing his video games. I was tired, so I rolled over and fell back asleep. When I woke up, it was after eleven in the morning. I thought it was pretty strange Jaxxon never came back in the room to check on me or to wake me up. I got up to go check on him.

When I walked out of my bedroom, I peered around the corner to look into the living room. Jaxxon was seated on the couch with his controller in his hand, and his phone was lying next to him. I walked into the living room, looked at him, and asked him if he was okay. He looked at me and told me he was fine, but the face he gave me said otherwise.

I asked him what the plans were for the day. He said he wanted to grab a case of beer, maybe a bottle of something else, and something to smoke from his plug. It was his typical thing to do on his days off. There was nothing suspicious about what he made plans to do. I left him to his game.

Jaxxon walked into the bedroom and told me he was stepping out. He told me he was going with his plug to go get some smoke. Again, it was something he had done before, so I didn't think anything of it. Jaxxon left my house wearing a pair of oversized blue-and-white swim trunks, a white T-shirt, and his flip-flops.

An hour went by, and I hadn't heard a word from Jaxxon. I was hungry and wanted to grab some takeout. I wanted to wait for Jaxxon to return before I left. To occupy my time waiting for Jaxxon, I started a movie. The movie started and ended. It was starting to get dark outside. I grabbed my phone to check the time as well as to see if Jaxxon had texted. It was almost seven in the evening, and there were no texts or missed calls from Jaxxon.

I grabbed the phone and dialed his number. It went straight to voicemail. I dialed it again, the same result. I texted him and told him to hit me up when he got a chance. I was worried, hoping nothing happened to him. I never received a reply.

Another hour or so went by, there was still no reply from Jaxxon. By this time, I was panicking. Something had to have happened. I tried Jaxxon's phone again. Still no response. I didn't know what to think, and I didn't want to think the worst. I checked his social media pages for activity; there was nothing there either.

After a while, I got dressed and went to get something to eat. When I got home, I made myself a plate, sat back on my bed, and put on another movie. One movie led to another and then another. I checked my phone every second looking for something from Jaxxon. Still, I received nothing.

It was six in the morning the next day when my phone beeped. It wasn't a call but a message. I was shocked to see it was Jaxxon. He was asking me if I was up and if I could come get him. There were no "I'm sorrys" or explanations for why he was gone for a whole damn day. I texted him back, telling him he had some nerve.

Jaxxon continued to play stupid, asking me what I meant.

I yelled into the phone, "You must think I'm the dumbest bitch on the planet not to realize my man wasn't at home all day, stayed out all night, and now he is calling me to pick him up from who knows where!"

Jaxxon said, "So, you're not going to come get me?"

I said, "No!" I hung the phone up, slamming it down. I rolled over in my bed and went back to sleep. I was extremely pissed. I didn't know what I wanted to do next or how I was going to handle the situation, but I knew I was going back to sleep. I knew I had some decisions to make.

Jaxxon was walking into my bedroom a couple of hours later. He had the same clothes he had on when he left my house yesterday morning. He looked like shit. He looked as if he hadn't slept in the past twenty-four hours.

I lifted my head from my pillow and stared at him as he approached my bed. Jaxxon and I made eye contact. I continued to ignore him. I laid my head back down on my pillow and moved away from the edge of the bed. He called my name repeatedly. After a couple of times of saying my name and me ignoring him, he stood up and whispered under his breath.

As he walked out of the room, he said, "You don't give a fuck about me."

I quickly jumped up from out of my bed in a rage. I followed behind him as he entered my living room. With anger in my voice, I said, "You got the nerve to come out your mouth to say some shit like that to me! I am always the one picking up your shit and making sure you are okay! You're selfish in everything you say and do! And you need to start taking responsibility for the shit you say and do, especially when it comes to destroying our relationship. Where in your head do you think you can up and disappear for a whole night, no call or text, and then just show up out the blue and think every-thing is okay? What woman do you know would sit back and take that, Jaxxon? Why do I always have to understand and excuse your issues?"

I continued to talk, and I started getting angrier. Jaxxon's bull-shit was getting the best of me, and I knew I wasn't going to be able to stop going off until I got it all off my chest. I'd overlooked so many things because I loved him. So many things I took and accepted, hoping he would get better. I continued being a good woman to him, hoping he would grow up and finally reach my level and stop playing games.

"The past few weeks, you have had some shit going on with you! Between not speaking to me for at least a day and you searching for women on Craigslist. I hoped your behavior was all about work and you having to do everything while there. I dismissed that thought because you told me you were going to talk to Shawn about it. I'm paying attention to the signs, Jaxxon—between you being distant, talking in your sleep, sweating like crazy throughout the night, and your attitude toward me becoming mean and aggressive. Whatever is going on with you, now is the time to get it out."

I stood directly in front of Jaxxon. I continued to speak. "If I didn't care about you, I wouldn't be telling you about yourself and your actions. I wouldn't be trying to help you better yourself. I wouldn't have you in my home, making sure you don't want for anything while you're with me. AND I WOULDN'T HAVE TAKEN YOUR ASS BACK! You're the one that said you were going to be an open book this time around."

I looked him directly in his eyes. "You still have a whole lot of work to do! You never think you do anything wrong, and then you try to play mister innocent to your own bullshit, always trying to act like you don't know what is going on. I'm not perfect, but I admit my truths, and I handle them, not run from them."

After the last word left my mouth, I turned around and went back into my bedroom, closed the door, and got back into bed. At that moment, I didn't care what Jaxxon chose to do next. I didn't care if he got all his shit and left. I wanted what I said to seep into his hard head.

I knew at that moment I was no longer equipped to keep going on this rollercoaster ride with Jaxxon. He needed to go straight or get away from me.

I got comfortable in my bed and went back to sleep.

After some much-needed sleep, I woke up to no plans. I didn't expect Jaxxon to still be at my house after everything I said, but when I got up to go to the bathroom, I noticed he was sitting on the couch in the living room playing his video game.

We made eye contact.

I continued with my intentions and headed for the bathroom. When I came out of the bathroom, I went about my business. I didn't say two words to Jaxxon as I went through most of the day.

I started a movie continuing to keep to myself. I was trying to stay stress-free from all things Jaxxon. As soon as the movie started, Jaxxon came in the room and lay next to me. He asked about the movie, trying to make small talk. My answers were short. The tension between us slowly subsided through half the movie. I was allowing him to playfully touch me.

Jaxxon never told me what happened the night he randomly disappeared. The only thing he ever said was he was home and got too high and drunk to do remember anything.

The weekend came and went, and we went to work as normal. After work, Jaxxon came to my house to sleep. A weird feeling came over me because I realized we haven't had sex. It was something we did on a regular, almost never going more than two days without it.

By the third morning of us not sexing, I was feeling the pressure. As he slept, I tried to entice him. I could tell by his body's reaction he was getting excited, but he didn't make a move back toward me. I tried enticing him a little longer, but I was denied. Jaxxon wasn't taking any of my sexual advances. I rolled back over to my side of the bed and went back to sleep.

Later in the day I texted Jaxxon while he was at work. I asked him if everything was all right with him. I brought up last night's attempts to seduce him, hoping he would offer some kind of explanation as to why he hadn't been making any moves on me, but he didn't.

I asked him straight up. "Why are you being stingy with your lovin'? I'm getting frustrated, waiting for you."

He laughed a little and said, "I guess I have to fix that, huh?"

"Are you not in need of a release?"

He didn't text back. I texted him back, "I'll wait!" being sarcastic.

His response came back defensive. "I have a lot on my mind, and I'm not in any rush getting out of my feelings. My day is already messed up, and it's going to get worse. I'm fed up with everything, and I'm tired of having to eat everyone else's shit."

"Hold up, where is all this coming from? What is going on, Jaxxon?"

Jaxxon never answered my questions.

We were going back and forth in text messages all day discussing when he was getting off. One minute he told me he was almost done, the next minute, he still had more to do. After a while, I stopped asking him what time he was going to be home.

I assumed Jaxxon took a detour to his house before coming to mine because he had his nephew drop him off, not his cousin Shawn. He told me they were riding around looking to score some weed.

Jaxxon got in the bed and went straight to sleep. I put on a movie, sat back in the bed, and chilled. Every so often, I'd looked beside me, at Jaxxon, as he slept. At times he slept peacefully, and other times he was sweating profusely. I thought he was possibly getting sick. I gently shook him awake. I said, "Are you okay?"

Jaxxon rolled over, looking in my direction. He said, "I'm fine!"

He went right back to sleep. We didn't have sex yet again, and I was on my second movie. I was feeling content. Every so often my relationship with Jaxxon would come to the forefront of my thoughts. I thought about the beginning of our relationship until now.

I wondered what he thought about when he did his dirt. I wondered what screwed a person up so much for them to hurt someone else, like Jaxxon had been doing to women for years. Jaxxon was damaged, and he left pain wherever his feet landed.

Jaxxon's phone started ringing, and the sound of it took me out of my train of thought. I glanced at the time on the TV screen, and I said, "Two in the morning!"

Jaxxon didn't move, and the ringing didn't faze him. I looked at the caller ID on the phone, and it displayed Trina's name.

I answered his phone assuming something was wrong with Jaxxon's son, especially at two in the morning. It dawned on me I had not once been introduced to her, and seeing how I was his girlfriend, it was well overdue.

When I said, hello, I heard the surprise in her response. Instead of saying hello back, she said, "Why are you answering my husband's phone? Where is my husband, and why do you have his phone?"

My heart skipped a thousand beats. I said, "Husband? I'm his girlfriend! And did you say husband?"

I thought she had the wrong number until she said, "Where is Jaxxon? And how do you have his phone?"

"He's asleep in my bed. That's how I have his phone!"

She quickly said, "You're lying! Put my husband on the phone. He told me he was out of town working, making deliveries. He said he doesn't come home until Monday. You must have found his phone somewhere."

I swung my body around in my bed to face Jaxxon's sleeping body. As she spoke, I was shaking my head. Heat was rising within me. My mind went on a tailspin. Something just happened, and I was the one that getting blindsided. The game just changed!

Her words were echoing in my head. Déjà vu hit me all over again. All I heard was "HUSBAND!" Did this shit just happen to me again? Was I involved with another lying-ass married man, who was lying in my bed, asleep? My mind circled back to his baby mama, or should I now say wife.

I said, "Sorry to inform you, but your husband is not on a work trip. He is at my house, sleeping in my bed."

By her comments, she still thought I was lying to her.

I said, "If you give me a second, I can prove it to you!"

I put her on hold, picked up my phone, and used my camera. I snapped a picture of me with Jaxxon in the background asleep and his phone in my left hand showing the time and date. I sent the picture to Jaxxon's phone and then sent it to her.

Her response to the picture pissed me off even more.

She was getting angry. She said, "This man moved me all the way to North Carolina just to cheat on me."

I said, "Hold up, wait. You're here in North Carolina?"

"Yes, I'm here in North Carolina, staying at his cousin's house, with his nephew. I have the kids with me too. He wanted us to be a family, so we moved here two weeks ago.

"Two weeks ago? What the hell! Now you're lying!"

I didn't want to believe Jaxxon was that extreme. I didn't want to think he could move his family into a house I frequented, let alone have a wife, while building a relationship with me. Jaxxon was the worst kind of man.

She said, "Yes, we're here, and we've been here!"

A few seconds after her response, a picture came through his phone. It was a picture of her sitting in his chair, in his room, on Perch Lane. I was done talking to her, but I was just getting started with Jaxxon. He was about to receive my wrath.

I told Trina I was done talking and I would gladly let Jaxxon know she called. Her response to me was petty as hell, but I was saving my anger for Jaxxon.

She said, "When you're done with my husband, you can send him on home. And tell him I still love him."

I laughed. "Trust me, you can have him! If I had known he was married this whole time, he wouldn't be in my bed now. I will gladly pass on your message!"

Then I hung up. I stood up from my bed. I grabbed my hair wrap and began to tie it around my head. I felt like I was about to go to war. I didn't need any distractions once I started in on Jaxxon. I paced around my bedroom floor a couple of times, watching him. I was trying to calm down and figure out my next move.

It was a little past three in the morning, and I stood at the end of my bed and called his name aloud.

I yelled, "Jaxxon!"

He didn't move. I called his name again. Still no movement. I called his name for the third time; this time I was shaking him awake. He slowly raised his head and looked at me. I guess with the look on my face he could tell something was wrong. He quickly rolled completely over so his body was facing me.

I said, "Your phone was ringing earlier!"

"Okay! Why didn't you answer it? You can answer my phone!"

I yelled, "I did answer your phone, Jaxxon, and I had a nice conversation with your WIFE!"

His eyes got big. "Who?"

I said, "Your wife! Not your baby mama like you've been calling her this whole time! She told me a lot of eye-opening shit! The main thing is she is here in North Carolina! Staying in your house! Kids and all!"

Jaxxon was speechless. Before I could say anything else, his phone started ringing again. I looked down on the nightstand to see who was interrupting our soon-to-be fight. It was Trina again. I picked up the phone and threw it at him. I told him to answer it. Jaxxon grabbed the phone, looked at the screen, and threw it to the side of the bed, away from me. He said, "Joss, she doesn't matter! I didn't know how to tell you she was here with my kids."

I looked at him. I was ready to put my hands on him, but I knew that wasn't going to solve anything. So I said, "How can you not know how to part your lips to say, 'I'm married, and my wife and kids are currently staying at my house?' All of this shit matters! You have taken disrespect to a whole other level. You got some nerve lying in my bed, asleep, with no cares in the world, and you have a whole wife with kids living at your house. A house I frequented, cleaned, slept, and cooked in. It all makes sense now why you disappeared the other day—the reason for the distance and the standoffish behavior."

By this time, I was fully broken. I was yelling my head off, shouting cuss words and "remember when" phrases at him. I said, "Remember the day you left and didn't answer the phone? You must have been showing her attention, acting like I didn't exist. Remember when you said you weren't in the mood to have sex? I guess that was because you were having sex with her while you were over there trying to be one big happy family. Your wife told me all about the twenty-four hours she had you at your house. Her story was one hundred percent different from yours!"

Jaxxon couldn't say anything. He finally said, "But I'm here with you though, Joss! You are who I want to be with, and now she knows."

I was ready to swing on Jaxxon. His wife wasn't making things any better because she was still calling his phone repeatedly as well as messaging me on FB Messenger. I didn't care what Jaxxon was saying, I wanted his lying ass to feel pain. I was yelling and moving closer to him, calling him all kinds of names, as everything started making sense in my head. Hell, it wasn't just me and Melissa. It was Trina and probably a whole lot more. Jaxxon was playing us all.

My phone was still connected to the TV, so every time Trina messaged my phone, the message popped up on the TV screen. Each time a message popped up, I would point my finger toward the TV screen saying, "Look at this bullshit."

Jaxxon grabbed my phone and tried to disconnect the two apps. I snatched my phone away from him before he could even try it. Her messages steadily coming in—pictures of the house, the room, and the kids and screenshots of their text conversations.

She reminded me, saying, "You're sleeping with a married man."

As soon as I read that message on my TV screen, I became irate. I told Jaxxon I wanted him to leave. Once he left for work or stepped foot out of my house, he was no longer allowed to return.

I told him loud and clear, "I don't fuck with married men!"

Jaxxon asked me if I loved him. I told him love had nothing to do with the situation. I quickly reminded him that he had a wife, whom he moved into his house without saying a mumbling word to me.

He said I was who he wanted to be with repeatedly. He was going to prove it to me by getting a divorce, and he wasn't leaving my house. These were his words for ten minutes straight. At the same time, messages from Trina continued popping up on my TV screen.

I was growing weary of it all. My anger was draining me. I said, "If you're not going to leave, fine! I'm over the whole situation, and I'm going to bed!"

Even though I was mad, my heart was breaking inside. Here was yet another man living a double life who invaded my life and broke my heart, giving me false hopes and promises for a future he had no right to promise.

I wanted to break down and cry. I wanted to fall apart, but not in front of Jaxxon. I didn't want him to know he had me messed up inside. He wasn't going to win this time. I grew and learned through this game they all played, and I *reigned* victory over them all.

I tried to become the positive in Jaxxon's life. Instead, I walked away with yet another story to tell about love and its betrayal. I blamed myself for being naive and thinking he was going to change. He had the charm and manipulation down packed.

I also applaud myself for not allowing myself to be the other woman.

I'm a true believer of the phrase "What God put together, let no man put asunder."

# Now Comes the Unique
# Part of Me in HER

My unique journey of heartbreak came after a five-year marriage that ended in divorce and another long-term relationship lasting almost ten years. After these two relationships, I had to figure out my worth. I had to figure out what I wanted for myself in order to have a successful relationship as well as love myself before I started dating again. I needed to take time to learn myself and my wants.

I took a look back at my two failed relationships, and I tried to see what I was doing wrong. I wanted to work on the part of myself that played a part in their failures. Over the years of being single, I did just that. I wanted to come into my next relationship with an open mind as well as a loving heart—a clear white canvas for me and my new loves to paint together.

I learned I loved hard. I did too much to make my relationships work. My definition of loving hard is me going out of my way to do things for a person thinking that is love. The more things I did, I felt it showed the other person how much I loved them. I did what I needed to do to satisfy my partners, and I made my feelings second to theirs.

I aimed to please, and I didn't like to fail. I gave everything I set my heart to, my all, and that included my relationships. That was my downfall. I became self-aware that *love* is my weakness. Love made me weak as well as blind.

I never professed to being the perfect woman, but I knew for sure I was a damn good one. I was good at making my men happy. I was too good to them because it drove them to lie to me to stay with me. Some of them are still reaching out with desires to be with me to this day.

I had high hopes for each of these guys. I tried with each relationship to not hold what the previous deceiver did to me against the next man. I was cautious, and I had my questions at the beginning of each relationship. They all knew the right things to say to get what they wanted from me and how to get me to trust them. All of them professed to one day make me their wife. Sadly, in the end, I could never be theirs when they obviously belonged to someone else—at least on paper. A handful of relationships were built on a thousand lies.

Ironically, this all started because someone didn't love me enough to marry me, to make me his wife. I ended up with men who loved me so much they were willing to hide their wives from their lives just to have me in theirs.

The journey to true love is never going to be easy, but it is up to us to recognize our worth and to figure out what we want and don't want in our lives so others will be able to recognize it and respect it.

Times are different for the dating world now. We have social media and a whole lot of cell phones to connect with people. Technology plays almost half a role in your relationship because it's the strongest form of communication in the world today. With that being said, people have gotten bolder in their actions to hiding their cheating behavior.

We still search the internet for answers as to why people cheat and do the things they do. It has nothing to do with you, the person who is heartbroken. It has everything to do with the deceivers. They have no self-worth. They should be the ones embarrassed. They are the ones that should be hurting.

That's the crazy thing about love. You can truly be head over heels for someone. You can eat, sleep, and breathe everything about that person, even become loyal to that person all the way down to a fault, wanting nothing but pure bliss for your relationship. And it only takes one text, one phone call, one picture, one telephone number, simply one wrong move to end the relationship you thought was solid in an instant.

With time, we all evolve. And so do the games that lead to a broken heart. The agenda doesn't change, just how they get there. I've come to the realization when a guy says if you don't like it, you can leave or you don't have to be here, believe what they say. They are showing you who they really are. Move on from them because they already have someone else to replace you. Most guys say this because they are testing you to see if you will actually leave. Others are waiting for you to just bounce. Neither comment meant "stay, don't leave."

If you feel like you are changing things to fit the person you are with and you are no longer doing things you love, you're losing yourself, and then the HER steps in.

Follow steps from your <u>h</u>urt to <u>e</u>mpowering yourself and others so you can then <u>r</u>eign over your life. Give yourself credit for who *you* are.

Yes, you want to give every relationship your all, and I did just that. I gave them my all, trusting and believing in them until it hurt. After these relationships, I believe trust is earned, not given.

The disbelief of being in a relationship where you are being betrayed has so many emotional demons conflicting with the real you. The pain, frustration, delusions, denial, and rage warring inside of you—all these emotions are true emotions. We want to act out, but we need to think without emotions but with logic.

You, the person, need to regain clarity and logically think about what you just found out or what you just experienced. We are sometimes able to regroup and think of a perfect way out of the drama we are in, and other times some of us just end up dealing with the drama repeatedly, only to end up with a lot of animosity toward the person who is hurting you.

I'm not a relationship expert, but my experiences qualify me to an opinion on love, lies, and manipulation. I know after five years of trying to date and coming across these different guys, it opened my eyes to how men can be deceitful and how us women fall for the hype of what's in front of our eyes.

I became unique more times than I would have desired for myself, but it was the wake-up call I needed to find myself. The world is full of individuals whose relationships take a unique turn, and that unique turn is how we all end up going through the same battle when it comes to love and with the same story in the end, which is heartbreak.

During one of these relationships, I remembered hearing on celebrity news about the actress from *Jumping the Broom* (she played in *Just Wright* as well) found out her boyfriend was living a double life with her. She found out he had a wife and kids. She is famous, has money, and she could have paid to get a background check before dating him. But she trusted him. And in the end, she became HER.

The North Carolina winner from *American Idol* was sued for alienation of affection (which is a law in many states). She fell in love with a married man. He didn't do what was right in the beginning, but he made it right in the end. He got a divorce, and then he married her. They are happy now, with kids. She empowered herself, and now she reigns.

I knew other women were dealing with the same kind of men. I was. I was far from being unique, far from being exempt from the pain of love's deception. I was no different from our mother's mothers when papa was a rolling stone, having a whole other family across town. Women before us went through the same lies and betrayals. I was unique in my experience! Coming across not one but four men who lied to build a life with me that wasn't theirs to share.

*****

I don't know why or how I let myself become so vulnerable, to allow a man to take advantage of me and make me insecure. I am that strong, independent woman who survived a lot of life's difficulties.

Making the mistake of loving these men made me weak. But I survived. I loved, and I survived love with my heart still intact.

Music is and was my therapy through these relationships and life. There was a different set of songs for each guy and each situation they put me through. The songs helped shape the many different emotions I developed while with these individuals. It kept me from making some dangerous decisions that I would have otherwise regretted.

I am that woman that gets in her car, turns on the most hurtful break-up song on a music-streaming app, and sings at the highest levels my vocals can reach, sometimes until I cried. There are so many songs that resonated to my pain on almost every level of heartbreak there is.

You should never be afraid to love someone because if it's true love, you shouldn't have any worries. Love is never meant to be easy in this world. *Love* is only pure through God.

Drew loved everything about me, from my booty to my hair. I have no doubt he loved me, and I know he loves me still. I believe if he could be with anyone in the world, it would be me. He never knew true love until he met me. I see Drew almost every year because he still comes back to the job to see me. I gave him everything, especially trust.

Sawyer loved my voice. He loved talking to me on the phone. He also loved my sex. I was what he wanted, but he was scared to trust his feelings. I think he was broken by women, and his wife was his safe haven, even though there was mental abuse in their relationship. Saw called twice a week every week for two years straight. Jaxxon answered the phone once when he called. He told him to stop calling, or he was going to find him and whoop his ass. Saw continued to call. I had to change my number, but I gave him all the comfort a woman could give.

Micah loved that I was a woman of worth. I do believe he wanted me for me. He loved my personality along with my determination to make things in life sweet. He wanted someone to love him and take care of him, even if he had to lie about his life to get it. Micah's last text to me was "Oh, so you're just going to ignore me?" I thought that was funny, especially after learning he and his wife welcomed another child nine months later. I gave him hope and determination for life.

Jaxxon loved everything about me. He loved me so hard it hurt him. He destroyed himself with each woman he was with because he, too, loved hard. He was greedy in love. He wanted all our love so bad he couldn't let any of us go. Whoever had the most love to give at the time was the one he ran to. I don't think he will ever be able to settle down with just one woman. He still checks in every so often as a friend. I know I will always have an impact on his life—on all of their lives. They will never meet another woman like Joss Love.

While going through these relationships, I wasn't always able to see what was going on right in front of my eyes. I was stupid, maybe even naive. I didn't want to believe the men I was loving didn't have the same respect for me as I had for them. I believed them when they said they loved me.

These guys knew me differently and personally in their own little way. Each had something special about them that made them different from the last guy. But in the end, they all ended up being the same. All having one common denominator—their wives.

As soon as I found out each of these men was married, I didn't hesitate to leave them. I knew my worth. I knew what I stood for, and I wasn't going to be the other woman. I adjusted myself and straightened my crown.

I became another part of HER in my own you-nique way!

I went through the heartbreak to endure the pain so I may hold my head up and reign as the queen that I know that I am. I survived so that I could become HER.

Hurt. Empower. Reign.

> There is *no fear* in love, but perfect love
> casteth out fear. (1 John 4:18)

# About the Author

A woman child of God, a survivor, mother, and wife!
An inspiration to everyone she meets and great to be around. She
writes about things most women wouldn't dare talk about—love
and its pain! A huge inspiration of love after knowing HER.
                                            —Sandy Banks, mother

Nakema, born in New Haven, Connecticut, now residing
in Snow Camp, North Carolina, has always had a lot
of ambition and many hidden talents, shaping her into
a beautiful, thoughtful, and tough daughter.
                                            —Abdul Qawi, father

Talented, creative, and has an amazing sense of storytelling! Readers
will experience her love for writing throughout the world!
                                            —Louis Guess

Once you get to know HER, you will quickly find
she will ride or die for you in every way. My sister, my
friend, is one of the most confident women I know.
She has never stopped believing in HER self.

—Anthony Banks

She always had a love for writing and pulled from life's
experiences to craft this novel. She enjoys spending time
with family, cooking, and watching movies. She loves art,
hates onions, and is hard at work on HER next project.

—Akeem Banks

Encouraging and always there for whoever may need her!

—Deraczi Martinez

She is my big sis!

—Muhammad Guess